LOW-FAT, HIGH-FLAVOR COOKBOOK

LOW-FAT, HIGH-FLAVOR
COOKBOOK

Low-Fat, High-Flavor Cookbook from the Today's Gourmet series

Book Division of Southern Progress Corporation
P.O. Box 2463, Birmingham, Alabama 35201

Library of Congress Catalog Card Number: 95-70356
ISBN: 0-8487-1454-7

Manufactured in the United States of America
First Printing 1995

Be sure to check with your health-care provider before making any changes in your diet.

Editor-in-Chief: Nancy Fitzpatrick Wyatt
Senior Foods Editor: Katherine M. Eakin
Senior Editor, Editorial Services: Olivia Kindig Wells
Art Director: James Boone

LOW-FAT, HIGH-FLAVOR COOKBOOK

Editor: Deborah Garrison Lowery
Assistant Editor: Kathryn L. Matuszak, R.D.
Copy Editors: Keri Bradford Anderson, Holly Ensor
Editorial Assistant: Alison Rich Lewis
Assistant Art Director: Cynthia R. Cooper

Director, Test Kitchens: Kathleen Royal Phillips
Assistant Director, Test Kitchens: Gayle Hays Sadler
Test Kitchen Home Economists: Susan Hall Bellows, Julie Christopher, Michele Brown Fuller, Natalie E. King, Elizabeth Tyler Luckett, Iris Crawley O'Brien, Jan A. Smith
Recipe Developers: Linda West Eckhardt, Linda Gassenheimer, Debby Maugans, Elizabeth J. Taliaferro
Text Consultants: Kathryn Coniff Link, Christin Loudon, R.D.

Photographer: Ralph Anderson
Photo Stylist: Virginia R. Cravens
Production and Distribution Director: Phillip Lee
Associate Production Manager: Theresa L. Beste
Production Assistants: Valerie Heard, Marianne Jordan Wilson

Cover: *Santa Fe Salsa (page 52)*
Page 1: *Herbed Pepper Rub (page 21)*
Page 2: *Citrus Vinegar (page 36); Peppered Citrus Oil (page 34)*
Page 3: *Mint Marinade over a lean lamb chop (page 16)*

CONTENTS

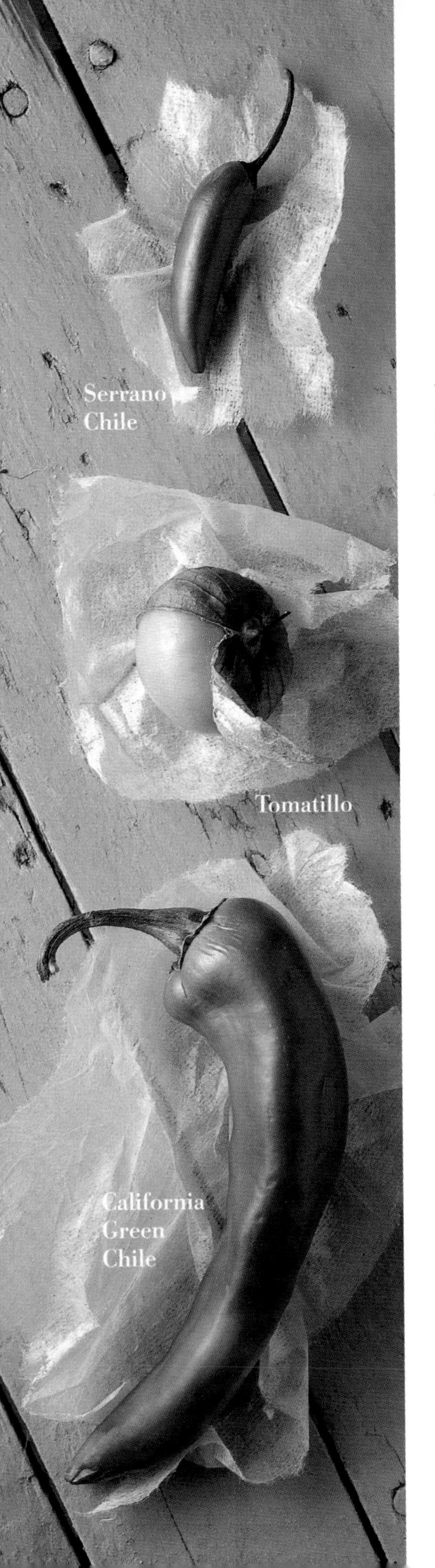

INTRODUCTION

YOU'VE JUST OPENED a cookbook unlike any other. What you hold in your hands isn't just another collection of recipes (although you'll find over 200 of them). The *Low-Fat, High-Flavor Cookbook* is also a virtual encyclopedia of easy ways to make low-fat recipes—yours and ours—taste as delicious and mouth-watering as they should.

Flip through the pages: You'll find almost as many tips as recipes. That's how important it is to us that we show you *how* to cook with flavor as well as *what* to cook. The many tips feature hints about buying, storing, and cooking with natural flavoring ingredients like cinnamon, chiles, fresh herbs, garlic, lemons, limes, and pungent spices.

And there's more. Here are a few other highlights to look for as you cook your way through the book:

- How-to photos on making homemade mustard, roasting peppers, making pesto, and grill-smoking.
- Color photo identification charts for ingredients like mushrooms, onions, spices, and various ethnic foods.
- Authentic ethnic and regional menus using recipes in the book, along with a description of each ethnic cuisine's most prominent ingredients and flavors.
- A pictorial glossary of flavorful ingredients and food terms.
- A handy mail order source for hard-to-find and regional ingredients.

One thing you can be sure of: If it wasn't terrific in taste-testing, then it didn't go in this book. We knew we'd met our goal of creating high-flavor recipes after one editor made Lemon-Lime Cake (page 207) as cupcakes. They were a hit with both adults and neighborhood kids; one 8-year-old boy even downed five of them before he left for home. (The editor had to give his mother the recipe ASAP.) A definite seal of approval. And we hope you'll give it yours.

How to Plan Healthy Meals—All of the recipes also fit within the calorie and fat guidelines of a healthy diet. As you use the nutrient grid to guide your eating plans, remember:

•It's more important to be aware of the number of fat grams you eat than the percentage of fat in an individual recipe. U.S. Department of Agriculture (USDA) guidelines suggest that a person's calories from fat should average 30 percent or less of total calories consumed during a day or period of days.

•Eat more carbohydrates and less fat and protein so you get at least half of your calories from carbohydrates (cereals, fruits, grains, pastas, and vegetables) and 20 percent or less of calories from protein sources (meat, cheese, and eggs). This 50-20-30 guideline is recommended by both the American Heart Association and the American Dietetic Association.

•To help you plan healthy meals, we calculated the percentage of calories from fat for all of the recipes in the "Cooking with Flavor" section. Because the recipes within the "Seasoning Secrets" section are intended to be used as an ingredient in another recipe or as a condiment (and wouldn't be eaten alone) we didn't include the percentage of fat there. You may notice that not every recipe in this book is less than 30 percent fat. That's okay; just serve these recipes with lower fat accompaniments, and you'll still create a balanced meal.

•Keep in mind that you can gain weight if the calories add up, even if the fat grams don't.

•Look for this nutrient grid after every recipe:

Per Serving		
Calories 185 (17% Calories from Fat)	Carbohydrate 10.4 g	Cholesterol 66 mg
Fat 3.4 g (Saturated Fat 0.7 g)	Protein 27.8 g	Sodium 284 mg

The values listed for each recipe come from a computer analysis program provided by the USDA.

Harissa, page 66

Seasoning Secrets

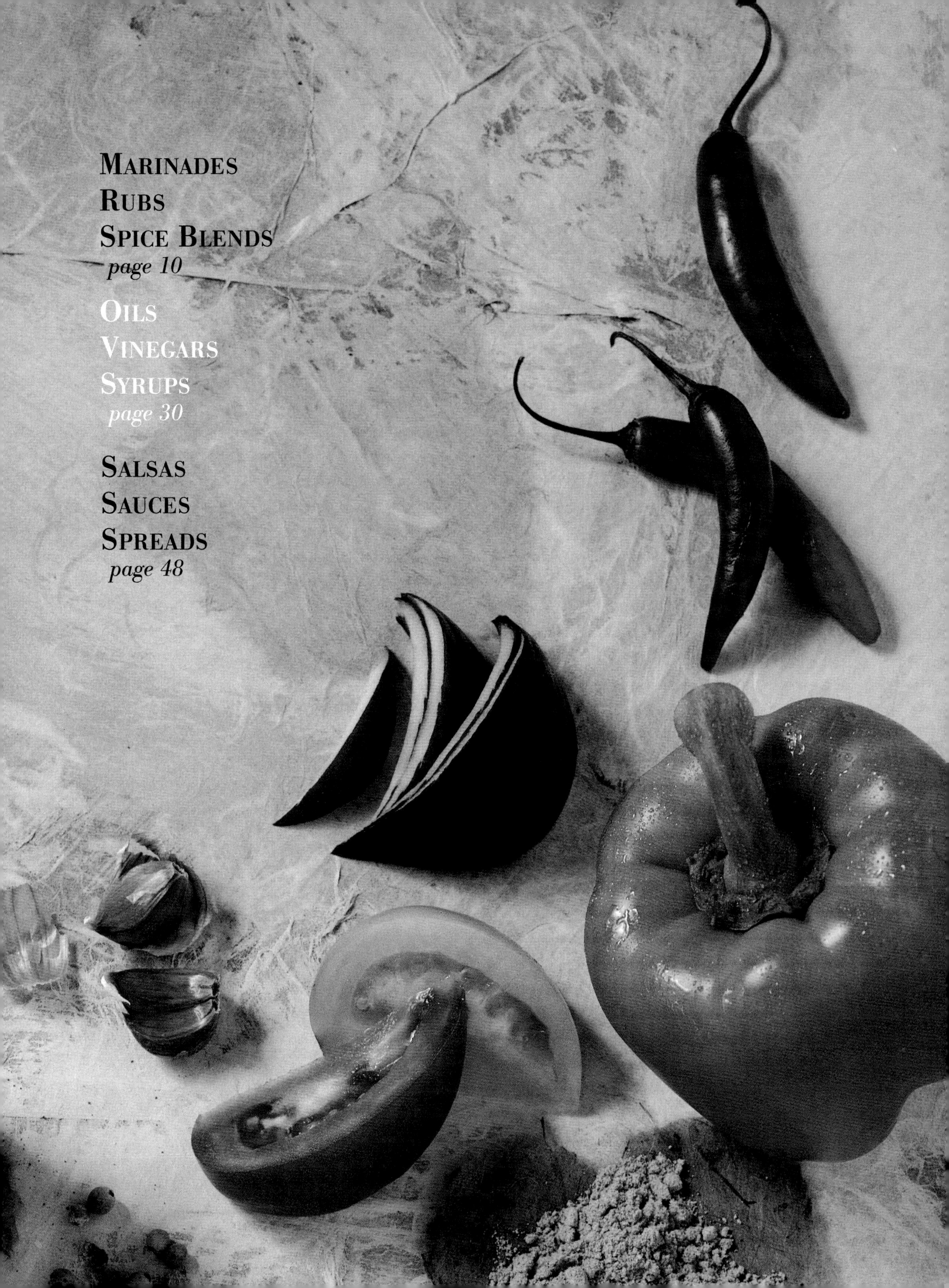

Port Wine Marinade

Lemon-Vanilla Sugar

Creole Seasoning Blend

MARINADES

For Jamaicans it's a wet jerk rub. In India, it's curry powder or garam masala. The French swear by their classic bouquet garni. And Louisiana natives stand by the fiery tabasco pepper, while Kentuckians season with a liberal splash of locally made bourbon.

Of course, those aren't all the secrets to making food taste better. Flavor sources are everywhere; take

RUBS

your pantry, for instance. Find any dried herbs, spices, horseradish, or mustards? How about the fridge—any fresh hot chiles, pungent cilantro, or juicy lemons? Congratulations. You've just found the tools for your own adventure into high-flavor cooking, all without adding a lot of fat.

SPICE BLENDS

Look over the recipes in this chapter, and you'll see that we've done the work of an Indian masalchi (someone who blends spices) for you. You'll find an array of marinades, dry spice rubs and coatings, and spice mixes, all intended for use in your own recipes or in recipes within this book.

Our personal favorite has to be Lemon-Vanilla Sugar (page 29). It's as easy to use as the sugar on your kitchen counter and twice as tasty. Use it as a replacement for regular sugar when you make tea, muffins, lemonade, or sugar cookies—delicious!

Buffalo Wings Marinade

Here's the marinade that made chicken drummettes (the tiny "drumsticks" from the wings) famous as Buffalo wings. The marinade tastes good on beef and pork, too.

½ cup canned low-sodium chicken broth, undiluted
1 tablespoon paprika
2 tablespoons fresh lime juice
1 tablespoon low-sodium soy sauce
1 tablespoon honey
1 teaspoon safflower oil
½ teaspoon salt
½ teaspoon hot sauce
¼ teaspoon ground red pepper
⅛ teaspoon black pepper

Combine all ingredients in a small bowl; stir well. Use immediately or store in refrigerator. Use to marinate chicken drummettes, chicken breasts, turkey, beef, or pork (see chart, page 19). Yield: ¾ cup.

Per Tablespoon

Calories 13	Carbohydrate 2.1 g	Cholesterol 16 mg
Fat 0.5 g (Saturated Fat 0.2 g)	Protein 0.2 g	Sodium 135 mg

Beer Marinade

Red beer actually is a medium dark beer or ale. The name comes from the reddish tint it gets from aging in redwood barrels.

1 (12-ounce) can red beer
¼ cup reduced-calorie ketchup
2 teaspoons dry mustard
¼ teaspoon salt
¼ teaspoon pepper
1 clove garlic, crushed

Combine all ingredients in a medium bowl; stir well. Use to marinate chicken or pork (see chart, page 19). Yield: 1¾ cups.

Per Tablespoon

Calories 7	Carbohydrate 0.7 g	Cholesterol 0 mg
Fat 0 g (Saturated Fat 0 g)	Protein 0.1 g	Sodium 22 mg

Citrus Marinade

- 1 teaspoon grated orange rind
- ½ cup fresh orange juice
- ⅓ cup fresh grapefruit juice
- 1 teaspoon grated lime rind
- 2 tablespoons fresh lime juice
- 2 tablespoons vegetable oil
- 2 tablespoons honey
- 1 tablespoon white wine vinegar
- 1 teaspoon white wine Worcestershire sauce
- ½ teaspoon Dijon mustard
- ¼ teaspoon ground red pepper

Combine all ingredients in a medium bowl; stir well. Use immediately or store in refrigerator. Use to marinate chicken, pork, lamb, or fish (see chart, page 19). Yield: 1⅓ cups.

Note: See Citrus-Marinated Orange Roughy with Corn Relish (page 152) and Grilled Chicken on Baby Greens (page 193).

Per Tablespoon

Calories 20	Carbohydrate 2.5 g	Cholesterol 0 mg
Fat 1.2 g (Saturated Fat 0.2 g)	Protein 0.1 g	Sodium 5 mg

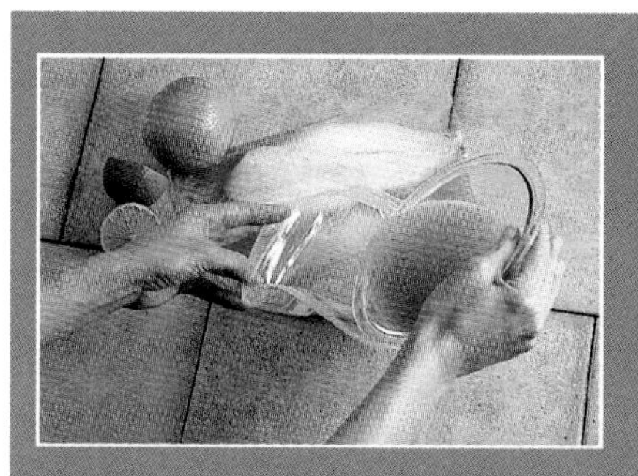

Bag the Marinade

One of the easiest ways to marinate food is in a zip-top bag. The bag takes little space in the refrigerator, and it's convenient to flip the bag over to make sure all of the food takes on the flavor. Use just enough marinade to cover the food. And remember that marinades made from acidic ingredients like vinegar, yogurt, wine, or citrus juice, as in Citrus Marinade (pictured), are good for tenderizing meat before cooking.

Curry Marinade

- ¼ cup canned no-salt-added chicken broth, undiluted
- ¼ cup low-sodium soy sauce
- 1 tablespoon curry powder
- 1 tablespoon safflower oil
- 2 teaspoons sugar
- 1 clove garlic, minced

Combine all ingredients in a medium bowl; stir well. Use immediately or store in refrigerator. Use to marinate chicken, beef, pork, or fish (see chart, page 19), or stir into cooked rice or lentils. Yield: ½ cup plus 2 tablespoons.

Per Tablespoon

Calories 21	Carbohydrate 1.3 g	Cholesterol 0 mg
Fat 1.5 g (Saturated Fat 0.1 g)	Protein 0.1 g	Sodium 156 mg

Fajita Marinade

Even if you've never eaten fajitas, you've probably heard them sizzling on platters as they're served in restaurants. Traditional fajitas, once considered Mexican peasant food, are made from marinated grilled flank steak cut into strips and rolled in tortillas.

½ cup fresh lime juice
1½ teaspoons ground cumin
1½ teaspoons pepper
6 cloves garlic, minced

Combine all ingredients in a bowl; stir well. Use immediately or store in refrigerator. Use to marinate chicken or beef (see chart, page 19). Yield: ½ cup.

Per Tablespoon

Calories 12	Carbohydrate 3.0 g	Cholesterol 0 mg
Fat 0.1 g (Saturated Fat 0 g)	Protein 0.4 g	Sodium 2 mg

Horseradish Marinade

¼ cup dry red wine
2 tablespoons minced fresh thyme
2 tablespoons low-sodium Worcestershire sauce
2 tablespoons red wine vinegar
2 tablespoons prepared horseradish
2 tablespoons tomato paste
1½ teaspoons freshly ground pepper
4 cloves garlic, minced

Combine all ingredients in a small bowl; stir well. Use to marinate beef (see chart, page 19). Yield: ¾ cup.

Per Tablespoon

Calories 11	Carbohydrate 1.5 g	Cholesterol 0 mg
Fat 0 g (Saturated Fat 0 g)	Protein 0.3 g	Sodium 70 mg

Horseradish Heat

This peppery hot root related to the familiar red radish on the produce counter can make you cry. So after you peel it, grate or shred it in a processor, if possible. Then use it quickly; the pungency lasts just a little while.

Indian Chutney Marinade

1/3 cup water
1/2 cup commercial mango chutney
1 teaspoon curry powder
1/2 teaspoon ground cardamom
1/2 teaspoon ground ginger
1/2 teaspoon ground cumin
1/4 teaspoon sugar
1/4 teaspoon pepper
1/8 teaspoon garlic powder

Combine all ingredients in container of an electric blender or food processor; cover and process until smooth, stopping once to scrape down sides. Use immediately or store in refrigerator. Use to marinate chicken, beef, pork, or lamb (see chart, page 19). Yield: 3/4 cup.

Per Tablespoon

Calories 27	Carbohydrate 6.8 g	Cholesterol 0 mg
Fat 0.1 g (Saturated Fat 0 g)	Protein 0.2 g	Sodium 21 mg

Maple-Bourbon Marinade

Add a flavor kick to breakfast by marinating low-fat sausage in this mixture one hour before cooking it.

1 cup plus 2 tablespoons maple syrup
2/3 cup bourbon
1 teaspoon coarsely ground black pepper
1/8 teaspoon ground red pepper

Combine all ingredients in a medium bowl; stir well. Use to marinate chicken, beef, or pork (see chart, page 19). Yield: 1 3/4 cups.

Per Tablespoon

Calories 34	Carbohydrate 8.6 g	Cholesterol 0 mg
Fat 0 g (Saturated Fat 0 g)	Protein 0 g	Sodium 1 mg

Mint Marinade

Spicy-sweet hoisin sauce, made from soybeans, spices, and chiles, punches up the flavor in this marinade. (We used it to marinate the lean lamb chop pictured on the next page.) Save the remaining sauce in the refrigerator to use as a basting sauce or at the table instead of ketchup with meat, poultry, or fish.

1/3 cup molasses
1/4 cup minced fresh spearmint
1 tablespoon peeled, grated gingerroot
3 tablespoons low-sodium soy sauce
3 tablespoons hoisin sauce
2 tablespoons water
2 cloves garlic, minced

Combine all ingredients in a small bowl; stir well. Use immediately or store in refrigerator. Use to marinate beef, pork, or lamb (see chart, page 19). Yield: 3/4 cup.

Per Tablespoon

Calories 31	Carbohydrate 7.5 g	Cholesterol 0 mg
Fat 0 g (Saturated Fat 0 g)	Protein 0 g	Sodium 118 mg

Molasses Marinade

1/4 cup plus 2 tablespoons molasses
2 tablespoons fresh lemon juice
2 tablespoons reduced-calorie ketchup
1 tablespoon vegetable oil
1 1/4 teaspoons dried crushed red pepper
1/2 teaspoon ground cumin
1/4 teaspoon salt
2 cloves garlic, minced

Combine all ingredients in a small bowl; stir well. Use to marinate chicken or pork (see chart, page 19). Yield: 3/4 cup.

Per Tablespoon

Calories 34	Carbohydrate 7.6 g	Cholesterol 0 mg
Fat 1.2 g (Saturated Fat 0.2 g)	Protein 0.1 g	Sodium 54 mg

Mint Marinade

Great Thai

Thai restaurants, barbecue, salads, stir-fries, and more have reached new levels of popularity. But if you're wondering what kind of flavor you'll get when eating Thai, think of hot (from pungent little chile peppers), curry, and saucy Oriental mixtures of meat and vegetables. Not all Thai food is hot, but it's all flavorful.

Thai-Style Marinade

- ½ cup firmly packed brown sugar
- ½ cup finely chopped green onions
- ½ cup low-sodium soy sauce
- 2 tablespoons white wine vinegar
- 1 teaspoon dried crushed red pepper
- ½ teaspoon ground ginger
- 12 cloves garlic, halved

Combine all ingredients in a small bowl; stir well. Use to marinate beef or fish (see chart, next page). Yield: 1 cup plus 1 tablespoon.

Per Tablespoon

Calories 32	Carbohydrate 7.3 g	Cholesterol 0 mg
Fat 0 g (Saturated Fat 0 g)	Protein 0.2 g	Sodium 187 mg

Red Wine-Mustard Marinade

- ½ cup dry red wine
- ¼ cup finely chopped shallot
- 3 tablespoons green peppercorn mustard with white wine
- 1 tablespoon freshly ground pepper
- 1 tablespoon balsamic vinegar
- 1½ teaspoons chopped fresh rosemary
- 1 large clove garlic, minced

Combine all ingredients in a small bowl; stir well. Use to marinate beef, pork, or lamb (see chart, next page). Yield: 1 cup.

Per Tablespoon

Calories 12	Carbohydrate 1.1 g	Cholesterol 0 mg
Fat 0 g (Saturated Fat 0 g)	Protein 0.2 g	Sodium 29 mg

Port Wine Marinade

- ½ cup port wine
- 1 tablespoon chopped fresh thyme
- 3 tablespoons low-sodium soy sauce
- ½ teaspoon pepper
- ½ teaspoon hot sauce
- ¼ teaspoon salt
- 1 clove garlic, halved
- 1 bay leaf

Combine all ingredients in a small bowl; stir well. Use to marinate beef, pork, or lamb (see chart, below). Yield: ¾ cup.

Per Tablespoon
Calories 3
Fat 0 g (Saturated Fat 0 g)
Carbohydrate 0.4 g
Protein 0.1 g
Cholesterol 0 mg
Sodium 148 mg

Marinating Made Easy

Need help deciding the best meat, poultry, or fish to pair with a particular marinade? Just use the chart below as a guide. But be sure to follow the recommended marinating times. Some meats require longer than others to absorb the flavor, while overmarinating causes other meats to become soft and mushy.

Recipe	Poultry	Beef	Pork	Lamb	Fish
Buffalo Wings Marinade	8 hrs	8 hrs	8 hrs		
Beer Marinade	2 hrs		8 hrs		
Citrus Marinade	2 hrs		2 hrs	2 hrs	1hr
Curry Marinade	8 hrs	8 hrs	8 hrs		1hr
Fajita Marinade	2 hrs	8 hrs			
Horseradish Marinade		8 hrs			
Indian Chutney Marinade	2 hrs	8 hrs	8 hrs	8 hrs	
Maple-Bourbon Marinade	2 hrs	8 hrs	8 hrs		
Mint Marinade		8 hrs	8 hrs	8 hrs	
Molasses Marinade	2 hrs		8 hrs		
Thai-Style Marinade		8 hrs			1hr
Red Wine-Mustard Marinade		8 hrs	8 hrs	8 hrs	
Port Wine Marinade		8 hrs	8hrs	8 hrs	

Herbed Pepper Rub

Wet Jerk Rub

- 4 cups coarsely chopped green onions
- 1/4 cup fresh thyme leaves
- 3 tablespoons peeled, grated gingerroot
- 1 tablespoon freshly ground pepper
- 1 tablespoon freshly ground coriander seeds
- 2 tablespoons vegetable oil
- 2 tablespoons fresh lime juice
- 2 teaspoons salt
- 2 teaspoons freshly ground allspice
- 1 teaspoon freshly ground nutmeg
- 1 teaspoon ground cinnamon
- 5 cloves garlic, peeled and halved
- 3 bay leaves
- 1 to 2 habañero peppers, halved and seeded

Position knife blade in food processor bowl; add all ingredients and process until smooth, scraping sides of bowl once. Use 1 to 2 tablespoons to rub or brush onto chicken or fish before grilling. Yield: 1 1/2 cups.

Note: See Hickory-Grilled Jerk Chicken (page 143).

Per Tablespoon

Calories 22	Carbohydrate 2.7 g	Cholesterol 0 mg
Fat 1.3 g (Saturated Fat 0.3 g)	Protein 0.5 g	Sodium 199 mg

What's a JERK?

Forget your ex-boyfriend and think Jamaica, because that's where you'll find the original jerk. It's the term for a style of barbecue that includes marinating the meat in a green pesto-like mixture of herbs, spices, and the hottest peppers in the world. A little oil and lime juice make it a sauce-like "wet rub."

For the most flavor, use freshly ground spices. (You can grind whole allspice and nutmeg in a coffee grinder.) For an authentic flavor, use potent Scotch Bonnet or habañero peppers, and cook the meat over a fire flavored with wood chips.

Herbed Pepper Rub

- 2 tablespoons coarsely ground pepper
- 1 tablespoon dried Italian seasoning
- 1 teaspoon dry mustard
- 1/2 teaspoon garlic powder
- 1/4 teaspoon salt

Combine all ingredients in a small bowl; stir well. Use to rub onto beef or pork before cooking. Yield: 1/4 cup.

Per Tablespoon

Calories 16	Carbohydrate 3.5 g	Cholesterol 0 mg
Fat 0.4 g (Saturated Fat 0.9 g)	Protein 0.7 g	Sodium 149 mg

Here's the Rub

Most meats benefit from a good rub. A dry one, such as Paprika Rub (pictured), is simply a blend of spices rubbed onto uncooked meat to season it. The rub often is left on the meat for a while before cooking to allow the flavors to penetrate. The longer you leave the rub on before cooking, the more flavor you'll get.

Paprika Rub

It can be sweet or hot, but Hungarian paprika is thought to be the best. Regular paprika can be used instead.

1½ teaspoons dried thyme
1 teaspoon dried oregano
1 teaspoon dried rosemary, crushed
2 teaspoons sweet Hungarian paprika
¼ teaspoon salt
¼ teaspoon ground white pepper
¼ teaspoon freshly ground black pepper
⅛ teaspoon ground red pepper
2 large cloves garlic, minced
1 teaspoon olive oil

Combine dried herbs, spices, garlic, and olive oil in a small bowl; stir well. Rub mixture onto chicken, beef, or pork before cooking. Yield: 3 tablespoons.

Per Tablespoon

Calories 27	Carbohydrate 2.8 g	Cholesterol 0 mg
Fat 1.9 g (Saturated Fat 0.3 g)	Protein 0.5 g	Sodium 197 mg

Garlic Herb Paste

A mortar and pestle will help you grind these ingredients into a smooth paste. Crush the dried herbs first; then add the remaining ingredients. If you don't have a mortar and pestle, mash them together with a fork on a cutting board or other smooth surface.

2 teaspoons dried thyme
1 teaspoon dried rosemary, crushed
1 teaspoon pepper
½ teaspoon salt
6 cloves garlic, minced

Combine all ingredients in a small bowl; mash into a smooth paste. Use to rub onto chicken, beef, pork, or lamb before cooking. Yield: 3 tablespoons.

Per Tablespoon

Calories 22	Carbohydrate 4.9 g	Cholesterol 0 mg
Fat 0.3 g (Saturated Fat 0 g)	Protein 0.8 g	Sodium 589 mg

Creole Seasoning Blend

1½ tablespoons garlic powder
1½ tablespoons dried basil
1½ tablespoons dried parsley flakes
1 tablespoon onion powder
2½ teaspoons paprika
2 teaspoons dry mustard
1 teaspoon ground red pepper
½ teaspoon freshly ground black pepper

Combine all ingredients in a small bowl; stir well. Store in an airtight container; shake well before each use. Use to season chicken, fish, salad dressings, dips, or vegetables. Yield: ½ cup.

Per Tablespoon

Calories 16	Carbohydrate 3.0 g	Cholesterol 0 mg
Fat 0.4 g (Saturated Fat 0 g)	Protein 0.8 g	Sodium 2 mg

Cajun Seasoning Blend

2 teaspoons dried basil
2 teaspoons crushed black peppercorns
1 teaspoon ground white pepper
1 teaspoon cumin seeds, crushed
1 teaspoon caraway seeds, crushed
1 teaspoon fennel seeds, crushed
1 teaspoon dried thyme
1 teaspoon dried oregano
½ teaspoon salt
½ teaspoon dried crushed red pepper
2 teaspoons paprika

Combine first 10 ingredients in a small skillet; place over medium-high heat. Cook 3 minutes or until seeds are lightly browned. Remove from heat; stir in paprika. Store in an airtight container; shake well before each use. Use to coat chicken, beef, pork, or fish, or sprinkle over grilled corn or baked potatoes. Yield: ¼ cup.

Note: See Cajun-Blackened Swordfish Steaks (page 153).

Per Tablespoon

Calories 17	Carbohydrate 3.4 g	Cholesterol 0 mg
Fat 0.6 g (Saturated Fat 0 g)	Protein 0.8 g	Sodium 296 mg

A Toast You'll Love

Toasting seeds and other dried spices is another no-fat way to bring extra flavor to recipes. All it requires is a hot skillet (no oil), seasonings, and constant stirring for just a few minutes.

Curry Seasoning Blend

Curry powder is a blend of a few or many spices, some of the standard ones being cumin, ginger, coriander, chiles, and turmeric (the source of the yellow color).

2 tablespoons ground ginger
1 tablespoon plus 2 teaspoons ground coriander
1 tablespoon plus 2 teaspoons ground turmeric
1 tablespoon plus 1 teaspoon ground cumin
2 teaspoons pepper
1 teaspoon ground cardamom
1 teaspoon ground fenugreek

Combine all ingredients in a small bowl; stir well. Store mixture in an airtight container; shake well before each use. Use to season chicken, beef, pork, lamb, fish, or shrimp, or stir into lentils or rice. Yield: ½ cup.

Note: See Seared Salmon Steaks (page 152).

Per Tablespoon
Calories 18 | Carbohydrate 3.3 g | Cholesterol 0 mg
Fat 0.5 g (Saturated Fat 0.1 g) | Protein 0.7 g | Sodium 4 mg

Fenugreek for Flavor

Bittersweet ground fenugreek (pronounced like it looks) is one of the seasonings often used in curry powder mixes. The pebbly seed makes a good addition to salads.

Italian Seasoning Blend

⅓ cup dried oregano
¼ cup dried basil
¼ cup dried parsley flakes
3 tablespoons rubbed sage
1 tablespoon garlic powder
1 teaspoon dried rosemary
½ teaspoon salt

Combine all ingredients in a small bowl; stir well. Store in an airtight container; shake well before each use. Use to season chicken, corn, tomatoes, tomato sauce, pizza, bread, or popcorn. Yield: 1 cup.

Per Tablespoon
Calories 11 | Carbohydrate 2.3 g | Cholesterol 0 mg
Fat 0.3 g (Saturated Fat 0 g) | Protein 0.5 g | Sodium 75 mg

Mexican Seasoning Blend

½ cup chili powder
¼ cup paprika
2 tablespoons ground cumin
2 teaspoons garlic powder
1 teaspoon ground red pepper
½ teaspoon salt

Combine all ingredients in a small bowl; stir well. Store in an airtight container; shake well before each use. Use to season chicken or turkey. Yield: 1 cup.

Note: See Chicken Enchiladas (page 139) and Mesquite-Smoked Turkey Breast (page 149).

Per Tablespoon

Calories 21	Carbohydrate 3.7 g	Cholesterol 0 mg
Fat 1.0 g (Saturated Fat 0.2 g)	Protein 0.9 g	Sodium 113 mg

Garam Masala

3 tablespoons cumin seeds
2 tablespoons coriander seeds
1 tablespoon cardamom seeds
1 tablespoon peppercorns
1½ teaspoons whole cloves
2 (3-inch) cinnamon sticks, crushed
3 bay leaves, crumbled
1½ teaspoons ground mace

Combine first 7 ingredients in a small skillet. Cook over medium-high heat 3 minutes or until seeds are lightly browned, stirring frequently. Remove from heat; let cool completely.

Place mixture in container of an electric blender or food processor; cover and process until ground. Stir in mace. Store in an airtight container. Stir well before each use. Use in Indian dishes, pilafs, and meat dishes. Yield: ½ cup.

Per Teaspoon

Calories 13	Carbohydrate 2.3 g	Cholesterol 0 mg
Fat 0.6 g (Saturated Fat 0 g)	Protein 0.5 g	Sodium 3 mg

Indian Hot Spice

A traditional Indian spice blend is garam masala, which means "hot spice mixture." Cumin, coriander, cardamom, and black pepper form the base of most garam masalas, but many other spices are included according to the dish they will season.

Chili or Chile?

If you're talking spice powders, there's a big difference. Chili powder is a blend of many spices like salt, oregano, and powdered pure red chile pepper. Chile powder is just that—pulverized dried red chiles.

Mixed Herb Coating

- 1 cup plus 2 tablespoons corn flake crumbs
- 2 tablespoons paprika
- 2 teaspoons sugar
- 2 teaspoons dried oregano
- 2 teaspoons dried thyme
- 2 teaspoons dried rosemary, crushed
- 2 teaspoons garlic powder
- ½ teaspoon salt
- ½ teaspoon ground white pepper
- ½ teaspoon ground red pepper

Combine all ingredients in a medium bowl; stir well. Store in an airtight container; shake well before each use. Use as a coating mix for chicken, turkey, pork, or lamb. Yield: 1½ cups.

Per Tablespoon

Calories 19	Carbohydrate 4.3 g	Cholesterol 0 mg
Fat 0.2 g (Saturated Fat 0 g)	Protein 0.5 g	Sodium 84 mg

Southwest Spice Coating

Vary the heat in this coating mix by using mild, medium, or hot chile powder.

- ⅔ cup yellow cornmeal
- ¼ cup crushed no-oil baked tortilla chips
- ¼ cup grated Parmesan cheese
- 1 tablespoon plus 1 teaspoon garlic powder
- 1 tablespoon plus 1 teaspoon ground red chile powder
- 1 tablespoon plus 1 teaspoon ground cumin
- 1 teaspoon sugar
- ½ teaspoon ground red pepper

Combine all ingredients in a medium bowl; stir well. Store in an airtight container in refrigerator; shake well before each use. Use as a coating mix for chicken, turkey, pork, or fish. Yield: 1¼ cups.

Per Tablespoon

Calories 38	Carbohydrate 7.1 g	Cholesterol 1 mg
Fat 0.7 g (Saturated Fat 0.2 g)	Protein 1.8 g	Sodium 25 mg

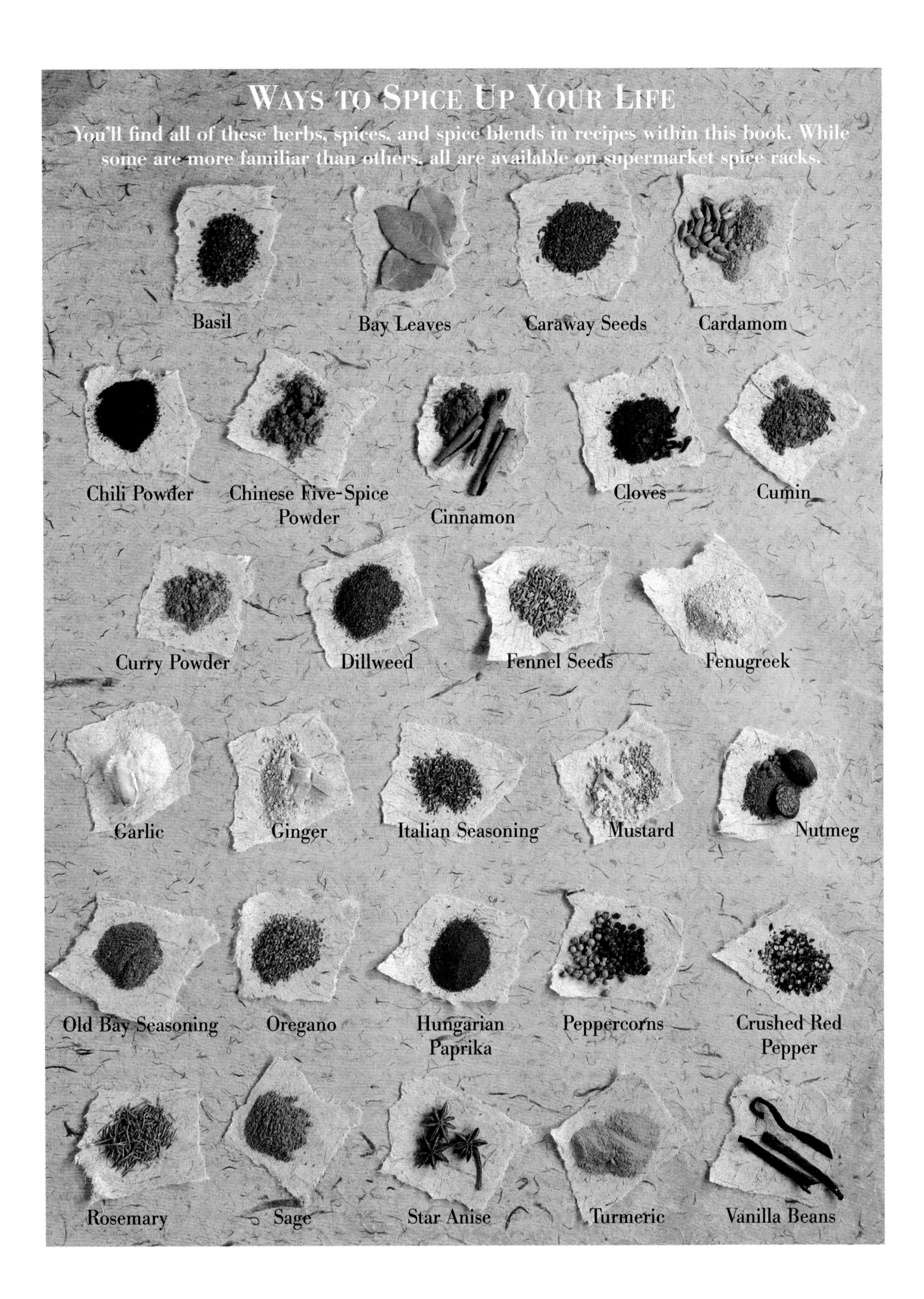
WAYS TO SPICE UP YOUR LIFE
You'll find all of these herbs, spices, and spice blends in recipes within this book. While some are more familiar than others, all are available on supermarket spice racks.
Basil
Bay Leaves
Caraway Seeds
Cardamom
Chili Powder
Chinese Five-Spice Powder
Cinnamon
Cloves
Cumin
Curry Powder
Dillweed
Fennel Seeds
Fenugreek
Garlic
Ginger
Italian Seasoning
Mustard
Nutmeg
Old Bay Seasoning
Oregano
Hungarian Paprika
Peppercorns
Crushed Red Pepper
Rosemary
Sage
Star Anise
Turmeric
Vanilla Beans

Bouquet Garni

Make several bouquet garnis, and freeze them in heavy-duty, zip-top plastic bags to keep an easy seasoning on hand. The flavor will stay fresh for up to one month.

Bag the Herbs

Wrap dried herbs in cheesecloth, or tie fresh herbs together to make bouquet garni, a seasoning generally made of thyme, parsley, and bay leaves. It's most often tossed into simmering broths, stews, or soups.

1 tablespoon fresh marjoram leaves
1 tablespoon fresh thyme leaves
1 tablespoon fresh oregano leaves
1½ teaspoons fresh whole sage leaves
1½ teaspoons fresh rosemary
3 cloves garlic, peeled and slightly crushed
2 bay leaves, halved

Combine all ingredients on an 8-inch square of cheesecloth; tie ends of cheesecloth securely. Add bouquet garni to soups, stews, or vegetables cooked in a small amount of water. Yield: one bouquet garni.

Per Bouquet Garni

Calories 31	Carbohydrate 6.8 g	Cholesterol 0 mg
Fat 0.6 g (Saturated Fat 0.2 g)	Protein 1.1 g	Sodium 3 mg

Gingered Cinnamon Sugar

1 (2.7-ounce) jar crystallized ginger
1 cup sugar
1 cup firmly packed brown sugar
1 tablespoon plus 2 teaspoons ground cinnamon

Position knife blade in food processor bowl; add all ingredients. Process 1 minute or until mixture is a fine powder. Store in an airtight container in a cool, dark place; shake well before each use. Sprinkle on cinnamon toast or French toast or over hot cereal, bananas, broiled grapefruit, baked apples, or pears; stir into low-fat or nonfat yogurt or sweet roll fillings. Yield: 2 cups.

Per Tablespoon

Calories 59	Carbohydrate 15.3 g	Cholesterol 0 mg
Fat 0 g (Saturated Fat 0 g)	Protein 0 g	Sodium 4 mg

Lemon-Vanilla Sugar

Look for vanilla beans in jars on spice racks in most supermarkets. Don't be surprised if there are only a couple of beans in each jar.

2 cups sugar
2 tablespoons grated lemon rind
1 (4-inch) vanilla bean, split lengthwise

Combine sugar and lemon rind in a bowl. Scrape vanilla bean seeds into sugar mixture; stir well. Store in an airtight container in refrigerator; stir well before each use. Stir into lemonade or hot tea, or use as a substitute for sugar in a favorite bread recipe. Yield: 2½ cups.

Note: See Lemon-Lime Cake (page 207) and Lemon 'n' Spice Apple Pie (page 212).

Per Tablespoon

Calories 39	Carbohydrate 10.0 g	Cholesterol 0 mg
Fat 0 g (Saturated Fat 0 g)	Protein 0 g	Sodium 0 mg

Not Just Plain Vanilla

Use the whole vanilla bean or a few drops of extract to enhance the flavor of almost any food. Here's how:

•Simmer a bean in the water with pasta or rice.
•Split a bean and add it to a bottle of olive oil to use (in small amounts) to sauté meats.
•Add extract to citrus-based salads to cut the sharp flavor.
•Stir it into recipes for vegetables, salad dressings, fish, poultry, and game to enhance the sweetness.

Mexican Mocha Spice Mix

2 cups unsweetened cocoa
1¾ cups sugar
¼ cup instant espresso powder
2 teaspoons ground cinnamon
1 teaspoon freshly grated nutmeg

Combine all ingredients in a large bowl; stir well. Store in an airtight container; shake well before each use. Use in mole sauce or stir into cake batters. Also, substitute for cocoa in chocolate pudding recipes, or use to make hot cocoa. Yield: 3½ cups.

Note: See Mocha-Cinnamon Cocoa (page 89) and Mexican Mocha Angel Food Cake (page 210).

Per Tablespoon

Calories 39	Carbohydrate 7.8 g	Cholesterol 0 mg
Fat 0.4 g (Saturated Fat 0.3 g)	Protein 1.0 g	Sodium 2 mg

Hot Thai Oil
Spiced Vinegar
Fresh Strawberry Syrup

OILS

Oils? In a low-fat cookbook! We thought recipes for flavored oils might cause a few raised eyebrows, but hear us out. In many low-fat recipes, you already use a little oil to sauté vegetables or to make vinaigrettes. So if you're going to use oil, why not use ones with the most powerful flavor—and make a little go a long way?

VINEGARS

These days there are lots of flavored oils, vinegars, and syrups available in stores, but you can make your own for a fraction of the cost. You won't believe the flavor you get by brushing a little of our jalapeño-spiked Spicy Southwest Chile Oil (page 33) on a slice

SYRUPS

of French bread and toasting it. Infused vinegars add a crisp, fresh flavor that your friends and family will love. Our foods staff certainly did at our annual Christmas party. When we played our traditional "Dirty Santa" game (where we opened gifts one at a time and then traded for any previously opened gift), everyone kept swapping for the bottle of tarragon vinegar made by Kate Matuszak, one of the editors of this book.

Homemade oils, vinegars, syrups, and liqueurs are also great ways to decorate. To impress a guest, just pull the jewel-toned bottles from their cool, dark storage places and line the counter to get a real "cook's kitchen" look.

Sun-Dried Tomato-Garlic Oil

Brush this oil on French bread slices, and then top them with diced tomato and Parmesan cheese. After placing the slices under the broiler for a minute or two, you'll have something better than plain garlic bread to serve with dinner.

8 large cloves garlic, halved
2 large cloves garlic
¼ cup white vinegar
20 sun-dried tomatoes, divided
2 cups extra virgin olive oil, divided
¼ teaspoon kosher salt

Combine halved garlic, whole cloves, and vinegar in a small glass bowl; cover and refrigerate at least 8 hours. Drain garlic, discarding vinegar; rinse and pat dry with paper towels. Set aside.

Cook tomatoes in boiling water to cover 2 minutes; drain well, and pat dry with paper towels.

Combine garlic halves, 15 tomatoes, 1 cup olive oil, and salt in container of an electric blender; cover and process until mixture is minced, stopping once to scrape down sides. Pour tomato mixture into a jar; add remaining 1 cup olive oil. Cover and refrigerate 24 hours.

Let oil stand at room temperature 2 hours. Pour mixture through a wire-mesh strainer lined with 2 layers of cheesecloth into a decorative bottle or jar, discarding solids. Thread 2 cloves garlic and remaining 5 tomatoes on a small wooden skewer; add to jar. Seal bottle with a cork or an airtight lid. Store in refrigerator up to 1 month.

Use in fresh tomato sauces, salad dressings, and marinades for beef; toss with pasta; or brush on bread cubes to toast for croutons. Yield: 1½ cups.

Note: See Vermicelli with Tomatoes and Fresh Herbs (page 113).

Per Teaspoon

Calories 50	Carbohydrate 0.3 g	Cholesterol 0 mg
Fat 5.5 g (Saturated Fat 0.8 g)	Protein 0.1 g	Sodium 13 mg

Garlic Warning

Combining fresh garlic (or any food grown in soil) and oil to make flavored oils can encourage the growth of botulin if you don't take precautions. To kill botulin spores, soak garlic in vinegar before combining with the oil, as we did in these recipes. For safekeeping, store the oils in the refrigerator.

Spicy Southwest Chile Oil

Pour this oil into a decorative bottle you can find at antique or flea markets or import stores, and then add chiles and a cork for a spicy gift.

4 cloves garlic
2 tablespoons white vinegar
1 jalapeño pepper
1 tablespoon coriander seeds
2 teaspoons cumin seeds
2 teaspoons dried oregano
2 cups extra virgin olive oil, divided
2 green chile peppers, cut in half
2 red chile peppers, cut in half

Combine garlic and vinegar in a small glass bowl; cover and refrigerate at least 8 hours. Drain garlic, discarding vinegar; rinse and pat dry with paper towels. Set garlic aside.

Remove stem from jalapeño pepper. Set pepper aside.

Heat a large skillet over medium heat 2 minutes; add coriander and cumin seeds. Cook, stirring constantly, 5 minutes or until lightly browned.

Transfer browned seeds to container of an electric blender; add garlic, jalapeño pepper, oregano, and 1 cup oil. Cover and process until minced, stopping once to scrape down sides. Pour mixture into a jar; add remaining 1 cup oil. Cover and refrigerate 24 hours.

Let oil stand at room temperature 2 hours. Pour mixture through a wire-mesh strainer lined with 2 layers of cheesecloth into a decorative bottle or jar, discarding solids. Add chiles. Seal bottle with a cork or an airtight lid. Store in refrigerator up to 1 month.

Use in salsas, fajitas, beans, and marinades for fish; or brush on vegetables before roasting. Yield: 1½ cups.

Note: See Thai Barbecue Beef Salad (page 192).

Per Teaspoon

Calories 54	Carbohydrate 0.1 g	Cholesterol 0 mg
Fat 6.0 g (Saturated Fat 0.8 g)	Protein 0 g	Sodium 0 mg

Hot Thai Oil

4 cloves garlic, halved
2 tablespoons white vinegar
2 tablespoons dried crushed red pepper
2 tablespoons peeled, minced gingerroot
12 (½-inch) strips tangerine rind, divided
2 cups peanut oil, divided
1 teaspoon dark sesame oil
2 dried red chile peppers

Combine garlic and vinegar in a small glass bowl; cover and refrigerate at least 8 hours. Drain garlic, discarding vinegar; rinse and pat dry with paper towels.

Combine garlic, crushed red pepper, gingerroot, 8 tangerine strips, and 1½ cups peanut oil in container of an electric blender; cover and process until minced, stopping once to scrape down sides. Pour mixture into a jar; add remaining ½ cup peanut oil and sesame oil. Cover and refrigerate 24 hours.

Let oil stand at room temperature 2 hours. Pour mixture through a wire-mesh strainer lined with 2 layers of cheesecloth into a decorative bottle or jar, discarding solids. Add remaining tangerine strips and red chiles. Seal bottle with a cork or an airtight lid. Store in refrigerator up to 1 month.

Use in marinades for beef and pork and in vinaigrettes; or brush on bread cubes to toast for croutons. Yield: 1½ cups.

Per Teaspoon

Calories 55	Carbohydrate 0.2 g	Cholesterol 0 mg
Fat 6.1 g (Saturated Fat 1.0 g)	Protein 0 g	Sodium 1 mg

Peppered Citrus Oil

2 tablespoons white peppercorns
8 (4- x ½-inch) strips lemon rind
4 bay leaves
¼ teaspoon kosher salt
2 cups extra virgin olive oil, divided
4 (4- x ¼-inch) strips lemon rind
2 or 3 bay leaves
1 tablespoon white peppercorns

Combine 2 tablespoons peppercorns, 8 lemon rind strips, 4 bay leaves, salt, and 1½ cups oil in container of an electric blender;

cover and process until rind is minced, stopping once to scrape down sides. Pour mixture into a jar; add remaining ½ cup oil. Cover and refrigerate 24 hours.

Curl 4 lemon rind strips tightly around a pencil; wrap with plastic wrap and refrigerate.

Let oil stand at room temperature 2 hours. Pour mixture through a wire-mesh strainer lined with 2 layers of cheesecloth into a decorative bottle or jar, discarding solids. Remove lemon rind curls from pencil; add to bottle. Add 2 or 3 bay leaves and peppercorns to bottle. Seal bottle with a cork or an airtight lid. Store in refrigerator up to 1 month.

Use in marinades for poultry and beef and in vinaigrettes or salad dressings; or brush on fish before cooking. Yield: 1½ cups.

Per Teaspoon

Calories 54	Carbohydrate 0.2 g	Cholesterol 0 mg
Fat 6.0 g (Saturated Fat 0.8 g)	Protein 0 g	Sodium 8 mg

Which Olive Oil?
The best oil comes from the first pressing of the olives and is labeled extra virgin. It generally has the deepest color and is the least acidic, most flavorful, and most expensive. The more the olives are pressed, the lighter the color, the greater the acidity, and the less you pay for the oil. Virgin olive oil comes from a later pressing. Use the most expensive type where you taste it most—in dressings or vinaigrettes. Other types work fine in cooked sauces.

Raspberry Vinegar

1 cup fresh raspberries
1¼ cups white wine vinegar
Additional fresh raspberries (optional)

Place 1 cup raspberries in a wide-mouth pint glass jar, and set aside. Pour vinegar into a nonaluminum saucepan; bring to a boil. Pour hot vinegar over raspberries in jar; cover with lid. Let stand at room temperature 2 weeks.

Pour mixture through a wire-mesh strainer lined with 2 layers of cheesecloth into a decorative bottle or jar, discarding raspberries. Add additional fresh raspberries, if desired. Seal bottle with a cork or an airtight lid.

Use in vinaigrettes and marinades, or serve over salad greens or fruit salads. Yield: 1¼ cups.

Per Tablespoon

Calories 3	Carbohydrate 0.2 g	Cholesterol 0 mg
Fat 0 g (Saturated Fat 0 g)	Protein 0 g	Sodium 2 mg

Vinegar Variations

Making your own flavored vinegar is as simple as pouring commercial vinegar over your favorite berries, herbs, or spices and storing the mixture for about 10 days. If you feel creative (or if you have an herb garden), use one of the herbed vinegar recipes on these pages and substitute the same amount of your favorite herb for the herb called for in the recipe.

The vinegar doesn't have to be heated when you pour it over the herbs, but when we made the vinegars in our kitchens, the final product was clearer when we used heated vinegar.

For flavor and color variations, pour cider, red wine, white wine, or champagne vinegar over the herbs.

Citrus Vinegar

10 (4-inch) strips orange rind
½ medium orange, peeled and sectioned
½ small grapefruit, peeled and sectioned
4 cups white wine vinegar

Combine first 3 ingredients in a wide-mouth quart glass jar; set aside.

Pour vinegar into a nonaluminum saucepan; bring to a boil. Pour hot vinegar over fruit and rind in jar; cover with lid. Let stand at room temperature 2 weeks.

Pour mixture through a wire-mesh strainer lined with 2 layers of cheesecloth into decorative bottles or jars, discarding fruit. Seal bottles with corks or airtight lids.

Use in vinaigrettes and in fruit or vegetable salads. Yield: 4 cups.

Per Tablespoon

Calories 2	Carbohydrate 0 g	Cholesterol 0 mg
Fat 0 g (Saturated Fat 0 g)	Protein 0 g	Sodium 2 mg

Spiced Vinegar

1 tablespoon whole cloves
1 tablespoon whole allspice
1 tablespoon black peppercorns
1 (2-inch) stick cinnamon
1 teaspoon cardamom seeds
1 whole nutmeg, cracked
4 cups red wine vinegar

Combine first 6 ingredients in a wide-mouth quart glass jar, and set aside. Pour vinegar into a nonaluminum saucepan; bring to a boil. Pour hot vinegar over spices in jar; cover with lid. Let stand at room temperature 2 weeks.

Pour mixture through a wire-mesh strainer lined with 2 layers of cheesecloth into decorative bottles or jars, discarding spices. Seal bottles with corks or airtight lids.

Use in vinaigrettes and in fruit or vegetable salads. Yield: 4 cups.

Per Tablespoon

Calories 3	Carbohydrate 0.7 g	Cholesterol 0 mg
Fat 0 g (Saturated Fat 0 g)	Protein 0 g	Sodium 0 mg

Mixed Herb Vinegar
Spiced Vinegar
Citrus Vinegar

How to Store Oils and Vinegars

Store flavored vinegars in sterilized glass bottles with airtight, nonmetallic lids in a cool, dark place. Store flavored oils in airtight bottles (the darker the better) in a cool, dark place or in the refrigerator. Oils flavored with garlic, herbs, or anything else that grows in the soil should be kept in the refrigerator. Some oils solidify when chilled, but they'll return to normal when allowed to come to room temperature. Oils become rancid quickly, so discard any that develop an off-flavor.

FRESH MINT VINEGAR

1 cup chopped fresh mint
2 cups white wine vinegar

Place mint in a wide-mouth pint glass jar, and set aside. Pour vinegar into a nonaluminum saucepan; bring to a boil. Pour hot vinegar over mint in jar and cover with lid. Let stand at room temperature 2 weeks.

Pour mixture through a wire-mesh strainer lined with 2 layers of cheesecloth into a decorative bottle or jar, discarding mint. Seal bottle with a cork or an airtight lid.

Use in vinaigrettes and in fruit or vegetable salads. Yield: 2 cups.

Per Tablespoon

Calories 2	Carbohydrate 0 g	Cholesterol 0 mg
Fat 0 g (Saturated Fat 0 g)	Protein 0 g	Sodium 1 mg

ITALIAN HERB VINEGAR

½ cup chopped fresh oregano
¼ cup chopped fresh rosemary
¼ cup chopped fresh basil
2 tablespoons chopped fresh sage
1 tablespoon chopped fresh parsley
1 tablespoon peppercorns
1 clove garlic, crushed
4 cups red wine vinegar
Additional sprigs of rosemary, basil, or sage (optional)

Combine first 7 ingredients in a wide-mouth quart glass jar, and set aside. Pour vinegar into a nonaluminum saucepan; bring to a boil. Pour hot vinegar over herbs in jar; cover with lid. Let stand at room temperature 2 weeks.

Pour mixture through a wire-mesh strainer lined with 2 layers of cheesecloth into decorative bottles or jars, discarding herbs. Add additional sprigs of rosemary, basil, or sage, if desired. Seal bottles with corks or airtight lids.

Use in vinaigrettes, marinades, or vegetable salads. Yield: 4 cups.

Per Tablespoon

Calories 2	Carbohydrate 0.5 g	Cholesterol 0 mg
Fat 0 g (Saturated Fat 0 g)	Protein 0 g	Sodium 0 mg

Mixed Herb Vinegar

½ cup chopped fresh thyme
¼ cup chopped fresh parsley
¼ cup chopped fresh rosemary
¼ cup chopped fresh sage
4 green onions, thinly sliced
1 clove garlic, crushed
9 peppercorns
3¾ cups white wine vinegar
Additional sprigs of thyme, rosemary, or sage (optional)

Combine first 7 ingredients in a wide-mouth quart glass jar, and set aside. Pour vinegar into a nonaluminum saucepan; bring to a boil. Pour hot vinegar over herbs in jar; cover with lid. Let stand at room temperature 2 weeks.

Pour mixture through a wire-mesh strainer lined with 2 layers of cheesecloth into decorative bottles or jars, discarding herbs. Add additional sprigs of thyme, rosemary, or sage, if desired. Seal bottles with corks or airtight lids.

Use in vinaigrettes, vegetable salads, soups, or stews. Yield: 3¾ cups.

Per Tablespoon

Calories 2	Carbohydrate 0 g	Cholesterol 0 mg
Fat 0 g (Saturated Fat 0 g)	Protein 0 g	Sodium 2 mg

Sesame Vinaigrette

2 tablespoons toasted sesame seeds
3 tablespoons low-sodium soy sauce
1 tablespoon plus 2 teaspoons white wine vinegar
1 tablespoon plus 1 teaspoon sesame oil

Combine all ingredients in a jar. Cover tightly, and shake vigorously. Cover and chill thoroughly; shake well before serving. Serve with sweet red peppers, green beans, or salad greens; or use in marinades for poultry or fish. Yield: ½ cup.

Per Tablespoon

Calories 33	Carbohydrate 0.2 g	Cholesterol 0 mg
Fat 3.2 g (Saturated Fat 0.5 g)	Protein 0.5 g	Sodium 147 mg

Why Balsamic's Best

Balsamic vinegar, made from the reduced juice of sweet grapes, is sweeter and more full-flavored than other vinegars. Like wine, it is aged in wooden barrels for several years to develop the flavor. And as with any fine, aged wine, it's expensive.

Chunky Tomato Vinaigrette

1¼ pounds tomatoes, peeled, seeded, and finely chopped (about 1½ cups)
¼ cup minced green onions
1 tablespoon chopped fresh basil
1 teaspoon minced fresh thyme
¾ teaspoon minced fresh oregano
¾ teaspoon minced fresh marjoram
⅛ teaspoon freshly ground pepper
3 tablespoons red wine vinegar
2 tablespoons balsamic vinegar
2 tablespoons olive oil
½ teaspoon sugar

Combine first 7 ingredients in a medium bowl; toss well. Combine vinegars, oil, and sugar, stirring well with a wire whisk. Pour over tomato mixture; toss gently. Let stand at room temperature 1 hour.

Serve with pasta, poultry, or fish, or use in marinades for poultry or vegetable salads. Yield: 2 cups.

Note: See Green Beans in Chunky Tomato Vinaigrette (page 163).

Per Tablespoon

Calories 11	Carbohydrate 0.7 g	Cholesterol 0 mg
Fat 0.9 g (Saturated Fat 0.1 g)	Protein 0.1 g	Sodium 1 mg

Spiced Applesauce Syrup

1 cup unsweetened applesauce
1 (10-ounce) jar apple jelly
¾ teaspoon ground cinnamon
Dash of ground cloves
Dash of salt

Combine all ingredients in a small saucepan. Cook over low heat, stirring occasionally, until jelly melts and mixture is blended.

Serve syrup with biscuits, French toast, pancakes, or waffles. Yield: 2 cups.

Per Tablespoon

Calories 30	Carbohydrate 7.9 g	Cholesterol 0 mg
Fat 0 g (Saturated Fat 0 g)	Protein 0.1 g	Sodium 8 mg

Maple-Honey-Cinnamon Syrup

- 1 cup sugar
- 2 tablespoons brown sugar
- ½ cup plus 1 tablespoon water
- ½ cup honey
- ½ teaspoon ground cinnamon
- ⅛ teaspoon imitation maple flavoring

Combine first 3 ingredients in a medium saucepan; bring to a boil. Remove from heat; stir in honey, cinnamon, and maple flavoring.

Serve with biscuits, French toast, pancakes, waffles, or nonfat frozen yogurt. Yield: 1¾ cups.

Per Tablespoon

Calories 50	Carbohydrate 13.1 g	Cholesterol 0 mg
Fat 0 g (Saturated Fat 0 g)	Protein 0 g	Sodium 1 mg

Flower Flavor

Pick a single-flower honey like clover, horsemint, lavender, rhododendron, locust, buckwheat, orange blossom, or rosemary for honey with a distinct flavor. A clear, runny honey works best for cooking. The darker the honey, the stronger the flavor.

Spiced Applesauce Syrup

Fresh Orange Syrup

9 oranges, cut in half
3/4 cup sugar
1/3 cup light-colored corn syrup

Using a juicer, extract juice from oranges. Pour juice through a wire-mesh strainer into a bowl; press with back of spoon against sides of strainer to squeeze out 3 1/3 cups juice. Discard pulp and seeds remaining in strainer.

Combine juice, sugar, and syrup in a large saucepan. Bring to a boil; reduce heat, and simmer, uncovered, 45 minutes, stirring frequently. Remove from heat, and skim off foam. Let cool. Cover and store in refrigerator up to 10 days. Serve with gingerbread or French toast or in sparkling water. Yield: 2 1/4 cups.

Note: See Raspberry-Orange Twist (page 86).

Per Tablespoon

Calories 35	Carbohydrate 8.9 g	Cholesterol 0 mg
Fat 0 g (Saturated Fat 0 g)	Protein 0.2 g	Sodium 0 mg

Fresh Strawberry Syrup

3 quarts fresh strawberries, hulled
1/2 cup sugar
1/4 cup light-colored corn syrup

Wash First . . .
. . . *then* cap the strawberries or you'll rinse away part of the flavor.

Slice strawberries; crush berries in a shallow pan, using a potato masher or fork. Pour berries through a wire-mesh strainer lined with 2 layers of cheesecloth into a bowl; press with back of spoon against the sides of the strainer to squeeze out 2 cups juice. Discard pulp remaining in strainer.

Combine juice, sugar, and syrup in a medium saucepan. Bring to a boil; reduce heat, and simmer, uncovered, 20 minutes, stirring frequently. Remove from heat, and skim off foam. Let cool. Cover and store in refrigerator up to 10 days. Serve with low-fat cheesecake, fruit, nonfat frozen yogurt, pancakes, or waffles. Yield: 1 3/4 cups.

Per Tablespoon

Calories 33	Carbohydrate 8.3 g	Cholesterol 0 mg
Fat 0 g (Saturated Fat 0 g)	Protein 0 g	Sodium 4 mg

Praline Liqueur

- 2 cups firmly packed dark brown sugar
- 1 cup sugar
- 2½ cups water
- 4 cups pecan pieces, lightly toasted
- 2 vanilla beans, split lengthwise
- 4 cups vodka

Combine first 3 ingredients in a medium saucepan, and cook over medium-high heat until sugars dissolve. Bring to a boil; reduce heat, and simmer 5 minutes. Place pecans and vanilla beans in a 1-gallon jar. Pour hot mixture into jar; let cool. Add vodka; stir well. Cover tightly, and store in a dark place at room temperature at least 2 weeks. Shake jar gently once daily.

Pour mixture through a wire-mesh strainer lined with 2 layers of cheesecloth into a bowl, discarding solids. Pour mixture through a wire-mesh strainer lined with a coffee filter into a bowl. Change filter often. (Mixture will drip slowly.) Pour mixture into jars; cover tightly. Store at room temperature.

Use in coffee, baked apples, or low-fat cakes. Yield: 4½ cups.

Note: See Caramel Peach Trifle (page 202).

Per Tablespoon
Calories 64
Fat 0 g (Saturated Fat 0 g)
Carbohydrate 8.7 g
Protein 0 g
Cholesterol 0 mg
Sodium 3 mg

Toast 'em

To toast pecans, spread them in a shallow pan and bake for 10 to 15 minutes at 350°, stirring occasionally. Toasting brings out a strong, rich flavor, so you can use fewer nuts and still have plenty of flavor.

Coffee Liqueur

- $1\frac{1}{2}$ **cups sugar**
- **1 cup firmly packed dark brown sugar**
- **2 cups water**
- $\frac{1}{2}$ **cup instant coffee granules**
- **3 cups vodka**
- $\frac{1}{4}$ **cup whole coffee beans**

Combine first 3 ingredients in a medium saucepan; cook over medium-high heat until sugars dissolve. Bring to a boil; reduce heat, and simmer 5 minutes. Remove from heat, and stir in coffee granules. Let cool. Combine coffee mixture, vodka, and coffee beans; pour into a 1-gallon jar. Cover tightly, and store in a dark place at room temperature at least 2 weeks. Shake jar gently once daily.

Pour mixture through a wire-mesh strainer lined with 2 layers of cheesecloth into jars, discarding coffee beans. Cover tightly. Store at room temperature.

Use in beverages, low-fat eggnog, or low-fat cake fillings and batters. Yield: 6 cups.

Per Tablespoon

Calories 38	Carbohydrate 5.4 g	Cholesterol 0 mg
Fat 0 g (Saturated Fat 0 g)	Protein 0 g	Sodium 1 mg

Guide to Java

If you don't know beans about coffee flavors, use this list to vary the taste of coffee desserts, beverages, and syrups. Remember that the darker the roast on the beans, the stronger the flavor.

- French Roast: a dark roast that gives a strong and slightly bitter flavor
- Continental Roast: the darkest roast of all which gives beans a burnt, bitter flavor
- Jamaican Blue Mountain: some of the world's most expensive beans which taste extremely smooth, mild, and a bit nutty
- Santos: smooth, sweet-tasting beans from Brazil
- Koni Kai: a rich, full-flavored, slightly acidic Hawaiian coffee
- Guatemalan: beans characterized by a rich, spicy, and smoky flavor
- Sumatra: Indonesian beans with a flavor somewhat like chocolate
- Java: Indonesian beans with a smooth, full, somewhat smoky taste

Coffee Liqueur
Raspberry Cordial
Praline Liqueur
Blueberry-Spice Cordial
Honey-Pineapple Cream Liqueur

Honey-Pineapple Cream Liqueur

2 cups coarsely chopped fresh pineapple
½ cup sugar
½ cup water
½ cup honey
1 tablespoon lemon juice
3 cups light rum
1 (14-ounce) can low-fat sweetened condensed milk

Combine pineapple, sugar, water, honey, and lemon juice in a medium saucepan. Bring to a boil; reduce heat, and simmer 3 minutes. Remove from heat, and let cool. Pour pineapple mixture into a 2-quart jar; add rum, stirring well. Cover tightly, and store in a dark place at room temperature at least 2 weeks. Shake jar gently once daily.

Pour pineapple mixture through a wire-mesh strainer into a large bowl, discarding pineapple. Add condensed milk, and stir mixture with a wire whisk. Pour mixture into jars, and cover tightly. Store in refrigerator.

Use in beverages, or serve over commercial low-fat pound cake, nonfat frozen yogurt, fresh pineapple, banana slices, or strawberries. Yield: 5½ cups.

Per Tablespoon
Calories 17
Fat 0.2 g (Saturated Fat 0.1 g)
Carbohydrate 5.4 g
Protein 0.3 g
Cholesterol 0 mg
Sodium 4.7 mg

Sweet 'n' Creamy

Sweetened condensed milk is a mixture of milk and sugar that has been cooked to a thick, creamy syrup. The new low-fat version is made from skim milk. You won't notice any difference in flavor, and you'll save some calories and fat.

Raspberry Cordial

2 (10-ounce) packages frozen raspberries in light syrup, thawed
1¾ cups sugar
¾ cup water
3½ cups brandy

Combine raspberries, sugar, and water in a medium saucepan; cook mixture over medium-high heat until sugar dissolves. Bring mixture to a boil; reduce heat, and simmer 5 minutes. Remove mixture from heat, and let cool. Pour raspberry mixture into a 1-gallon jar. Add brandy, and stir well. Cover mixture tightly, and store in a dark place at room temperature at least 2 weeks. Shake jar gently once daily.

Pour mixture through a wire-mesh strainer lined with 2 layers of cheesecloth into jars, discarding raspberries. Cover tightly. Store at room temperature.

Use in beverages, trifles, or sauces. Yield: 4¾ cups.

Per Tablespoon

Calories 44	Carbohydrate 4.8 g	Cholesterol 0 mg
Fat 0 g (Saturated Fat 0 g)	Protein 0 g	Sodium 0 mg

Blueberry-Spice Cordial

1 (16-ounce) package frozen blueberries, thawed
1½ cups sugar
½ cup water
6 whole cloves
1 (3-inch) stick cinnamon
1 whole nutmeg, cut in half
3 cups brandy

Combine first 6 ingredients in a medium saucepan; cook over medium-high heat until sugar dissolves. Bring to a boil; reduce heat, and simmer 5 minutes. Remove from heat, and let cool. Pour blueberry mixture into a 2-quart jar. Add brandy; stir well. Cover tightly, and store in a dark place at room temperature at least 2 weeks. Shake jar gently once daily.

Pour mixture through a wire-mesh strainer lined with 2 layers of cheesecloth into jars, discarding solids. Cover tightly. Store at room temperature.

Use in beverages, or serve with apple wedges or gingersnaps. Yield: 3¾ cups.

Per Tablespoon

Calories 48	Carbohydrate 5.2 g	Cholesterol 0 mg
Fat 0 g (Saturated Fat 0 g)	Protein 0 g	Sodium 0 mg

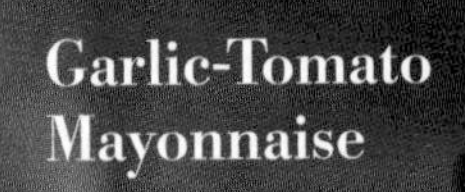

Garlic-Tomato Mayonnaise

Papaya Salsa

Grilled Corn Salsa

SALSAS

You know that little corner grill or cafe that's known for its "secret recipe" for spicy honey mustard that it spreads on its sandwiches? Well, that "secret recipe" concept is the whole idea of this chapter.

SAUCES

In fact, Mesquite Smoked Salsa is a secret we finagled from company foods photographer Charles Walton. He came up with the recipe after tasting a similar salsa during his travels. "I tasted this fantastic salsa once in Santa Fe. When I found out that the flavor came from just smoking the tomatoes, I kept trying to make one that tasted like it," he says. To savor it for yourself, just turn to page 53.

SPREADS

Don't miss Charles's Fiery Smoked Ketchup recipe on page 65, either. He used the same grill-smoking technique to make the hot seasoning that's a staple in his refrigerator. But don't tease him about his affection for ketchup. This gourmet cook quickly defends himself: "There's nothing low-brow about using ketchup." One taste of his smoke-seasoned version, and you'll agree.

Fresh Tomato Salsa

2 cups finely chopped tomato
1/4 cup chopped green onions
1 tablespoon finely chopped fresh cilantro
1 tablespoon fresh lime juice
1 teaspoon minced fresh jalapeño pepper
1/4 teaspoon salt

Combine all ingredients in a medium bowl; stir well. Cover and chill at least 3 hours. Serve with chicken or turkey or as a dip with no-oil baked tortilla chips. Yield: 2 cups.

Note: See Texas-Grilled Sirloin with Fresh Tomato Salsa (page 131).

Per Tablespoon

Calories 3	Carbohydrate 0.7 g	Cholesterol 0 mg
Fat 0 g (Saturated Fat 0 g)	Protein 0.1 g	Sodium 20 mg

What's a Salsa?

It's a fresh, usually uncooked vegetable or fruit mixture that sometimes looks more like a relish than a sauce, even though "salsa" is the Spanish word for "sauce." Mixtures with everything from grilled corn kernels and chiles to black beans and even watermelon can be called a salsa, but the most traditional ones are simple combos of tomatoes, onions, peppers, cilantro, and lime juice.

The most popular ways to serve salsa are as an appetizer with dippers; as a sauce spooned over a meat, poultry, or fish entrée; or as a soup topper, a side dish, or a garnish.

Two-Tomato Salsa

2 cups diced plum tomato
1 cup diced green tomato
1/2 cup diced green pepper
1/4 cup diced purple onion
1 tablespoon seeded, minced serrano chile
1 tablespoon chopped fresh cilantro
2 tablespoons fresh lime juice
1 tablespoon olive oil
1 teaspoon sugar
1/2 teaspoon salt
1/4 teaspoon coarsely ground pepper
1 clove garlic, minced

Combine all ingredients in a medium bowl; stir well. Cover and chill at least 3 hours. Serve with chicken or fish or as a dip with no-oil baked tortilla chips. Yield: 3 1/2 cups.

Per Tablespoon

Calories 6	Carbohydrate 0.8 g	Cholesterol 0 mg
Fat 0.3 g (Saturated Fat 0 g)	Protein 0.1 g	Sodium 22 mg

Black Bean Salsa

Two-Tomato Salsa

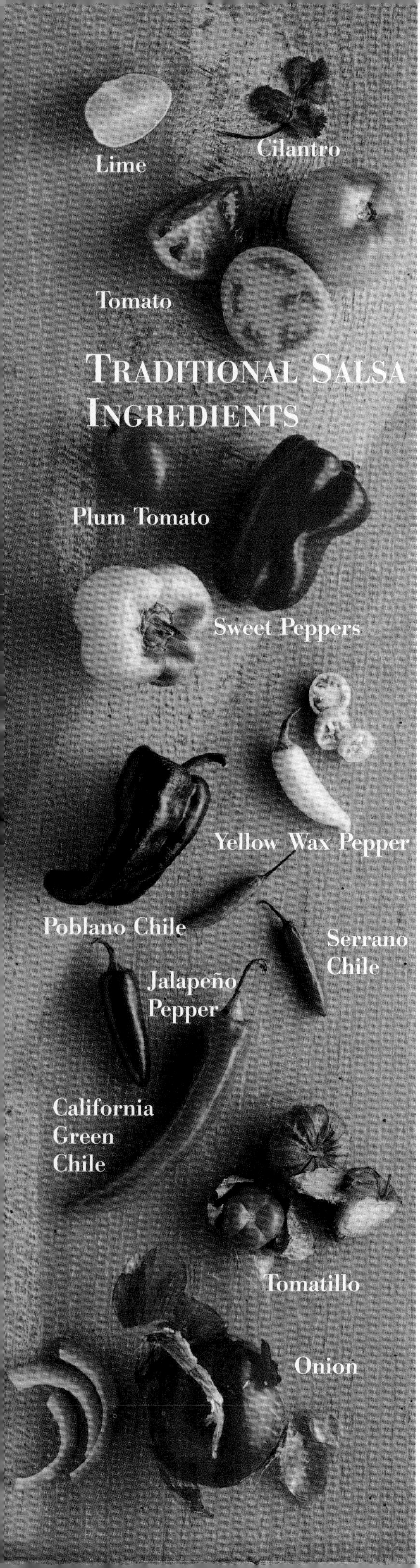

Santa Fe Salsa

This salsa's traditional blend of tomato, onion, and chiles can't be beat.

1 cup finely chopped tomato
1/2 cup finely chopped purple onion
1/8 teaspoon salt
1 (4-ounce) can chopped green chiles, undrained
1 large clove garlic, minced

Combine all ingredients in a small bowl; stir well. Cover and chill at least 2 hours. Serve with chicken or pork or as a dip with no-oil baked tortilla chips. Yield: 1 3/4 cups.

Note: See Southwest Crab Cakes (page 84) and Southwestern Pasta Toss (page 111).

Per Tablespoon

Calories 3	Carbohydrate 0.8 g	Cholesterol 0 mg
Fat 0 g (Saturated Fat 0 g)	Protein 0.1 g	Sodium 27 mg

Tomatillo Salsa

Tomatillos look like green cherry tomatoes in papery husks, but they have a lemon-like taste. Buy firm ones with husks attached.

1/2 pound fresh tomatillos
1/4 cup diced purple onion
1/4 cup chopped sweet yellow pepper
2 tablespoons chopped fresh cilantro
1 tablespoon unsweetened orange juice
1 teaspoon sugar
1/8 teaspoon salt
1 small jalapeño pepper, seeded and finely chopped
1 small clove garlic, minced

Remove husks from tomatillos; rinse and dice. Combine diced tomatillo, onion, and remaining ingredients in a small bowl; stir well. Cover and chill at least 30 minutes. Serve with chicken or as a dip with no-oil baked tortilla chips. Yield: 1 1/2 cups.

Per Tablespoon

Calories 5	Carbohydrate 1.0 g	Cholesterol 0 mg
Fat 0.1 g (Saturated Fat 0 g)	Protein 0.1 g	Sodium 12 mg

Mesquite Smoked Salsa

- 2 cups mesquite chips
- 1 head garlic
- 5 plum tomatoes, seeded and cut in half lengthwise
- 1 medium onion, peeled and separated into rings
- 2 large shallots, peeled and cut in half lengthwise
- ½ jalapeño pepper, seeded and cut in half lengthwise
- Vegetable cooking spray
- ¼ cup chopped fresh cilantro
- ¼ cup fresh lime juice
- ¼ teaspoon salt

Soak mesquite chips in water 30 minutes; drain.

Peel outer skin from garlic; cut off and discard top one-third of garlic head. Place garlic (cut side up), tomato halves (cut side down), and next 3 ingredients in a grill basket.

Pile charcoal on each side of grill, leaving center empty. Place a drip pan between coals. Prepare fire; let burn 10 to 15 minutes. Place half of mesquite chips on hot coals. Coat grill rack with cooking spray, and place over coals. Place grill basket on rack over drip pan; cover and cook 30 minutes. Turn vegetables, and add remaining mesquite chips to hot coals. Cover and cook 30 minutes or until vegetables are tender and lightly browned.

Remove vegetables from grill. Squeeze out pulp from each clove of garlic. Position knife blade in food processor bowl; add garlic pulp and vegetables. Process until coarsely chopped, scraping sides of processor bowl once. Transfer vegetables to a small bowl; add cilantro, lime juice, and salt, stirring well. Serve at room temperature or chilled. Use as a dip with no-oil baked tortilla chips or as a topping for tacos or other Mexican recipes. Yield: 1¼ cups.

Gas Grill Directions:

Soak mesquite chips in water 30 minutes; drain. Wrap chips in heavy-duty aluminum foil, and make several holes in foil.

Light gas grill on one side; place foil-wrapped chips directly on hot coals. Coat grill rack on opposite side with cooking spray. Place rack over cool lava rocks; let grill heat 10 to 15 minutes. Place grill basket on rack on opposite side from hot coals; cover and cook 30 minutes. Turn vegetables; cover and cook 30 minutes or until vegetables are tender and lightly browned.

Per Tablespoon

Calories 15	Carbohydrate 3.4 g	Cholesterol 0 mg
Fat 0.1 g (Saturated Fat 0 g)	Protein 0.5 g	Sodium 33 mg

Try This Trick

Freeze Mesquite Smoked Salsa in ice cube trays, and then stir a couple of thawed cubes into a jar of commercial salsa for a quick dip that tastes homemade.

A Hot Tip
What's the hottest chile? Generally, the hottest ones have the darkest green skins and pointed tips rather than blunt ones.

Black Bean Salsa

2 (15-ounce) cans black beans, drained
½ cup diced sweet red pepper
¼ cup diced purple onion
¼ cup diced cucumber
2 tablespoons diced celery
2 tablespoons minced jalapeño pepper
1 tablespoon chopped fresh basil
2 tablespoons olive oil
2 tablespoons tomato juice
2 tablespoons red wine vinegar
1 tablespoon fresh lemon juice
1½ teaspoons chopped fresh thyme
½ teaspoon ground cumin
½ teaspoon chili powder
¼ teaspoon salt
¼ teaspoon freshly ground pepper
1 clove garlic, pressed

Combine all ingredients in a medium bowl; stir well. Cover and chill at least 4 hours. Serve with pork or as a dip with no-oil baked tortilla chips. Yield: 3½ cups.

Per Tablespoon

Calories 17	Carbohydrate 2.3 g	Cholesterol 0 mg
Fat 0.6 g (Saturated Fat 0.1 g)	Protein 0.8 g	Sodium 36 mg

Jicama Salsa

1 cup diced jicama
½ cup chopped tomato
2 tablespoons chopped green onions
2 tablespoons fresh lime juice
1 tablespoon white wine vinegar
¼ teaspoon chili powder
2 cloves garlic, crushed

Combine all ingredients; stir well. Cover; let stand at room temperature 2 hours. Store in refrigerator. Serve with fish. Yield: 1½ cups.

Per Tablespoon

Calories 4	Carbohydrate 1.0 g	Cholesterol 0 mg
Fat 0 g (Saturated Fat 0 g)	Protein 0.1 g	Sodium 1 mg

Grilled Corn Salsa

This smoky-tasting salsa makes a great salad, too. Just serve it in a mound over torn salad greens.

6 ears fresh corn
1 large sweet red pepper
2 teaspoons vegetable oil
Vegetable cooking spray
½ cup finely chopped purple onion
¼ cup diced California green chile
¼ cup fresh lime juice
1 teaspoon vegetable oil
¼ teaspoon salt

Remove and discard husks and silks from corn; set corn aside. Cut red pepper into quarters; remove and discard seeds and membrane. Brush corn and pepper quarters with 2 teaspoons oil.

Coat grill rack with cooking spray; place on grill over medium-hot coals (350° to 400°). Place corn on rack; grill, covered, 20 minutes or until tender, turning every 5 minutes. Let cool; cut corn from cob. Place red pepper on rack; grill, covered, 5 minutes on each side. Let cool; dice red pepper.

Combine corn, red pepper, onion, and remaining ingredients in a medium bowl; stir well. Serve at room temperature with chicken or pork or as a dip with no-oil baked tortilla chips. Yield: 3½ cups.

Note: See Black Bean Tostadas with Grilled Corn Salsa (page 117).

Per Tablespoon
Calories 13
Fat 0.4 g (Saturated Fat 0.1 g)
Carbohydrate 2.5 g
Protein 0.3 g
Cholesterol 0 mg
Sodium 12 mg

Cranberry-Kumquat Salsa

2 cups fresh or frozen cranberries
6 kumquats, unpeeled and coarsely chopped
3 tablespoons minced crystallized ginger
2 jalapeño peppers, seeded and finely chopped
3/4 cup sugar
1/4 cup minced fresh mint

Position knife blade in food processor bowl; drop cranberries through food chute with processor running, and process 15 seconds or until minced. Transfer cranberries to a small bowl.

Cranberry-Kumquat Salsa

Position knife blade in processor bowl; add kumquats, ginger, and pepper. Pulse 3 to 5 times or until mixture is finely chopped.

Add kumquat mixture to cranberries. Stir in sugar and mint. Cover and store in refrigerator. Flavor intensifies the longer salsa is chilled. Serve with chicken, pork, or turkey or as a spread over nonfat cream cheese; or stir into low-fat yogurt. Yield: 1¾ cups.

Note: See Amaretto-Cranberry Pear Wedges (page 74).

Per Tablespoon

Calories 30	Carbohydrate 7.7 g	Cholesterol 0 mg
Fat 0 g (Saturated Fat 0 g)	Protein 0.1 g	Sodium 1 mg

Say What?

A kumquat (rhymes with "squat") looks like a miniature orange, but you can eat the whole sweet thing–skin and all. They're in season during winter months, like most citrus fruits.

No kumquats in your store's produce section? Then just use one small peeled orange in place of six kumquats.

Three-Melon Salsa

1½ cups seeded, diced watermelon
½ cup chopped fresh cilantro
½ cup peeled, diced jicama
¼ cup diced cantaloupe
¼ cup diced honeydew melon
2 tablespoons finely chopped purple onion
1 tablespoon finely chopped jalapeño pepper
2 tablespoons fresh lime juice
2 tablespoons maple syrup
¼ teaspoon salt

Combine all ingredients in a medium bowl; stir well. Cover and store in refrigerator. Serve with grilled fish. Yield: 2½ cups.

Per Tablespoon

Calories 6	Carbohydrate 1.6 g	Cholesterol 0 mg
Fat 0 g (Saturated Fat 0 g)	Protein 0.1 g	Sodium 15 mg

Southwest Melon Salsa

1½ cups diced cantaloupe
1½ cups diced honeydew
½ cup chopped green pepper
½ cup chopped purple onion
2 tablespoons fresh cilantro
2 serrano chiles, seeded and chopped
1 clove garlic, minced
3 tablespoons fresh lime juice
1 tablespoon white wine vinegar
1 teaspoon vegetable oil
¼ teaspoon ground cumin

Combine first 7 ingredients in a large bowl; stir well. Combine lime juice and remaining ingredients; stir well with a wire whisk. Pour over melon mixture, and toss gently. Cover and store in refrigerator. Serve with chicken or fish. Yield: 4 cups.

Per Tablespoon

Calories 4	Carbohydrate 0.8 g	Cholesterol 0 mg
Fat 0.1 g (Saturated Fat 0 g)	Protein 0.1 g	Sodium 1 mg

Canned Heat

Keep a jar of pickled jalapeños on the shelf for emergencies. They'll substitute for the same amount of fresh serranos or jalapeños. And don't worry, they don't taste "pickled."

Pineapple-Kiwifruit Salsa

1⅓ cups chopped fresh pineapple
2 kiwifruit, peeled and chopped
1 jalapeño pepper, seeded and minced
2 tablespoons minced fresh mint
1 tablespoon minced fresh cilantro
1 teaspoon sugar
½ teaspoon ground ginger
1½ teaspoons fresh lemon juice

Combine all ingredients in a medium bowl; stir well. Cover and store in a glass container in refrigerator. Serve with chicken, pork, fish, or low-fat cheese. Yield: 2 cups.

Per Tablespoon

Calories 12	Carbohydrate 2.9 g	Cholesterol 0 mg
Fat 0.1 g (Saturated Fat 0 g)	Protein 0.1 g	Sodium 0 mg

Papaya Salsa

3 cups peeled, seeded, and diced papaya
¾ cup peeled, diced kiwifruit
2 tablespoons chopped sweet red pepper
1½ tablespoons chopped shallot
1½ tablespoons chopped fresh cilantro
1½ tablespoons fresh lime juice
⅛ teaspoon ground allspice

Combine all ingredients in a medium bowl; toss well. Cover and store in refrigerator. Serve with beef, pork, venison, or fish or as a dip with baked flour tortilla wedges. Yield: 3½ cups.

Note: See Bourbon Chicken Kabobs (page 81).

Per Tablespoon

Calories 6	Carbohydrate 1.3 g	Cholesterol 0 mg
Fat 0 g (Saturated Fat 0 g)	Protein 0.1 g	Sodium 0 mg

Fresh Mint Relish

1½ cups tightly packed fresh mint leaves
1 California green chile, seeded and minced
1 tablespoon minced onion
2 tablespoons water
1 tablespoon lemon juice
¾ teaspoon sugar
½ teaspoon peeled, grated gingerroot
¼ teaspoon salt

Position knife blade in food processor bowl; add all ingredients, and process 30 seconds or until mixture is finely chopped. Transfer to a small bowl. Cover and chill 1 hour. Yield: ½ cup plus 1 tablespoon.

Per Tablespoon

Calories 4	Carbohydrate 1.0 g	Cholesterol 0 mg
Fat 0 g (Saturated Fat 0 g)	Protein 0.2 g	Sodium 65 mg

Chilled Heat

The longer a hot chile-spiced salsa sits before you serve it (even if it's chilled), the hotter the flavor becomes.

Maple-Molasses Barbecue Sauce

Vegetable cooking spray
½ cup finely chopped onion
2 cloves garlic, minced
1 tablespoon cornstarch
½ cup plus 1 tablespoon maple syrup
½ cup water
¼ cup low-sodium soy sauce
¼ cup molasses
3 tablespoons cider vinegar
1 teaspoon dried crushed red pepper
1 teaspoon peeled, minced gingerroot
¼ cup creamy reduced-fat peanut butter

Coat a medium saucepan with cooking spray; place over medium heat until hot. Add onion and garlic; cook, stirring constantly, 3 minutes or until tender.

Combine cornstarch and next 7 ingredients; stir well. Add to onion mixture; bring to a boil. Cook 3 minutes, stirring frequently. Add peanut butter; cook, stirring constantly, 2 minutes or until peanut butter melts. Use to baste while cooking and/or to serve with chicken or pork. Yield: 1¾ cups.

Per Tablespoon

Calories 40	Carbohydrate 8.0 g	Cholesterol 0 mg
Fat 0.9 g (Saturated Fat 0.1 g)	Protein 0.6 g	Sodium 68 mg

Good and Sticky

Molasses, the cooked-down syrup from sugar cane or sugar beets, adds the characteristic flavor to gingerbread. But this sweet syrup with its acidic taste is also a good flavoring for savory sauces and meat glazes.

Spicy Barbecue Sauce

1 cup reduced-sodium ketchup
¾ cup minced onion
½ cup water
¼ cup cider vinegar
2 tablespoons dark brown sugar
2 tablespoons molasses
1 tablespoon low-sodium Worcestershire sauce
2 teaspoons dry mustard
1 teaspoon garlic powder
1 teaspoon chili powder

Combine all ingredients in a small saucepan, and bring to a boil, stirring constantly. Reduce heat, and simmer, uncovered, 20 minutes, stirring frequently. Use to baste while cooking and/or to serve with chicken, pork, or beef. Yield: 1¾ cups.

Per Tablespoon

Calories 26	Carbohydrate 3.9 g	Cholesterol 0 mg
Fat 0.1 g (Saturated Fat 0 g)	Protein 0.1 g	Sodium 73 mg

A Cool Head

Keep tightly wrapped heads of roasted garlic in the refrigerator—they'll be ready to use when you need them.

Roasted Garlic-Lemon Sauce

Want a simple entrée with great flavor? Just spoon this sauce over plain grilled chicken or pork.

3 large heads garlic
2 tablespoons fresh lemon juice
1 tablespoon low-sodium soy sauce
1½ teaspoons white wine vinegar
⅛ teaspoon salt
⅛ teaspoon freshly ground pepper

Peel outer skin from each garlic head and discard. Cut off top one-third of each garlic head. Place garlic, cut side up, in center of a piece of heavy-duty aluminum foil. Fold foil over garlic, sealing tightly. Bake at 350° for 1 hour or until garlic is soft. Remove from oven; cool 10 minutes. Remove and discard papery skin from garlic. Squeeze pulp from each clove or scoop out with a spoon.

Combine garlic pulp, lemon juice, and remaining ingredients in container of a small food processor; process until smooth. Serve at room temperature with chicken, pork, or vegetables. Yield: ½ cup.

Per Tablespoon

Calories 38	Carbohydrate 8.3 g	Cholesterol 0 mg
Fat 0.1 g (Saturated Fat 0 g)	Protein 1.5 g	Sodium 88 mg

Spicy Peanut Sauce

Spicy Peanut Sauce

½ cup plain low-fat yogurt
1 teaspoon all-purpose flour
Vegetable cooking spray
½ cup finely chopped onion
⅓ cup finely chopped green pepper
½ cup canned low-sodium chicken broth, undiluted
⅓ cup creamy reduced-fat peanut butter
½ teaspoon chili powder
⅛ teaspoon salt
⅛ teaspoon pepper
⅛ teaspoon ground red pepper

Combine yogurt and flour in a bowl; stir well, and set aside.

Coat a saucepan with cooking spray, and place over medium heat until hot. Add onion and green pepper; cook, stirring constantly, 4 minutes. Add yogurt mixture, broth, and remaining ingredients; stir well. Reduce heat, and cook, uncovered, 20 minutes; stir occasionally. Serve warm with chicken, pork, or Chinese noodles. Yield: 1¼ cups.

Per Tablespoon
Calories 29 | Carbohydrate 3.0 g | Cholesterol 0 mg
Fat 1.8 g (Saturated Fat 0.3 g) | Protein 1.5 g | Sodium 39 mg

Pesto Sauce

4 cloves garlic
2 tablespoons pine nuts
1½ cups tightly packed fresh basil leaves
½ cup chopped fresh parsley
⅓ cup freshly grated Parmesan cheese
½ cup commercial oil-free Italian dressing

Position knife blade in food processor bowl. Drop garlic and pine nuts through food chute with processor running; process 5 seconds or until garlic is minced. Add basil and parsley; process 10 seconds or until minced. Add cheese; process until blended. Slowly pour Italian dressing through food chute with processor running, blending until smooth. Spread on chicken or fish before cooking, use as a stuffing for mushroom caps, spread on fresh tomato slices or baguette slices, or serve on hot pasta. Yield: 1 cup plus 2 tablespoons.

Note: See Pesto-Stuffed Pasta Shells (page 115).

Per Tablespoon

Calories 22	Carbohydrate 1.7 g	Cholesterol 1 mg
Fat 1.5 g (Saturated Fat 0.4 g)	Protein 1.0 g	Sodium 101 mg

Cucumber and Yogurt Raita

This cool, yogurt-based side dish complements spicy Indian cuisine. *See the Indian menu on page 222.*

2 medium cucumbers, peeled, seeded, and finely chopped
1 medium tomato, seeded and finely chopped
1 serrano chile, seeded and minced
1½ cups plain nonfat yogurt
¼ cup finely chopped fresh mint
½ teaspoon cumin seeds, toasted
½ teaspoon salt

Combine all ingredients in a medium bowl; stir well. Cover and chill 1 hour. Yield: 3½ cups.

Per Tablespoon

Calories 5	Carbohydrate 0.8 g	Cholesterol 0 mg
Fat 0 g (Saturated Fat 0 g)	Protein 0.4 g	Sodium 26 mg

Presto–Pesto!

If you have a processor, fre basil, and a bottle of salad dre ing, you can make pesto in a f minutes. Pesto is the flavor Italian herb sauce usually ma from basil, garlic, olive oil, a pine nuts. Our low-fat version just as good—we substituted Itali salad dressing for the oil.

Make it ahead of time, a freeze it in ice cube trays. It w darken a bit in the freezer, b the flavor won't change. Th thaw it to use to spread on brea tomato slices, fish, and potato to stuff in mushrooms or squas or to mix with pasta. Here's ho

Step 1: Drop garlic and pine nu through food chute with proce sor running until the ingredien are finely chopped.

Step 2: Add basil and parsley, a process until they're finely mince

Step 3: Add the dressing with t processor running.

A Crushing Experience

To crush spice seeds with a mortar and pestle, just work the rounded end of the pestle against the seeds in the bowl of the mortar, rolling it as you press.

HERBED TOMATO SAUCE

- **1 teaspoon olive oil**
- **1 cup chopped onion**
- **1 large clove garlic, minced**
- **¼ cup chopped fresh basil**
- **1 tablespoon chopped fresh oregano**
- **½ teaspoon fennel seeds, crushed**
- **1 (14.5-ounce) can no-salt-added whole tomatoes, undrained and chopped**
- **½ cup water**
- **1 tablespoon no-salt-added tomato paste**
- **⅛ teaspoon salt**
- **⅛ teaspoon pepper**

Heat olive oil in a medium saucepan over medium-high heat until hot. Add onion and garlic; cook, stirring constantly, 4 minutes or until tender. Add basil, oregano, and fennel seeds; cook, stirring constantly, 1 minute. Add tomatoes and remaining ingredients; bring to a boil. Reduce heat, and simmer, uncovered, 15 minutes. Serve with pasta. Yield: 2¼ cups.

Note: See Pesto-Stuffed Pasta Shells (page 115).

Per Tablespoon
Calories 5
Fat 0.1 g (Saturated Fat 0 g)
Carbohydrate 0.9 g
Protein 0.2 g
Cholesterol 0 mg
Sodium 10 mg

Fiery Smoked Ketchup

- 2 cups mesquite chips
- 1 head garlic
- 5 plum tomatoes, seeded and cut in half lengthwise
- 1 small yellow onion, peeled and separated into rings
- 2 small shallots, peeled and cut in half lengthwise
- ½ jalapeño pepper, seeded and cut in half lengthwise
- Vegetable cooking spray
- 2 (8-ounce) cans no-salt-added tomato sauce
- ¼ cup ground mild red chile pepper
- ½ teaspoon salt
- ¼ teaspoon pepper

Soak mesquite chips in water at least 30 minutes; drain.

Peel outer skins from garlic; cut off and discard top one-third of garlic head. Place garlic (cut side up), tomato halves (cut side down), and next 3 ingredients in a grill basket.

Pile charcoal on each side of grill, leaving center empty. Place a drip pan between coals. Prepare fire; let burn 10 to 15 minutes. Place half of mesquite chips on hot coals. Coat grill rack with cooking spray, and place over coals. Place grill basket on rack over drip pan; cover and cook 30 minutes. Turn vegetables, and add remaining mesquite chips to hot coals. Cover and cook 30 minutes or until vegetables are tender and lightly browned.

Remove vegetables from grill. Squeeze out pulp from each clove of garlic. Position knife blade in food processor bowl; add garlic pulp, vegetables, tomato sauce, and remaining ingredients. Process until smooth, scraping sides of processor bowl twice. Serve with meat loaf, turkey burgers, turkey franks, and sloppy joes. Yield: 3 cups.

Gas Grill Directions:

Soak mesquite chips in water 30 minutes; drain. Wrap chips in heavy-duty aluminum foil, and make several holes in foil.

Light gas grill on one side; place foil-wrapped chips directly on hot coals. Coat grill rack on opposite side with cooking spray. Place rack over cool lava rocks; let grill heat 10 to 15 minutes. Place grill basket on rack on opposite side from hot coals; cover and cook 30 minutes. Turn vegetables; cover and cook 30 minutes or until vegetables are tender and lightly browned.

Per Tablespoon

Calories 10	Carbohydrate 2.2 g	Cholesterol 0 mg
Fat 0.1 g (Saturated Fat 0 g)	Protein 0.4 g	Sodium 28 mg

Turn Up the Heat

Substitute serrano chile for jalapeño pepper to get a hotter salsa.

Hot, Hot Harissa

Some call this red chile paste "violently hot." One taste and you won't argue. In Middle Eastern cuisine, harissa traditionally is served with couscous as a condiment. The heat is from the dried red chiles, which are soaked and ground into paste with a mortar and pestle or in a food processor. Typical seasonings include garlic, coriander, caraway, cumin, mint, and cilantro. Harissa lasts several months in the refrigerator if kept tightly covered. To use harissa, stir it into nonfat mayonnaise for a spicy dollop to serve with fish, or add it to soups, stews, or tomato sauce for extra zip.

HARISSA

This traditional North African condiment is so hot you need only a small amount.

5 dried hot New Mexico chiles
1 cup hot water
1 tablespoon all-purpose flour
¼ teaspoon ground cumin
¼ teaspoon ground coriander
¼ teaspoon ground red pepper
⅛ teaspoon sugar
⅛ teaspoon caraway seeds, crushed
½ cup finely chopped onion
1 large clove garlic, minced
1 tablespoon vegetable oil
2 tablespoons no-salt-added tomato paste
⅛ teaspoon salt
2 teaspoons fresh lime juice

Using rubber gloves, remove and discard stems and seeds from chile peppers. Wash chiles in cold water; drain. Tear chiles into strips; place in a small bowl. Add hot water; let stand 20 minutes.

Pour chile mixture into container of an electric blender; cover and process until smooth, stopping once to scrape down sides. Set mixture aside.

Combine flour and next 5 ingredients in a small bowl; set aside.

Cook onion and garlic in oil in a small skillet over medium-high heat, stirring constantly, 5 minutes or until onion is tender. Add flour mixture; stir well. (Mixture will be dry.) Cook, stirring constantly, 1 minute. Gradually add chile mixture; cook over medium heat, stirring constantly, until mixture is thickened and bubbly. Stir in tomato paste and salt. Let cool slightly.

Pour mixture into container of electric blender; cover and process until smooth, stopping once to scrape down sides. Stir in lime juice. Store in refrigerator. Serve as a condiment with couscous, soups, or stews, or spread on bread. Yield: 1 cup plus 2 tablespoons.

Note: Dried California green chiles or ancho chiles may be substituted for dried New Mexico chiles. See Vegetable Garden Couscous (page 120).

Per Teaspoon

Calories 10	Carbohydrate 1.2 g	Cholesterol 0 mg
Fat 0.6 g (Saturated Fat 0.1 g)	Protein 0.2 g	Sodium 13 mg

Lemon Herbed Aioli

Aioli (pronounced ay–OH–lee) is a dressed-up version of mayonnaise generally flavored with garlic. Use aioli as you would mayonnaise–as a sandwich spread or, as they do in France, served aside vegetables, meat, or fish.

½ cup canned low-sodium chicken broth, undiluted
1 tablespoon cornstarch
2 tablespoons water
1 egg yolk, beaten
½ cup chopped fresh parsley
¼ cup loosely packed fresh basil leaves
2 cloves garlic, minced
¼ teaspoon grated lemon rind
2 teaspoons Dijon mustard
¼ teaspoon salt
⅛ teaspoon freshly ground pepper

Combine first 3 ingredients a small saucepan, stirring well. Cook over medium-high heat, stirring constantly, until mixture comes to a boil. Cook an additional minute or until thickened; remove from heat. Gradually stir about one-fourth of hot mixture into egg yolk; add to remaining hot mixture, stirring constantly. Cook mixture over low heat, stirring constantly, until thickened. Transfer mixture to a small bowl; let cool to room temperature.

Position knife blade in food processor bowl. Add parsley and basil; process until finely chopped. Add garlic, lemon rind, and mustard; process until smooth.

Combine cooled broth mixture and parsley mixture in a small bowl; stir well. Stir in salt and pepper. Cover and chill thoroughly. Serve with fish or steamed vegetables. Yield: ¾ cup.

Per Tablespoon

Calories 11	Carbohydrate 1.1 g	Cholesterol 18 mg
Fat 0.6 g (Saturated Fat 0.2 g)	Protein 0.4 g	Sodium 78 mg

Lemon Herbed Aioli

Mad About Mustard

This is the condiment that adds zing to sandwiches, pretzels, vegtable and fruit dips, and sauces. To make your own mustard, start with whole, partially ground, or powdered yellow or brown mustard seeds. Just follow the three steps below.

Step 1: Soak the seeds in the flavorful liquids such as vinegar, wine, champagne, or beer.

Step 2: Pour soaked seeds and remaining ingredients in a food processor.

Step 3: Process until smooth.

Garlic-Tomato Mayonnaise

½ cup nonfat mayonnaise
3 tablespoons no-salt-added tomato sauce
2 cloves garlic, minced
¼ cup plus 2 tablespoons seeded, finely chopped tomato
1 tablespoon chopped fresh parsley

Combine mayonnaise, tomato sauce, and garlic; stir well. Cover and chill at least 3 hours. Stir in tomato and parsley. Store in refrigerator. Serve with steamed vegetables, or use as a sandwich spread. Yield: 1 cup.

Note: For extra flavor, use 2 teaspoons commercial roasted garlic instead of 2 cloves minced garlic.

Per Tablespoon

Calories 9	Carbohydrate 2.1 g	Cholesterol 0 mg
Fat 0 g (Saturated Fat 0 g)	Protein 0.1 g	Sodium 96 mg

Spicy Mustard with Cumin

1 (2.5-ounce) jar brown mustard seeds
¼ cup yellow mustard seeds
¾ cup red wine vinegar
½ cup light beer
2 teaspoons dried crushed red pepper
4 cloves garlic, minced
1½ tablespoons ground cumin
1 tablespoon plus 1 teaspoon red wine vinegar
1 tablespoon plus 1 teaspoon light beer
1 teaspoon hot sauce
½ teaspoon celery seeds
½ teaspoon salt

Combine first 6 ingredients in a small bowl or glass jar, stirring well; cover and let stand 48 hours.

Position knife blade in food processor bowl; add seed mixture, cumin, and remaining ingredients. Process 5 minutes or until smooth. Store in refrigerator. Serve with chicken, fish, breadsticks, or pretzels. Yield: 2 cups.

Per Tablespoon

Calories 21	Carbohydrate 1.9 g	Cholesterol 0 mg
Fat 1.1 g (Saturated Fat 0.1 g)	Protein 1.0 g	Sodium 39 mg

Sweet Potato Chutney

2¾ cups peeled, diced sweet potato (about 1 pound)
1 tablespoon grated orange rind
1½ cups fresh orange juice
⅔ cup chopped onion
¼ cup sugar
¼ cup raisins
1 teaspoon ground ginger
¼ teaspoon ground cinnamon
¼ teaspoon ground allspice
⅛ teaspoon ground cardamom

Cook sweet potato in boiling water to cover 30 minutes or until tender; drain.

Combine sweet potato and remaining ingredients in a large saucepan; stir well. Bring to a boil; cover, reduce heat, and simmer 40 minutes. Uncover and simmer 1 hour and 30 minutes or until liquid is absorbed, stirring frequently. Let cool. Serve at room temperature, or chilled thoroughly. Serve with beef, pork, or low-sodium ham. Yield: 2 cups.

Note: See Sweet Potato Crostini (page 80).

Per Tablespoon

Calories 28	Carbohydrate 6.7 g	Cholesterol 0 mg
Fat 0 g (Saturated Fat 0 g)	Protein 0.3 g	Sodium 119 mg

Pricey Spice

It's no wonder cardamom is one of the world's three most expensive spices; every pod must be harvested by hand. But a little goes a long way. And it's so versatile, it's worth paying extra to get the pungent mix of pepper, lime, camphor, and ginger flavors. The peppery sweet spice adds just the right seasoning to many sweets, breads, wines, and spice blends. (By the way, the other two most expensive spices are vanilla beans and saffron.)

COOKING WITH FLAVOR

Cider Tea

White Bean
Bruschetta

Sparkling
Strawberry
Lemonade

APPETIZERS

It kept happening. We'd buy the freshest mussels at the seafood market early in the mornings, but by the time the home economist was ready to cook them, more than half of the shellfish were ready for the trash. Really frustrating.

Soon we hit on a trick that keeps those shells shut until cooking time. Here's what we do: As soon as we come in from our market trip with the mussels, we cover them with water and then pour ice on top. Lots of ice. Now only a few shells open before we're ready to cook. Try it for yourself when you make Mussels Antipasto on page 85.

BEVERAGES

Once we solved our mussel problem, we turned our attention to the rest of the recipes for this chapter. That wasn't hard to do because most of them commanded attention (the good kind). Every day that we sampled appetizers and beverages, the ooohhh's, aaahhh's, and mmmm's intensified at the tasting table. Maybe it's because these aren't your run-of-the-mill party fare recipes. Not a single ingredient is unusual, but the creative combinations of ordinary foods provide a "wow" factor. The key to our success is the use of high-flavor foods like blue cheese, sweet potatoes, amaretto, curry, and raspberries.

So if you want sausage balls or plain ol' chips and dip, grab another cookbook. These recipes are for cooks who want to make an impression—and then take all the honors.

Amaretto-Cranberry Pear Wedges

Cut pears into halves rather than quarters for a delicious side dish.

3 firm ripe Bartlett pears
1/3 cup amaretto
1 tablespoon lemon juice
3/4 cup Cranberry-Kumquat Salsa (page 56)
3 tablespoons slivered almonds, toasted

Liquid Almond Flavor

Spice up food with amaretto, an almond-flavored liqueur. You'll get the almond flavor without all the fat from the almonds.

Peel and core pears; quarter each lengthwise. Using a melon baller, carve out a well in center of each quarter. Place pears in a heavy-duty, zip-top plastic bag; pour amaretto and lemon juice over pears. Chill at least 1 hour.

Drain pears, discarding liquid. Place on a serving platter. Spoon Cranberry-Kumquat Salsa into pear cavities, and sprinkle with almonds. Yield: 1 dozen appetizers.

Per Appetizer

Calories 68 (12% Calories from Fat)	Carbohydrate 14.1 g	Cholesterol 0 mg
Fat 0.9 g (Saturated Fat 0 g)	Protein 0.5 g	Sodium 1 mg

No-Cook Appetizers to Make in No Time

Try these ideas for fruit appetizers to make in a matter of minutes.

- Layer thin slices of honeydew or cantaloupe on a plate, and place a few fresh blueberries or raspberries over the centers of the slices.
- Arrange peeled, sliced oranges and kiwifruit over lettuce leaves, and sprinkle with pomegranate seeds.
- Serve fresh strawberries in a compote with a splash of champagne, balsamic vinegar, or an orange-flavored liqueur.
- Mix cinnamon and honey to use as a dip for banana and apple slices. (Great for kids!)
- For an appetizer buffet, cut a whole pineapple in half, and remove pineapple, leaving a 1/2-inch thick shell. Cut pineapple into bite-size pieces, and toss with a mixture of fresh berries. Fill pineapple halves with fruit mixture. Serve with wooden picks and a dip of low-fat poppyseed dressing or low-fat vanilla yogurt mixed with orange marmalade.
- Thread chunks of any combination of strawberries, unpeeled apple pieces, and pineapple, melon, banana, and orange segments onto small kabob skewers. Spear the kabobs into a whole pineapple to serve as a buffet centerpiece.

Curried Fruit Kabobs

With just 2 teaspoons of curry powder, you get the benefit of a blend of many spices—sometimes as many as 20.

- **½ fresh pineapple, cut into 1-inch cubes**
- **4 medium plums, pitted and quartered**
- **3 kiwifruit, peeled and quartered**
- **2 small bananas, peeled and cut into 1-inch slices**
- **¼ cup frozen pineapple-orange-banana juice concentrate, thawed and undiluted**
- **¼ cup light rum**
- **2 tablespoons honey**
- **2 teaspoons curry powder**
- **½ teaspoon ground ginger**
- **Vegetable cooking spray**
- **1 (8-ounce) carton vanilla low-fat yogurt**

Place first 4 ingredients in a large bowl. Combine juice concentrate, rum, honey, curry, and ginger; stir well. Pour juice mixture over fruit, and toss gently. Cover and chill 3 hours, stirring occasionally.

Soak 12 (6-inch) wooden skewers in water for 30 minutes. Drain fruit mixture, reserving 2 tablespoons juice. Thread fruit alternately onto skewers. Place kabobs on a baking sheet coated with cooking spray. Broil 3 inches from heat (with electric oven door partially opened) 3 to 4 minutes on each side or until fruit is lightly browned.

Combine 2 tablespoons reserved juice mixture and yogurt; stir well. Serve kabobs with yogurt sauce. Yield: 1 dozen appetizers.

Per Appetizer

Calories 91 (8% Calories from Fat)	Carbohydrate 20.5 g	Cholesterol 1 mg
Fat 0.8 g (Saturated Fat 0.2 g)	Protein 1.7 g	Sodium 180 mg

Blue Cheese Potato Tarts

Blue Cheese Potato Tarts

The fat-free tortillas used in these tarts are made with modified potato starch instead of lard, a staple ingredient in traditional tortillas.

9 small round red potatoes
½ cup light process cream cheese, softened
¼ cup (1 ounce) crumbled blue cheese
2 teaspoons minced fresh rosemary
½ teaspoon freshly ground pepper
1 cup seeded and finely chopped tomato
¼ cup finely chopped ripe olives
1 tablespoon balsamic vinegar
3 (8-inch) fat-free flour tortillas
Olive oil-flavored vegetable cooking spray
3 tablespoons minced fresh chives

Cook potatoes in a large saucepan in boiling water to cover 15 minutes or until tender. Drain and cool. Cut potatoes into 1/8-inch-thick slices; set aside.

Combine cream cheese and next 3 ingredients in a small bowl, mixing well. Set aside. Combine tomato, olives, and vinegar in a small bowl; toss gently. Set aside. Cut 2 circles from each flour tortilla, using a 4-inch round cookie cutter. Spread cheese mixture evenly over tortilla circles. Overlap potato slices around edges of tortillas to form circles. Coat potato slices with cooking spray.

Place a baking sheet in a 400° oven for 5 minutes. Remove from oven; immediately arrange tarts on hot baking sheet, and bake 8 to 10 minutes or until hot and tortillas are crisp. Spoon tomato mixture evenly onto centers of tarts; sprinkle with chives. Serve immediately. Yield: 6 appetizers.

Per Appetizer
Calories 160 (28% Calories from Fat) Carbohydrate 24.3 g Cholesterol 15 mg
Fat 5.0 g (Saturated Fat 2.9 g) Protein 6.0 g Sodium 227 mg

Sing the Blues
Blue cheese is strong tasting. That's great for low-fat cooking because you can use just a little and still get a lot of flavor.

Cheese and Tomato Quesadillas

3/4 cup seeded and diced tomato
1/4 cup thinly sliced green onions
2 pickled jalapeño peppers, chopped
6 (8-inch) fat-free flour tortillas
3/4 cup (3 ounces) shredded reduced-fat sharp Cheddar cheese
Vegetable cooking spray
3/4 cup no-salt-added tomato salsa

Divide first 3 ingredients evenly among tortillas, arranging just off center of each. Top each evenly with cheese.

Coat a medium-size nonstick skillet with cooking spray; place over medium-high heat until hot. Place one tortilla in skillet. Cook 1 minute or until bottom of tortilla is golden. Fold tortilla in half; cook 30 seconds or until cheese melts. Repeat procedure with remaining tortillas. Cut each quesadilla into 4 wedges. Top wedges with salsa. Yield: 2 dozen appetizers.

Per Appetizer
Calories 43 (17% Calories from Fat) Carbohydrate 7.1 g Cholesterol 2 mg
Fat 0.8 g (Saturated Fat 0.4 g) Protein 2.0 g Sodium 397 mg

Roasted Garlic and Pepper Dip

Put roasted heads of garlic in a zip-top plastic bag in the refrigerator, and it will be easier to squeeze the pulp from the cloves. That's because the pulp shrinks from the skin as it chills.

2 large heads garlic
Olive oil-flavored vegetable cooking spray
2 large sweet red peppers
1 cup nonfat cottage cheese
2 ounces goat cheese
¼ cup nonfat sour cream
½ teaspoon hot sauce

Peel outer skin from each garlic head, and discard. Cut off top one-third of each garlic head. Place garlic, cut side up, in center of a piece of heavy-duty aluminum foil. Fold foil over garlic, sealing tightly. Bake at 350° for 1 hour or until garlic is soft. Remove from oven; cool 10 minutes. Remove and discard papery skin from garlic. Squeeze pulp from each clove, or scoop out with a spoon; set pulp aside.

Cut peppers in half lengthwise; remove and discard seeds and membranes. Place peppers, skin side up, on a large baking sheet; flatten peppers with palm of hand. Broil 5½ inches from heat (with electric oven door partially opened) 15 to 20 minutes or until charred. Place peppers in ice water until cool. Remove from water; peel and discard skins.

Combine garlic pulp, peppers, cottage cheese, and remaining ingredients in container of an electric blender; cover and process until smooth, stopping once to scrape down sides. Spoon mixture into a small bowl; cover and chill at least 2 hours. Serve with fresh raw vegetables, breadsticks, or unsalted crackers. Yield: 2¼ cups.

Garlic in a Jar
Don't have time to roast a head of garlic? Buy a jar of roasted garlic to keep on hand.

Per Tablespoon

Calories 13 (28% Calories from Fat)	Carbohydrate 1.1 g	Cholesterol 2 mg
Fat 0.4 g (Saturated Fat 0.2 g)	Protein 1.4 g	Sodium 45 mg

White Bean Bruschetta

This recipe calls for a baguette, a crispy-crusted long, thin loaf of French bread. You can substitute a loaf of regular French bread instead.

24 (½-inch-thick) slices French baguette
Olive oil-flavored vegetable cooking spray
¼ cup plus 2 tablespoons sun-dried tomatoes (packed without oil)
¼ cup boiling water
¼ cup finely chopped plum tomato
¼ cup plus 2 tablespoons chopped ripe olives
½ teaspoon dried basil
1 clove garlic, minced
1 (15-ounce) can cannellini beans, drained and mashed
2 teaspoons lemon juice
Fresh basil sprigs (optional)

Lightly coat both sides of bread slices with cooking spray; arrange in a single layer on a baking sheet. Bake at 350° for 10 to 12 minutes or until lightly browned, turning once.

Combine sun-dried tomatoes and water in a small bowl; cover and let stand 15 minutes. Drain and finely chop tomatoes. Combine sun-dried tomato, plum tomato, and next 3 ingredients. Cover and let stand 1 hour.

Combine mashed beans and lemon juice. Spread bean mixture evenly over bread slices. Broil 5½ inches from heat (with electric oven door partially opened) 1 to 1½ minutes or until thoroughly heated. Spoon tomato mixture evenly over bean mixture. Garnish with basil sprigs, if desired. Serve immediately. Yield: 2 dozen appetizers.

Per Appetizer

Calories 40 (23% Calories from Fat)	Carbohydrate 6.4 g	Cholesterol 0 mg
Fat 1.0 g (Saturated Fat 0.2 g)	Protein 1.4 g	Sodium 93 mg

Roasted Bread??

Bruschetta comes from the Italian word *bruscare,* which means to roast over coals. These days, however, most of us roast it in the oven.

Sweet Potato Crostini

12 (½-inch-thick) slices Italian bread
Olive oil-flavored vegetable cooking spray
2½ ounces goat cheese
1½ cups Sweet Potato Chutney (page 69)
1 tablespoon minced fresh thyme
24 thin strips roasted red pepper
Fresh thyme sprigs (optional)

Lightly coat both sides of bread slices with cooking spray; arrange in a single layer on a baking sheet. Bake at 350° for 10 to 12 minutes or until lightly browned, turning once.

Spread goat cheese evenly on each slice. Spoon Sweet Potato Chutney evenly onto cheese; sprinkle with minced thyme. Bake at 425° for 5 minutes. Top with red pepper strips. Garnish with thyme sprigs, if desired. Yield: 1 dozen appetizers.

Note: You can save a little time if you buy strips of roasted red pepper in a jar. To roast your own, follow instructions on page 170.

Per Appetizer

Calories 131 (11% Calories from Fat)	Carbohydrate 25.3 g	Cholesterol 6 mg
Fat 1.6 g (Saturated Fat 0.9 g)	Protein 3.9 g	Sodium 243 mg

Tomato-Pesto Stuffed Mushrooms

24 large fresh mushrooms
Olive oil-flavored vegetable cooking spray
15 sun-dried tomatoes (packed without oil)
¾ cup boiling water
⅓ cup nonfat cream cheese
¼ cup minced fresh basil
¼ cup minced pecans, toasted
1 (8-ounce) carton nonfat sour cream
1 clove garlic, minced
¼ cup fine, dry breadcrumbs

Clean mushrooms with damp paper towels. Remove stems, reserving stems for another use.

Coat a large nonstick skillet with cooking spray, and place over medium-high heat until hot. Add mushroom caps, and sauté 10 minutes. Remove mushroom caps from skillet, and drain on paper towels.

Micro-toast Nuts

To toast nuts in the microwave, spread them in a shallow dish, and microwave for a few minutes at HIGH, stopping every 30 seconds to stir and sample the nuts.

Combine tomatoes and boiling water in a small bowl; cover and let stand 15 minutes. Drain and finely dice tomatoes. Combine tomato, cream cheese, and next 4 ingredients; stir well.

Spoon 1 heaping tablespoon of tomato mixture into each mushroom cap; sprinkle each with ½ teaspoon breadcrumbs. Arrange on a baking sheet coated with cooking spray. Bake at 375° for 10 to 15 minutes or until thoroughly heated. Yield: 2 dozen appetizers.

Per Appetizer
Calories 35 (28% Calories from Fat) Carbohydrate 4.3 g Cholesterol 1 mg
Fat 1.1 g (Saturated Fat 0 g) Protein 2.2 g Sodium 73 mg

Bourbon Chicken Kabobs

6 (4-ounce) skinned, boned chicken breast halves
¼ cup reduced-sodium teriyaki sauce
1 tablespoon peeled, grated gingerroot
3 tablespoons bourbon
2 tablespoons honey
2 teaspoons dark sesame oil
2 cloves garlic, minced
6 green onions, cut into 1-inch pieces
Vegetable cooking spray
Papaya Salsa (page 59)

Place chicken between 2 sheets of heavy-duty plastic wrap; flatten to ¼-inch thickness, using a meat mallet or rolling pin. Cut chicken into ½-inch-wide strips. Combine teriyaki sauce and next 5 ingredients in a heavy-duty, zip-top plastic bag. Add chicken strips and green onions; seal bag, and shake until well coated. Marinate in refrigerator 3 hours, turning bag occasionally.

Soak 16 (6-inch) bamboo skewers in water 30 minutes; set aside.

Remove chicken and green onions from marinade; discard marinade. Thread chicken and green onions alternately onto soaked skewers. Coat grill rack with cooking spray; place on grill over medium-hot coals (350° to 400°). Place skewers on rack; grill, covered, 1 to 2 minutes on each side or until done. Serve with Papaya Salsa. Yield: 16 appetizers.

Per Appetizer
Calories 71 (18% Calories from Fat) Carbohydrate 3.3 g Cholesterol 27 mg
Fat 1.4 g (Saturated Fat 0.4 g) Protein 10.2 g Sodium 81 mg

Phyllo Adds Crunch
Phyllo dough is a great low-fat way to add crispy texture to appetizers. Find the paper-thin dough in boxes in the freezer section of the supermarket or even fresh in some Greek or ethnic markets. As you work with the dough layers, remember that it dries quickly. Covering it with a damp paper towel will keep it fresh.

Oriental Firecrackers

12 green onions
1¼ cups shredded cooked chicken
1½ tablespoons reduced-sodium teriyaki sauce
1½ tablespoons hot horseradish mustard
1 tablespoon peeled, minced gingerroot
2 teaspoons white wine vinegar
1 teaspoon sesame oil
½ teaspoon sugar
16 sheets frozen phyllo pastry, thawed
Butter-flavored vegetable cooking spray
½ cup hot horseradish mustard

Remove tops of green onions; set aside white portion of onions. Cut green onion tops into very thin strips; place in a bowl of ice water, and set aside. Slice white portion of 3 onions; set aside. Reserve remaining onion for another use.

Position knife blade in food processor bowl; add chicken and next 6 ingredients. Process 30 seconds, stopping once to scrap down sides. Stir sliced onion into chicken mixture.

Place 1 phyllo sheet on a damp towel (keeping remaining phyllo covered). Lightly coat phyllo with cooking spray. Layer 3 phyllo sheets on first sheet, lightly coating each sheet with cooking spray. Cut phyllo stack in half lengthwise; cut stack crosswise into thirds to make 6 stacks. Keep phyllo stacks covered.

Spoon 1 tablespoon chicken mixture into center of 1 phyllo stack to within 1½ inches from each end, parallel with long edge. Roll up phyllo, jellyroll fashion, starting with long side; twist 1½ inches from each end. Place "firecracker," seam side down, on a baking sheet coated with cooking spray. Repeat procedure with remaining phyllo and chicken mixture.

Bake at 400° for 15 minutes or until golden. Tie each end of firecrackers with a green onion strip. Serve with hot horseradish mustard. Yield: 2 dozen appetizers.

Per Appetizer

Calories 62 (23% Calories from Fat)	Carbohydrate 7.6 g	Cholesterol 7 mg
Fat 1.6 g (Saturated Fat 0.3 g)	Protein 3.5 g	Sodium 115 mg

Taco Chicken Spread

You can chop the chicken into bigger chunks to serve it as a salad.

1½ tablespoons taco seasoning mix
2 teaspoons olive oil
1 large clove garlic
¾ cup nonfat sour cream
2 cups finely chopped cooked chicken
1 (4-ounce) can chopped green chiles, drained
¼ cup minced onion

Place first 3 ingredients in a mortar and pestle or miniature food processor; mash until a smooth paste forms. Spoon mixture into a medium bowl; add sour cream, and stir well. Stir in chicken, chiles, and onion. Cover and chill 2 hours. Serve with fresh raw pepper slices or other raw vegetables, Melba toast, or unsalted crackers; or use as a sandwich spread. Yield: 2¼ cups.

Per Tablespoon

Calories 19 (24% Calories from Fat)	Carbohydrate 0.7 g	Cholesterol 6 mg
Fat 0.5 g (Saturated Fat 0.1 g)	Protein 2.6 g	Sodium 23 mg

Tips for Tasty Chicken

Add a little flavor to chicken that you cook to chop for salads or spreads: just toss ingredients such as herbs, spices, onions, or chiles in the water while it simmers. Be sure the flavors complement those in the recipe. And if you let the chicken cool for a few minutes in the cooking water before you remove it, the chicken will be juicier.

Southwest Crab Cakes

- 1/2 cup frozen whole-kernel corn
- 1/2 cup nonfat sour cream
- 1 egg white, lightly beaten
- 1/3 cup minced poblano chile
- 1 teaspoon chili powder
- 1/2 to 1 teaspoon ground cumin
- 1/4 teaspoon ground red pepper
- 3/4 cup soft breadcrumbs
- 1 pound fresh lump crabmeat, drained
- Vegetable cooking spray
- 16 radicchio leaves
- Santa Fe Salsa (page 52)

Cook corn according to package directions, omitting salt and fat. Drain well. Combine sour cream and egg white in a large bowl, and mix well; add corn, poblano chile, and next 3 ingredients, stirring well. Add breadcrumbs and crabmeat, stirring well. Shape mixture into 16 (1/2-inch-thick) patties.

Coat a large nonstick skillet with cooking spray; place over medium heat until hot. Add crab cakes, in batches, and cook 3 to 4 minutes on each side or until golden.

Arrange radicchio leaves on a serving platter; place a crab cake in center of each leaf. Spoon Santa Fe Salsa evenly over crab cakes. Yield: 16 appetizer servings.

Per Serving

Calories 56 (13% Calories from Fat)	Carbohydrate 5.1 g	Cholesterol 28 mg
Fat 0.8 g (Saturated Fat 0.1 g)	Protein 7.1 g	Sodium 120 mg

Root for Ginger

In a knobby piece of gingerroot, the best flavor is just under the skin. So carefully peel away only the tough outer skin. The freshest gingerroot has smooth skin; wrinkled skin means the root is old, and the flesh will be dry. Wrapped tightly, it will keep for a week in the refrigerator or up to 2 months in the freezer.

Thai Barbecued Oysters

- Rock salt
- 1 dozen fresh oysters (in the shell)
- 2 tablespoons commercial low-sodium barbecue sauce
- 1/4 cup fine, dry breadcrumbs
- 1/4 cup minced fresh cilantro
- 3 tablespoons minced green onion
- 1 tablespoon peeled, grated gingerroot

Sprinkle a layer of rock salt in a 15- x 10- x 1-inch jellyroll pan; set pan aside.

Scrub oyster shells, and open, discarding tops. Arrange oysters over rock salt. Brush oysters on half shells with barbecue sauce.

Combine breadcrumbs and remaining ingredients in a small bowl; stir well. Sprinkle evenly over oysters. Bake at 425° for 12 minutes or until oysters begin to curl. Yield: 12 appetizers.

Note: Shelled fresh oysters sold in plastic tubs may be substituted for oysters in shells. Prepare recipe in shell-shaped baking dishes found at gourmet kitchen shops.

Per Appetizer

Calories 30 (24% Calories from Fat)	Carbohydrate 2.7 g	Cholesterol 15 mg
Fat 0.8 g (Saturated Fat 0.2 g)	Protein 2.2 g	Sodium 70 mg

Mussels Antipasto

Tightly shut shells mean that the mussels are fresh and still alive. Select small ones for the most tender mussels.

2 pounds fresh mussels
½ cup water
⅓ cup dry white wine
3 tablespoons diced carrot
3 tablespoons diced celery
2 tablespoons chopped fresh parsley
⅛ teaspoon dried crushed red pepper
1 clove garlic, sliced
1 bay leaf
2 tablespoons sliced green onions

Mussels Antipasto

Remove beards on mussels, and scrub shells with a brush. Discard opened, cracked, or heavy mussels (they're filled with sand). Set aside remaining mussels.

Combine water and next 7 ingredients in a large saucepan; bring to a boil. Reduce heat, and simmer 2 to 3 minutes. Add mussels; bring to a boil. Cover and cook 3 to 4 minutes or until shells open. Remove and discard bay leaf and any unopened mussels. Remove from heat; stir in green onions. Ladle mixture evenly into individual serving bowls. Yield: 4 servings.

Per Serving

Calories 118 (20% Calories from Fat)	Carbohydrate 6.0 g	Cholesterol 32 mg
Fat 2.6 g (Saturated Fat 0.5 g)	Protein 13.8 g	Sodium 220 mg

Sweet Mangoes
Mangoes are juicy, sweet, and—if they're ripe—as soft as bananas. The seed inside is large, so choose a big mango to get more of the sweet orange flesh.

Tropical Piña Colada Shake

- **1 medium-size ripe banana, peeled and cut into 1-inch slices**
- **2 teaspoons lemon juice**
- **1 medium mango (10 ounces), peeled, pitted, and cut into ½-inch pieces**
- **1½ cups pineapple-orange juice, chilled**
- **1 cup vanilla nonfat frozen yogurt**
- **1 teaspoon coconut extract**

Toss banana slices with lemon juice in a small bowl. Place slices on a baking sheet, reserving lemon juice; freeze until banana is solid.

Combine banana, reserved lemon juice, mango, and remaining ingredients in container of an electric blender; cover and process until smooth. Pour into chilled glasses, and serve immediately. Yield: 4 (1-cup) servings.

Per Serving

Calories 150 (0% Calories from Fat)	Carbohydrate 35.7 g	Cholesterol 0 mg
Fat 0.2 g (Saturated Fat 0 g)	Protein 2.8 g	Sodium 42 mg

Raspberry-Orange Twist

- **4 cups coarsely crushed ice**
- **1½ cups fresh raspberries**
- **1 cup cranberry-raspberry juice cocktail**
- **¾ cup Fresh Orange Syrup (page 42)**
- **⅔ cup fresh lime juice**
- **3 tablespoons sugar**
- **12 fresh raspberries**

Combine half each of first 6 ingredients in container of an electric blender; cover and process until slushy. Repeat procedure with remaining half of ingredients. Pour into glasses. Top each serving with 2 raspberries. Yield: 6 (1-cup) servings.

Per Serving

Calories 144 (1% Calories from Fat)	Carbohydrate 37.0 g	Cholesterol 0 mg
Fat 0.2 g (Saturated Fat 0 g)	Protein 0.8 g	Sodium 10 mg

Ruby Spiced Mint Tea

Ruby Spiced Mint Tea

4½ cups water
1 cup loosely packed fresh mint leaves
3 tablespoons sugar
3 whole cloves
1 (3-inch) stick cinnamon
6 cranberry-flavored tea bags

Combine first 5 ingredients in a large saucepan. Bring to a boil; cover, remove from heat, and let cool to room temperature. Add tea bags. Bring to a boil; cover, remove from heat, and let cool to room temperature. Remove and discard tea bags. Strain and serve over ice. Yield: 4 (1-cup) servings.

Per Serving
Calories 43 (4% Calories from Fat) Carbohydrate 10.7 g Cholesterol 0 mg
Fat 0.2 g (Saturated Fat 0 g) Protein 0.3 g Sodium 2 mg

Nice over Ice

When you brew tea to be served over ice, brew it extra strong so the melting ice cubes won't dilute the taste.

Sparkling Strawberry Lemonade

1 (12-ounce) package frozen unsweetened strawberries, thawed
2 (12-ounce) cans frozen pink lemonade concentrate, thawed and undiluted
2 cups water
4 cups berry-flavored sparkling mineral water, chilled
Lemon slices (optional)

Place strawberries in container of an electric blender; cover and process until smooth, stopping once to scrape down sides. Pour strawberry puree through a wire-mesh strainer into a large freezer-proof container, discarding pulp and seeds. Add lemonade and water to container; stir well. Cover and freeze 4 hours or until slushy.

To serve, transfer lemonade mixture to a large pitcher or a small punch bowl. Stir in mineral water, and serve immediately. Garnish with lemon slices, if desired. Yield: 10 (1-cup) servings.

Per Serving

Calories 135 (1% Calories from Fat)	Carbohydrate 35.1 g	Cholesterol 0 mg
Fat 0.2 g (Saturated Fat 0 g)	Protein 0.3 g	Sodium 23 mg

Cider Tea

2 cups unsweetened apple cider
2 cups water
1/4 cup sugar
4 whole allspice
4 whole cloves
4 regular-size red zinger tea bags

Combine first 5 ingredients in a large saucepan; let stand 1 hour. Bring to a boil. Add tea bags; remove from heat. Cover and steep 10 minutes. Pour tea through a wire-mesh strainer into mugs, discarding spices and tea bags. Serve warm. Yield: 4 (1-cup) servings.

Per Serving

Calories 107 (0% Calories from Fat)	Carbohydrate 27.0 g	Cholesterol 0 mg
Fat 0.1 g (Saturated Fat 0 g)	Protein 0.1 g	Sodium 4 mg

Apple Rum Toddy

3 cups unsweetened apple cider
2 tablespoons dark brown sugar
1 tablespoon reduced-calorie margarine
3 whole cloves
2 (3-inch) sticks cinnamon
1 whole nutmeg, halved
6 lemon slices
½ cup spiced rum
2 tablespoons amaretto
Lemon slices (optional)

How to Crack a Nutmeg
In our kitchens we use a hammer and an unbreakable cutting surface. It's a little bit of trouble, but you get the strongest fresh spice flavor just after cracking a whole nutmeg.

Combine first 6 ingredients in a heavy saucepan; bring to a boil, and cook, stirring constantly, until sugar dissolves. Add 6 lemon slices; reduce heat, and simmer, uncovered, 5 minutes, stirring occasionally. Remove and discard cloves, cinnamon sticks, nutmeg, and lemon. Remove from heat; stir in rum and amaretto. Garnish each serving with a lemon slice, if desired. Serve immediately. Yield: 6 (¾-cup) servings.

Per Serving
Calories 145 (9% Calories from Fat) Carbohydrate 20.8 g Cholesterol 0 mg
Fat 1.4 g (Saturated Fat 0 g) Protein 0.3 g Sodium 24 mg

Mocha-Cinnamon Cocoa

3½ cups instant nonfat dry milk powder
1 cup Mexican Mocha Spice Mix (page 29)
1 cup sifted powdered sugar
13½ cups hot water

Combine first 3 ingredients; stir well. Store mixture in an airtight container. To serve, spoon ¼ cup cocoa mix into each individual mug. Add ¾ cup hot water to each mug, and stir well. Yield: 18 (1-cup) servings.

Per Serving
Calories 145 (3% Calories from Fat) Carbohydrate 26.0 g Cholesterol 5 mg
Fat 0.5 g (Saturated Fat 0.4 g) Protein 9.3 g Sodium 127 mg

Chili Breadsticks

Rosemary Currant Focaccia

Apple-Walnut Country Bread

Fruited Streusel Muffins

MUFFINS

The bread bakers and tasters at our taste-testing table have shown no mercy. And for that, we're sure you'll be glad. That's because only the best, most flavorful breads made it onto the pages that follow. From tender lemon-buttermilk muffins with crunchy streusel

ROLLS

on top to spiraled basil-cheese rolls to a round loaf of bread flavored with apples and walnuts—all had to pass our lips and garner an affirmative answer to the oft-repeated question: "Is it good enough for a *high-flavor* cookbook?"

And we're proud to say we achieved our mission. We did it with ginger, cinnamon, apples, cilantro, chili powder, Parmesan cheese, sweet potatoes, molasses, orange rind, fresh rosemary, walnuts, and jalapeños.

LOAVES

And for even more flavor and texture variety, we included breads made with lime-seasoned blue cornmeal, earthy-flavored yellow cornmeal, nutty-tasting whole wheat flour, and distinctive rye flour.

Our favorite? Well, it's hard to say. It would have to be a toss-up among Fruited Streusel Muffins, Basil-Cheese Rolls, and Apple-Walnut Country Bread. But we'll let you make the final decision.

TRIPLE GINGER PANCAKES

Pancakes spiced with three flavors of ginger scream for a topping of applesauce, powdered sugar, or sliced strawberries and bananas.

Three-Flavored Ginger
You can't substitute one form of ginger for another and get the same flavor. That's because freshly grated gingerroot tastes hot, ground ginger gives a sweet but peppery flavor, and crystallized ginger is spicy sweet.

1 cup all-purpose flour
1½ teaspoons baking powder
¼ teaspoon salt
1 tablespoon brown sugar
½ teaspoon ground ginger
¼ teaspoon ground cinnamon
2 tablespoons finely chopped crystallized ginger
1 tablespoon peeled, grated gingerroot
1 cup skim milk
2 teaspoons vegetable oil
1 egg, lightly beaten
Vegetable cooking spray
1 teaspoon sifted powdered sugar

Combine first 6 ingredients in a medium bowl; stir in crystallized ginger and freshly grated gingerroot. Combine milk, oil, and egg in a bowl; stir well. Add milk mixture to flour mixture, stirring just until blended. (Mixture will be slightly lumpy.)

Coat a nonstick griddle with cooking spray, and preheat to 350°. For each pancake, pour ¼ cup batter onto hot griddle. Cook pancakes until tops are covered with bubbles and edges look cooked; turn pancakes, and cook other side. Sprinkle pancakes with powdered sugar. Serve immediately. Yield: 8 (4-inch) pancakes.

Per Pancake
Calories 107 (18% Calories from Fat) Carbohydrate 18.5 g Cholesterol 28 mg
Fat 2.1 g (Saturated Fat 0.5 g) Protein 3.5 g Sodium 100 mg

Cinnamon-Apple Waffles

We reached for Rome apples—a good cooking variety—when we made these waffles. But it's okay to use any apples you happen to have in the refrigerator.

1 cup all-purpose flour
2/3 cup whole wheat flour
2 teaspoons baking powder
1/4 teaspoon salt
2 tablespoons sugar
2 tablespoons brown sugar
1 1/2 teaspoons ground cinnamon
1 2/3 cups low-fat buttermilk
1 tablespoon vegetable oil
1/2 teaspoon vanilla extract
3/4 cup peeled, finely chopped apple
2 egg whites
1/8 teaspoon cream of tartar
Vegetable cooking spray

Combine first 7 ingredients in a large bowl; make a well in center of mixture. Combine buttermilk and oil; stir with a wire whisk. Add to dry ingredients, stirring just until dry ingredients are moistened. Stir in vanilla and apple.

Beat egg whites and cream of tartar at high speed of an electric mixer until stiff peaks form; gently fold beaten egg white mixture into batter.

Coat an 8-inch square waffle iron with cooking spray; allow waffle iron to preheat. For each waffle, spoon 1 1/4 cups batter onto hot waffle iron, spreading batter to edges. Bake 4 to 5 minutes or until steaming stops. Repeat procedure with remaining batter. Cut each waffle into 4 squares. Yield: 12 (4-inch) waffles.

Per Waffle
Calories 111 (16% Calories from Fat) Carbohydrate 19.8 g Cholesterol 0 mg
Fat 2.0 g (Saturated Fat 0.4 g) Protein 3.8 g Sodium 76 mg

Nuts About Whole Wheat

If you've given up nuts because of the fat content, you can still enjoy a nut-like flavor when you use whole wheat flour, which is made from entire grains of wheat.

Carrot-Pineapple Muffins

- 1 (8-ounce) can crushed pineapple in juice, undrained
- 1 cup all-purpose flour
- 1 cup whole wheat flour
- 1 tablespoon baking powder
- ½ teaspoon baking soda
- ¼ teaspoon salt
- ½ cup firmly packed brown sugar
- 1 cup skim milk
- ½ cup frozen egg substitute, thawed
- ¼ cup unsweetened applesauce
- 2 tablespoons vegetable oil
- 1 cup finely shredded carrot
- ½ cup golden raisins
- Vegetable cooking spray

Drain pineapple, reserving juice for another use. Press pineapple between paper towels to remove excess moisture; set aside.

Combine all-purpose flour and next 5 ingredients in a medium bowl; make a well in center of mixture. Combine milk and next 3 ingredients; add to dry ingredients, stirring just until dry ingredients are moistened. Stir in pineapple, carrot, and raisins. Spoon batter into muffin pans coated with cooking spray, filling three-fourths full. Bake at 400° for 20 to 22 minutes or until golden. Remove from pans immediately. Yield: 18 muffins.

Per Muffin

Calories 113 (16% Calories from Fat)	Carbohydrate 21.9 g	Cholesterol 0 mg
Fat 2.0 g (Saturated Fat 0.4 g)	Protein 3.0 g	Sodium 90 mg

Fruited Streusel Muffins

2 cups all-purpose flour
2 teaspoons baking powder
¼ teaspoon baking soda
¼ teaspoon salt
½ cup sugar
2 teaspoons grated lemon rind
1 egg, lightly beaten
¾ cup plus 1 tablespoon nonfat buttermilk
3 tablespoons vegetable oil
Vegetable cooking spray
Fruited Streusel Topping

Combine first 6 ingredients in a medium bowl; make a well in center of mixture. Combine egg, buttermilk, and oil; add to dry ingredients, stirring just until dry ingredients are moistened.

Spoon batter into muffin pans coated with cooking spray, filling two-thirds full. Sprinkle evenly with Fruited Streusel Topping. Bake at 400° for 15 minutes or until golden. Remove from pans immediately. Yield: 15 muffins.

Fruited Streusel Topping

2½ tablespoons regular oats, uncooked
1½ tablespoons brown sugar
1 tablespoon all-purpose flour
¼ teaspoon ground allspice
½ tablespoon reduced-calorie stick margarine
2 tablespoons dried blueberries
1 tablespoon chopped almonds
½ tablespoon grated lemon rind

Position knife blade in food processor bowl. Add first 4 ingredients; pulse 2 or 3 times or until mixed. Add margarine, and pulse 5 times or until mixture resembles coarse meal. Transfer to a small bowl, and stir in blueberries, almonds, and lemon rind. Yield: ½ cup.

Per Muffin

Calories 169 (26% Calories from Fat)	Carbohydrate 28.1 g	Cholesterol 19 mg
Fat 4.9 g (Saturated Fat 0.9 g)	Protein 3.6 g	Sodium 102 mg

Mind Your Rind

When you grate rind from lemon or any other citrus fruit, be sure to grate just the colored part of the skin. The white part beneath the outer skin is bitter.

Spicy Apple Butter Bread

Yogurt-Rye Breadsticks

Cilantro-Pepper Biscuits

Squash-Corn Muffins

1 1/4 cups all-purpose flour
3/4 cup yellow cornmeal
2 teaspoons baking soda
1/4 teaspoon salt
2 1/2 teaspoons brown sugar
1 teaspoon chili powder
1 cup nonfat buttermilk
2 1/2 tablespoons olive oil
1 egg, lightly beaten
3/4 cup shredded yellow squash (about 1 small)
1/4 cup frozen whole-kernel corn, thawed
1/4 cup diced sweet red pepper
Vegetable cooking spray

The Color of Cornmeal
The only difference between white and yellow cornmeal is the color of the kernel from which the meal is ground.

Combine first 6 ingredients in a medium bowl; make a well in center of mixture. Combine buttermilk, oil, and egg; add to dry ingredients, stirring just until moistened. Gently stir in squash, corn, and red pepper. Spoon batter into muffin pans coated with cooking spray, filling three-fourths full. Bake at 400° for 15 minutes or until golden. Remove from pans immediately. Yield: 12 muffins.

Per Muffin

Calories 125 (29% Calories from Fat)	Carbohydrate 19.2 g	Cholesterol 19 mg
Fat 4.0 g (Saturated Fat 0.6 g)	Protein 3.5 g	Sodium 289 mg

Buttermilk Raisin Biscuits

2 cups all-purpose flour
3/4 teaspoon baking soda
1/2 teaspoon salt
1/3 cup sugar
2 tablespoons margarine
3/4 cup plus 1 tablespoon nonfat buttermilk
1/2 cup raisins
1 tablespoon all-purpose flour
Vegetable cooking spray
1 tablespoon skim milk

Combine first 4 ingredients in a large bowl; cut in margarine with a pastry blender until mixture resembles coarse meal. Add buttermilk, stirring with a fork just until dry ingredients are moistened. Stir in raisins.

Sprinkle 1 tablespoon flour evenly over work surface. Turn dough out onto floured surface, and knead 4 or 5 times. Pat dough to ¾-inch thickness; cut into rounds with a 2-inch biscuit cutter. Place rounds on a baking sheet coated with cooking spray. Brush tops of rounds with skim milk. Bake at 425° for 11 minutes or until golden. Serve immediately. Yield: 12 biscuits.

Per Biscuit

Calories 143 (14% Calories from Fat)	Carbohydrate 28.0 g	Cholesterol 1 mg
Fat 2.2 g (Saturated Fat 0.5 g)	Protein 3.1 g	Sodium 218 mg

Cilantro-Pepper Biscuits

1 tablespoon cornmeal
1¾ cups all-purpose flour
1½ teaspoons baking powder
½ teaspoon cracked pepper
3 tablespoons minced fresh cilantro
2 tablespoons margarine
2 egg whites, lightly beaten
¾ cup 1% low-fat cottage cheese
1 tablespoon all-purpose flour
Vegetable cooking spray
2 teaspoons grated Parmesan cheese

Sprinkle a baking sheet with 1 tablespoon cornmeal; set aside.

Combine 1¾ cups flour and next 3 ingredients in a large bowl; cut in margarine with a pastry blender until mixture resembles coarse meal. Stir in egg whites and cottage cheese just until flour mixture is moistened.

Sprinkle 1 tablespoon flour onto work surface. Turn dough out onto floured surface, and knead 4 or 5 times. Roll dough to ¾-inch thickness; cut into rounds with a 2-inch biscuit cutter. Place rounds on prepared baking sheet. Coat tops of rounds lightly with cooking spray; sprinkle with Parmesan cheese. Bake at 450° for 14 minutes or until golden. Serve immediately. Yield: 12 biscuits.

Per Biscuit

Calories 105 (22% Calories from Fat)	Carbohydrate 15.6 g	Cholesterol 1 mg
Fat 2.6 g (Saturated Fat 0.6 g)	Protein 4.5 g	Sodium 95 mg

Pepper for Punch

Cracked pepper gives bread a bite of pungent flavor. The spice is found in jars on supermarket spice racks, but the kind from your pepper mill will also work.

Blue Cornbread

When Blue Is Best

Blue cornmeal is best when you want an authentic Southwestern flavor. The rich tradition of the lime-flavored corn started when native American tribes stored their blue corn in limestone caves. When the corn was stored there, it took on the limestone flavor that is now a characteristic flavor of the region's cuisine. Blue cornmeal has a coarser texture than blue corn flour, which is fine and powdery.

Blue Cornbread

- Vegetable cooking spray
- 1 cup finely chopped sweet red pepper
- ½ cup finely chopped onion
- ¼ cup minced jalapeño pepper
- 1⅓ cups blue cornmeal
- ⅔ cup all-purpose flour
- 1½ teaspoons baking powder
- ½ teaspoon baking soda
- ½ teaspoon salt
- 2 tablespoons sugar
- 1 cup nonfat buttermilk
- ⅓ cup evaporated skimmed milk
- ¼ cup frozen egg substitute, thawed
- 3 tablespoons reduced-calorie margarine, melted

Coat a nonstick skillet with cooking spray; place over medium-high heat until hot. Add chopped red pepper, onion, and jalapeño pepper; sauté until tender.

Combine cornmeal and next 5 ingredients in a large bowl; make a well in center of mixture.

Combine buttermilk, skimmed milk, egg substitute, and melted margarine in a small bowl; add buttermilk mixture to cornmeal mixture, stirring just until dry ingredients are moistened. Stir in vegetable mixture.

Pour batter into a 9-inch square pan coated with cooking spray. Bake at 425° for 25 minutes or until golden. Cut into squares to serve. Yield: 9 squares.

Note: Blue corn flour may be substituted for blue cornmeal. When using corn flour, reduce the buttermilk to ¾ cup; then prepare as directed.

Per Square

Calories 160 (19% Calories from Fat)	Carbohydrate 28.3 g	Cholesterol 1 mg
Fat 3.4 g (Saturated Fat 0.5 g)	Protein 5.1 g	Sodium 294 mg

Chili Breadsticks

- 1 cup plus 2 tablespoons water
- 2 teaspoons olive oil
- 3 cups bread flour, divided
- 1 package rapid-rise yeast
- 1 teaspoon salt
- 1 teaspoon sugar
- 1/4 cup instant nonfat dry milk powder
- 3 tablespoons cumin seeds
- 2 tablespoons bread flour
- Vegetable cooking spray
- 3 tablespoons chili powder
- 3 tablespoons yellow cornmeal
- 1 egg white, beaten

Combine water and oil in a small saucepan; heat to 120° to 130°.

Combine 1 cup flour and next 5 ingredients in a large bowl; stir well. Gradually add liquid mixture to flour mixture, beating well at low speed of an electric mixer. Beat 2 additional minutes at medium speed. Gradually stir in enough of the remaining 2 cups flour to make a stiff dough.

Sprinkle 2 tablespoons flour over work surface. Turn dough out onto floured surface, and knead until smooth and elastic (about 8 minutes). Place in a bowl coated with cooking spray, turning to coat top. Cover dough, and let rise in a warm place (85°), free from drafts, 45 minutes or until doubled in bulk.

Combine chili powder and cornmeal; set aside. Punch dough down, and divide into 20 equal portions. Roll each portion into a 14-inch rope. Brush each rope with egg white, and sprinkle with cornmeal mixture. Place 1 inch apart on a large baking sheet coated with cooking spray. Bake at 400° for 12 to 14 minutes or until done. Yield: 20 breadsticks.

Per Breadstick

Calories 99 (10% Calories from Fat)	Carbohydrate 18.3 g	Cholesterol 0 mg
Fat 1.1 g (Saturated Fat 0.2 g)	Protein 3.7 g	Sodium 134 mg

How to Pick a Flour

If you want soft biscuits or tender cakes or cookies, use a soft wheat flour. For yeast bread, use bread or all-purpose flour. Bread flour has a higher protein content and helps develop the elastic texture needed for yeast doughs.

Yogurt-Rye Breadsticks

1 package active dry yeast
1 cup warm water (105° to 115°)
1½ tablespoons sugar
2½ cups bread flour, divided
1 cup medium rye flour
1 tablespoon yellow cornmeal
1 teaspoon salt
¾ cup plain nonfat yogurt
2 tablespoons margarine, softened
1½ teaspoons caraway seeds
1 tablespoon bread flour
Vegetable cooking spray
1 egg white
1 tablespoon water
1 teaspoon caraway seeds

Sprinkle on Flavor

One little trick to making breads taste extra good is to put the most flavorful ingredient on the outside. Sprinkle seeds, herbs, or cheese on top of muffins, loaves, rolls, or breadsticks. It's a great way to get the flavor of higher fat ingredients such as nuts and cheese without all the fat and calories.

Combine first 3 ingredients in a 1-cup liquid measuring cup; let stand 5 minutes.

Combine yeast mixture, 2 cups bread flour, rye flour, cornmeal, and salt in a large mixing bowl; beat at medium speed of an electric mixer until ingredients are well blended. Add yogurt, margarine, and 1½ teaspoons caraway seeds; mix well. Gradually stir in enough of remaining ½ cup bread flour to make a soft dough.

Sprinkle 1 tablespoon bread flour evenly over work surface. Turn dough out onto floured surface, and knead until smooth and elastic (about 8 minutes). Place in a large bowl coated with cooking spray, turning to coat top. Cover and let rise in a warm place (85°), free from drafts, 1 hour or until doubled in bulk.

Punch dough down, and divide into 16 equal portions; shape each portion into a 16-inch rope. Place on baking sheets coated with cooking spray.

Cover and let rise in a warm place, free from drafts, 15 minutes or until puffy. Combine egg white and 1 tablespoon water; brush breadsticks evenly with mixture. Sprinkle evenly with 1 teaspoon caraway seeds. Bake at 400° for 17 to 20 minutes or until golden. Yield: 16 breadsticks.

Per Breadstick

Calories 131 (14% Calories from Fat)	Carbohydrate 23.7 g	Cholesterol 0 mg
Fat 2.0 g (Saturated Fat 0.4 g)	Protein 4.3 g	Sodium 175 mg

Sweet Potato Rolls

- 1 medium-size sweet potato
- 1 package active dry yeast
- 2 tablespoons brown sugar
- 2¾ cups bread flour, divided
- 3 tablespoons instant nonfat dry milk powder
- ½ teaspoon salt
- 1 egg
- 1 teaspoon vegetable oil
- 2 tablespoons bread flour
- Vegetable cooking spray

Scrub potato; prick several times with a fork. Place in a medium saucepan; add water to cover. Bring to a boil; reduce heat, and simmer 20 to 30 minutes or until tender. Drain potato, reserving ¾ cup water. Let potato cool slightly. Peel and mash potato, reserving ⅔ cup. Reserve remaining potato for another use.

Cool reserved ¾ cup water to 105° to 115°. Combine water, yeast, and brown sugar in a 1-cup liquid measuring cup; let stand 5 minutes. Combine yeast mixture, 1½ cups flour, dry milk, and salt in a large mixing bowl; beat at medium speed of an electric mixer until well blended. Add potato, egg, and oil, beating well. Gradually stir in enough of remaining 1¼ cups flour to make a soft dough.

Sprinkle 2 tablespoons flour evenly over work surface. Turn dough out onto floured surface, and knead until smooth and elastic (about 5 minutes). Place in a bowl coated with cooking spray, turning to coat top. Cover and let rise in a warm place (85°), free from drafts, 45 minutes or until doubled in bulk.

Punch dough down, and divide into 24 equal portions. Shape each portion into a ball, and place balls on a baking sheet coated with cooking spray.

Cover and let rise in a warm place, free from drafts, 30 minutes or until doubled in bulk. Bake at 400° for 10 minutes or until golden. Yield: 24 rolls.

Per Roll

Calories 71 (9% Calories from Fat)	Carbohydrate 13.4 g	Cholesterol 9 mg
Fat 0.7 g (Saturated Fat 0.2 g)	Protein 2.5 g	Sodium 58 mg

Which Yeast to Use?

Rapid-rise, active dry, and bread machine yeasts all are interchangeable. But just remember that anytime you use active dry yeast, you must first dissolve it in warm liquid, unlike rapid-rise or bread machine yeasts which can be mixed in with the dry ingredients. The advantage to rapid-rise and bread machine yeasts is that the bread generally rises only one time, instead of two.

Basil-Cheese Rolls

Basil-Cheese Rolls

Pesto is the flavorful filling for these rolls. Just process together the fresh basil, Parmesan, olive oil, and garlic for our low-fat version.

1 package active dry yeast
1 cup warm water (105° to 115°)
2½ cups bread flour
½ teaspoon salt
1 tablespoon bread flour, divided
Vegetable cooking spray
1 cup loosely packed fresh basil
½ cup chopped onion
3 tablespoons grated Parmesan cheese
1 tablespoon olive oil
1 egg white
¼ teaspoon salt
4 cloves garlic

Combine yeast and warm water in a 1-cup liquid measuring cup; let stand 5 minutes. Position dough blade in food processor bowl; add yeast mixture, 2½ cups bread flour, and ½ teaspoon salt. Process 1 minute or until well blended, stopping once to scrape down sides.

Sprinkle 1½ teaspoons flour evenly over work surface. Turn dough out onto floured surface, and knead until smooth and elastic (about 10 minutes). Place dough in a large bowl coated with cooking spray, turning to coat top. Cover and let rise in a warm place (85°), free from drafts, 45 minutes or until doubled in bulk.

Punch dough down. Sprinkle remaining 1½ teaspoons flour evenly over work surface. Turn dough out onto floured surface, and roll into an 11- x 14-inch rectangle.

Position knife blade in food processor bowl; add basil and remaining ingredients. Process 1 minute or until finely chopped, scraping sides of processor bowl twice. Spread pesto mixture evenly over dough. Roll up, starting at long side. Pinch seam to seal (do not seal ends). Cut into 18 (¾-inch) slices. Place slices on a baking sheet coated with cooking spray.

Cover and let rise in a warm place, free from drafts, 20 minutes. Bake at 400° for 15 to 18 minutes or until golden. Yield: 18 rolls.

Per Roll

Calories 86 (15% Calories from Fat)	Carbohydrate 15.0 g	Cholesterol 1 mg
Fat 1.4 g (Saturated Fat 0.3 g)	Protein 3.1 g	Sodium 114 mg

Apple-Walnut Country Bread

½ cup unsweetened apple cider
½ cup dried apples, chopped
1 cup peeled and coarsely shredded Granny Smith apple
2½ teaspoons active dry yeast
¼ cup warm water (105° to 115°)
2¾ cups bread flour
¾ teaspoon salt
¼ teaspoon ground ginger
1 teaspoon ground cinnamon
3 tablespoons honey
1 tablespoon margarine, softened
1 egg
1 cup medium rye flour
2 tablespoons bread flour
Vegetable cooking spray
½ cup walnut pieces, lightly toasted
1 egg white, lightly beaten

What's a Wash?

A "wash" is what you call any liquid mixture you brush on bread doughs before you bake them to create a special appearance. Brushing water or milk on the dough gives a dark, crusty look. For shiny bread crusts, combine beaten egg white and a little water (or use just beaten egg white). An egg wash also helps seeds or chopped herbs to stick on the surface of the dough.

Combine cider and dried apples in a measuring cup. Microwave at HIGH 1½ minutes. Stir in shredded apple, and set aside.

Combine yeast and warm water; let stand 5 minutes.

Combine apple mixture, yeast mixture, 2¾ cups bread flour, and next 5 ingredients in a large bowl; beat at medium speed of an electric mixer until ingredients are well blended. Gradually stir in egg and enough rye flour to make a soft dough.

Sprinkle 2 tablespoons bread flour evenly over work surface. Turn dough out onto floured surface, and knead until smooth and elastic (about 5 minutes). Place in a bowl coated with cooking spray, turning to coat top. Cover and let rise in a warm place (85°), free from drafts, 55 minutes or until doubled in bulk.

Punch dough down; turn out onto work surface, and flatten slightly. Sprinkle walnuts over dough; knead gently to incorporate walnuts. Shape into a 7-inch round loaf. Place loaf on a baking sheet coated with cooking spray. Cover and let rise in a warm place, free from drafts, 40 minutes or until doubled in bulk. With a sharp knife, make 4 crisscross slashes (¼-inch deep) across top of loaf. Brush loaf with egg white. Bake at 350° for 35 minutes or until loaf sounds hollow when tapped. Remove bread from baking sheet immediately; let cool on a wire rack. Cut into wedges. Yield: 24 wedges.

Per Wedge
Calories 118 (20% Calories from Fat) Carbohydrate 20.9 g Cholesterol 9 mg
Fat 2.6 g (Saturated Fat 0.3 g) Protein 3.3 g Sodium 86 mg

Spicy Apple Butter Bread

Want your bread to look like the loaves in the window of a French bakery? Just sprinkle a little flour on top after it bakes. That's what we did in the photo on page 96.

1 tablespoon active dry yeast
1 teaspoon brown sugar
1 cup warm water (105° to 115°)
1 tablespoon honey
½ cup apple butter
2½ cups bread flour
1 cup whole wheat flour
1 teaspoon ground cinnamon
½ teaspoon salt
¼ cup toasted honey-flavored wheat germ
Vegetable cooking spray
1 tablespoon skim milk

Combine first 4 ingredients in a 2-cup liquid measuring cup; let stand 5 minutes. Stir in apple butter. Combine yeast mixture, bread flour, and next 3 ingredients in a large mixing bowl; beat at medium speed of an electric mixer until well blended.

Sprinkle wheat germ evenly over work surface. Turn dough out onto surface, and knead until smooth and elastic (about 10 minutes). Place in a bowl coated with cooking spray, turning to coat top. Cover and let rise in a warm place (85°), free from drafts, 50 minutes or until doubled in bulk.

Punch dough down, and shape into an 8-inch round loaf. Place loaf on a baking sheet coated with cooking spray. Cover and let rise in a warm place, free from drafts, 30 minutes or until doubled in bulk. Brush loaf with milk. Bake at 425° for 10 minutes. Reduce oven temperature to 375°, and bake 10 additional minutes or until loaf sounds hollow when tapped. Remove loaf from baking sheet immediately; cool on a wire rack. Cut loaf into wedges. Yield: 24 wedges.

Per Wedge

Calories 89 (5% Calories from Fat)	Carbohydrate 18.6 g	Cholesterol 0 mg
Fat 0.5 g (Saturated Fat 0.1 g)	Protein 2.9 g	Sodium 50 mg

Rosemary Currant Focaccia

For a little extra flavor, use lemon olive oil in this recipe. Find it in well-stocked supermarkets on the specialty oils and vinegars aisles.

2¾ cups bread flour, divided
1 package rapid-rise yeast
1 teaspoon salt
¾ cup plus 3 tablespoons water
2 tablespoons olive oil
Vegetable cooking spray
¼ cup currants
2 tablespoons chopped fresh rosemary
1 tablespoon cornmeal
1 teaspoon olive oil
½ teaspoon kosher salt

Combine 2 cups flour, yeast, and 1 teaspoon salt in a large mixing bowl, stirring well. Combine water and 2 tablespoons olive oil in a saucepan; place over medium heat until mixture is very warm (120° to 130°).

Gradually add liquid mixture to flour mixture, beating well at low speed of an electric mixer. Beat 2 additional minutes at medium speed. Gradually stir in enough of the remaining ¾ cup bread flour to make a soft dough.

Turn dough out onto work surface, and knead until smooth and elastic (about 10 minutes). Place dough in a large bowl coated with cooking spray, turning to coat top. Cover and let rise in a warm place (85°), free from drafts, 40 minutes or until doubled in bulk.

Punch dough down; turn out onto work surface, and flatten slightly. Sprinkle currants and rosemary over dough; knead gently to incorporate currants and rosemary. Cover and let dough rest 15 minutes.

Roll dough into an 11-inch circle; place on a baking sheet sprinkled with cornmeal. Let dough rest 10 minutes. Brush dough with 1 teaspoon olive oil, and sprinkle evenly with kosher salt. Poke holes in dough at 1-inch intervals with handle of a wooden spoon. Bake at 500° for 10 to 12 minutes or until golden. Cut into wedges. Yield: 12 wedges.

Per Wedge
Calories 152 (20% Calories from Fat) Carbohydrate 26.0 g Cholesterol 0 mg
Fat 3.4 g (Saturated Fat 0.4 g) Protein 4.2 g Sodium 295 mg

A Tip for Rosemary

To use fresh rosemary, first strip the leaves from the woody stems by sliding your thumb and forefinger the length of the stem. Then crush the leaves with a mortar and pestle, or finely chop them on a cutting board with a sharp knife.

Roasted Red Pepper Lasagna

MEATLESS

Our dilemma? We needed harissa to serve with Vegetable Garden Couscous (page 120), a recipe that became one of our favorites in this chapter. In the Middle East, harissa is to couscous as Tabasco sauce is to red beans and rice down in Cajun country. A must. But when we finally found it, it was on an obscure shelf in an ethnic food market.

Since we had such a hard time tracking down harissa, we worried that you might have trouble finding it, too. Then home economist Julie Christopher hit on an idea. "Gee, I think it would be pretty easy to make," she said. So she grabbed a bag of dried red chiles with a mission in mind. A few experiments later Julie had a homemade harissa that tasted and looked just like the commercial canned one. And was it hot! Of course, any really hot chile sauce would be a good

DISHES

substitute for harissa. But if you want to be authentic you can find Julie's recipe on page 66, or check out our mail-order source on page 230.

So now you have the key to the best tasting meatless entrées. It's that there is no "secret" ingredient to these recipes—just flavor from hot peppers, roasted vegetables, spices, herb-flavored pesto sauce, and even cheeses like feta and Parmesan.

Roasted Red Pepper Lasagna

Although fresh roasted is best, you can speed up preparation time by using already-roasted peppers in a jar. They're on the canned vegetable aisle in supermarkets.

3 large sweet red peppers
12 sun-dried tomatoes
1 cup boiling water
¾ cup fresh basil leaves
1 tablespoon lemon juice
½ teaspoon salt
½ teaspoon freshly ground pepper
2 cloves garlic
1 (8-ounce) can no-salt-added tomato sauce
2 tablespoons water
1 (8-ounce) carton light process cream cheese, softened
¾ cup nonfat ricotta cheese
½ cup nonfat sour cream
¼ cup frozen egg substitute, thawed
¼ cup freshly grated Parmesan cheese
2 teaspoons dried oregano
Vegetable cooking spray
3 cups sliced fresh mushrooms
2¼ cups shredded carrot
2 cups chopped zucchini
1 cup chopped onion
6 cooked lasagna noodles (cooked without salt or fat)
2 cups (8 ounces) shredded part-skim mozzarella cheese

Cut peppers in half lengthwise; remove and discard seeds and membranes. Place peppers, skin side up, on a baking sheet, and flatten with palm of hand. Broil 5½ inches from heat (with electric oven door partially opened) 15 to 20 minutes or until charred. Place in ice water until cool; peel and discard skins. Coarsely chop peppers.

Combine tomatoes and 1 cup boiling water in a small bowl; let stand 5 minutes. Drain.

Position knife blade in food processor bowl; add chopped pepper, tomatoes, basil, and next 4 ingredients. Process until smooth, scraping sides of processor bowl once. Combine pepper mixture, tomato sauce, and 2 tablespoons water; stir well. Set aside.

Beat cream cheese at medium speed of an electric mixer until creamy. Add ricotta cheese, sour cream, egg substitute, Parmesan cheese, and oregano, beating until smooth. Set aside.

Shear Cooking
To chop lots of fresh herbs the quick way, pack the leaves in a measuring cup and snip them with kitchen shears.

Coat a large nonstick skillet with cooking spray; place over medium-high heat until hot. Add mushrooms, carrot, zucchini, and onion; sauté 8 minutes or until tender.

Spread ¾ cup pepper mixture over bottom of a 13- x 9- x 2-inch baking dish coated with cooking spray. Place 3 lasagna noodles over sauce; top with half of cream cheese mixture, half of vegetable mixture, and half of remaining pepper mixture. Repeat layers with remaining noodles, cream cheese mixture, vegetable mixture, and pepper mixture.

Cover and bake at 350° for 30 minutes. Uncover; sprinkle with mozzarella cheese. Bake 5 additional minutes or until cheese melts. Let stand 10 minutes before serving. Yield: 10 servings.

Per Serving
Calories 248 (31% Calories from Fat) Carbohydrate 27.7 g Cholesterol 29 mg
Fat 8.5 g (Saturated Fat 4.9 g) Protein 16.4 g Sodium 477 mg

Southwestern Pasta Toss

½ (8-ounce) package rotini (corkscrew pasta), uncooked
1¾ cups Santa Fe Salsa (page 52)
Vegetable cooking spray
1 teaspoon olive oil
1 clove garlic, minced
½ teaspoon ground cumin
1 cup frozen whole kernel corn, thawed
1 (15-ounce) can black beans, drained
¼ cup chopped fresh cilantro
2 tablespoons grated Parmesan cheese
1 tablespoon lime juice

Cook pasta according to package directions, omitting salt and fat; drain. Place pasta in a serving bowl. Add Santa Fe Salsa, and toss gently. Set aside.

Coat a medium nonstick skillet with cooking spray; add oil. Place over medium heat until hot. Add garlic and cumin, and sauté 30 seconds. Stir in corn and beans. Cook, stirring constantly, until thoroughly heated. Add corn mixture, cilantro, cheese, and lime juice to pasta mixture, and toss gently. Serve immediately. Yield: 4 (1¼-cup) servings.

Per Serving
Calories 300 (11% Calories from Fat) Carbohydrate 56.1 g Cholesterol 2 mg
Fat 3.7 g (Saturated Fat 1.0 g) Protein 13.1 g Sodium 221 mg

Spicy Sauté

Stir dried spices for a few minutes in a hot skillet (with or without oil) to bring out a toasted, more pronounced flavor.

Roasted Asparagus Lasagna

1½ cups water
¼ cup plus 2 tablespoons instant nonfat dry milk powder
2 tablespoons reduced-calorie margarine
3 tablespoons all-purpose flour
⅛ teaspoon ground white pepper
¼ teaspoon salt
⅛ teaspoon ground cloves
Olive oil-flavored vegetable cooking spray
2 teaspoons olive oil, divided
2 large purple onions (about 1½ pounds), thinly sliced
2 cloves garlic, minced
2 pounds fresh asparagus
1 cup sliced fresh mushrooms
12 cooked lasagna noodles (cooked without salt or fat)
1½ cups (6 ounces) shredded part-skim mozzarella cheese
1 cup grated Parmigiano Reggiano cheese

Combine water and milk powder, stirring until powder dissolves. Set milk aside.

Melt margarine in a small heavy saucepan over medium heat; add flour and pepper. Cook 1 minute, stirring constantly with a wire whisk. Gradually add milk, stirring constantly. Cook, stirring constantly, 12 additional minutes or until thickened and bubbly. Add salt and cloves; stir well. Set aside.

Coat a large nonstick skillet with cooking spray; add 1 teaspoon oil. Place over medium-high heat until hot. Add onion and garlic; sauté until tender. Set aside.

Snap off tough ends of asparagus. Remove scales from asparagus spears with a knife or vegetable peeler, if desired. Place asparagus and mushrooms in a large roasting pan coated with cooking spray. Add remaining 1 teaspoon oil, tossing well. Bake asparagus mixture at 500° for 8 minutes. Cool. Slice asparagus, diagonally, into thin slices. Add asparagus and mushrooms to onion mixture. Set mixture aside.

Coat a 13- x 9- x 2-inch baking dish with cooking spray. Place 4 lasagna noodles in bottom of dish. Top with one-third of onion mixture, one-third of white sauce, ½ cup mozzarella cheese, and ⅓ cup Parmigiano Reggiano cheese. Repeat layers twice with remaining noodles, onion mixture, white sauce, and cheeses.

Prince of Parmesan

The name is Parmigiano Reggiano. It's aged longer than regular Parmesan to make a strong-flavored cheese that melts in your mouth.

Cover and bake at 350° for 30 to 40 minutes or until thoroughly heated. Uncover and bake 10 additional minutes. Let lasagna stand 15 minutes before serving. Yield: 8 servings.

Per Serving
Calories 345 (27% Calories from Fat) Carbohydrate 45.1 g Cholesterol 21 mg
Fat 10.3 g (Saturated Fat 4.2 g) Protein 18.9 g Sodium 407 mg

Vermicelli with Tomatoes and Fresh Herbs

Olive oil-flavored vegetable cooking spray
2 teaspoons Sun-Dried Tomato-Garlic Oil (page 32) or garlic-flavored olive oil, divided
½ cup chopped onion
½ cup shredded carrot
2 cloves garlic, minced
6 cups peeled, seeded, and chopped tomato
2 (8-ounce) cans no-salt-added tomato sauce
½ cup chopped fresh basil
¼ cup chopped fresh marjoram
1 teaspoon coarsely ground pepper
½ teaspoon salt
1½ tablespoons chopped walnuts
10 ounces vermicelli, uncooked
2½ ounces basil-tomato (or regular) feta cheese

Coat a Dutch oven with cooking spray; add 1 teaspoon Sun-Dried Tomato-Garlic Oil. Place over medium-high heat until hot. Add onion, carrot, and garlic, and sauté until tender. Add tomato and next 5 ingredients; bring mixture to a boil. Reduce heat, and simmer, uncovered, 15 minutes or until thickened. Set mixture aside, and keep warm.

Heat remaining 1 teaspoon Sun-Dried Tomato Garlic Oil in a small skillet over medium heat; add walnuts. Cook until lightly browned, stirring frequently. Set walnuts aside.

Cook pasta according to package directions, omitting salt and fat; drain. Place pasta on a serving platter; spoon tomato mixture over pasta. Sprinkle with walnuts and cheese. Yield: 5 servings.

Per Serving
Calories 375 (20% Calories from Fat) Carbohydrate 64.4 g Cholesterol 13 mg
Fat 8.2 g (Saturated Fat 2.7 g) Protein 13.2 g Sodium 447 mg

Crumble for Feta

The soft, tangy chunks of cheese in Greek salads are feta. This cheese made from sheep, goat, or cow's milk is strong, but not bitter. Still, a little goes a long way.

Pesto-Stuffed Pasta Shells

Pesto-Stuffed Pasta Shells

You can use commercial pesto sauce instead of making your own, but look for a low-fat brand since traditional pesto is high in fat.

2 (10-ounce) packages frozen chopped spinach, thawed
½ cup Pesto Sauce (page 63)
2 cups 1% low-fat cottage cheese
3 tablespoons freshly grated Parmesan cheese, divided
⅛ teaspoon pepper
⅛ teaspoon freshly grated nutmeg
20 jumbo pasta shells, uncooked
2¼ cups Herbed Tomato Sauce (page 64)
Vegetable cooking spray

Drain spinach, and press between paper towels to remove excess moisture. Combine spinach, Pesto Sauce, cottage cheese, 2 tablespoons Parmesan cheese, pepper, and nutmeg; stir well.

Cook pasta shells according to package directions, omitting salt and fat; drain. Stuff cheese mixture evenly into cooked shells.

Spoon 1 cup Herbed Tomato Sauce into a 13- x 9- x 2-inch baking dish coated with cooking spray. Place filled shells over sauce. Pour remaining Herbed Tomato Sauce over shells. Cover and bake at 375° for 20 minutes or until hot and bubbly. Remove from oven, and sprinkle with remaining 1 tablespoon Parmesan cheese. Serve immediately. Yield: 5 servings.

Per Serving
Calories 365 (19% Calories from Fat) Carbohydrate 49.2 g Cholesterol 11 mg
Fat 7.6 g (Saturated Fat 2.9 g) Protein 25.3 g Sodium 800 mg

Grate Taste

The strongest flavor is released when whole nutmeg is freshly grated. You can find a nutmeg grater or nutmeg grinder in most kitchen shops.

WHAT'S A CHIPOTLE?

The powerful little chipotle (chih-POHT-lay) chile is smoke-seasoned during the drying process. The smoked chile is sold dried, but it is also sold canned in adobo sauce (which is a spicy chile-vinegar marinade) on the ethnic food aisle.

Chipotle Red Beans and Rice

Some recipes, like this one, taste better with bitters, a flavoring made from distilled herbs, barks, and roots.

1 pound dried kidney beans
8 cups water, divided
Vegetable cooking spray
2 cups chopped onion
2 cups chopped green pepper
1 cup finely chopped celery
2 cloves garlic, minced
2 teaspoons dried basil
1 teaspoon dried oregano
1 teaspoon ground cumin
½ teaspoon dried thyme
2 bay leaves
2 cups canned vegetable broth, undiluted
1 cup dry red wine
3 canned chipotle peppers in adobo sauce, drained and chopped
1½ tablespoons low-sodium Worcestershire sauce
1 tablespoon bitters
¼ teaspoon pepper
9 cups cooked brown rice (cooked without salt or fat)
1 cup chopped fresh cilantro
¼ teaspoon salt
2 cups diced fresh tomato

Sort and wash beans; place beans in a large Dutch oven. Cover with water to a depth of 2 inches above beans. Bring to a boil; cover, remove from heat, and let stand for 1 hour.

Drain beans, and return to Dutch oven. Add 6 cups water; bring to a boil. Cover; reduce heat, and simmer 30 minutes. Set aside.

Coat a large skillet with cooking spray; place over medium heat until hot. Add onion and next 3 ingredients; cook, stirring constantly, 7 to 9 minutes or until tender. Add basil and next 4 ingredients; cook, stirring constantly, 1 to 2 minutes.

Add onion mixture, remaining 2 cups water, broth, and next 4 ingredients to bean mixture; bring to a boil. Cover; reduce heat, and simmer 1 hour.

Pour 2 cups bean mixture into container of an electric blender; cover and process until smooth. Return mixture to Dutch oven; bring to a boil. Reduce heat; simmer, uncovered, 2 hours or until thickened, stirring occasionally. Remove and discard bay leaves. Stir in pepper.

Combine rice, cilantro, and salt; stir well. Spoon 1 cup rice mixture into each of 9 individual serving bowls; top each with 1 cup bean mixture. Sprinkle evenly with tomato. Yield: 9 servings.

Per Serving

Calories 404 (6% Calories from Fat)	Carbohydrate 76.0 g	Cholesterol 0 mg
Fat 2.9 g (Saturated Fat 0.5 g)	Protein 15.3 g	Sodium 233 mg

Black Bean Tostadas with Grilled Corn Salsa

2 cloves garlic
2 (15-ounce) cans no-salt-added black beans, drained
1 cup canned vegetable broth, undiluted
3 tablespoons finely chopped onion
1/4 teaspoon salt
1/4 cup plus 2 tablespoons nonfat sour cream
3 tablespoons chopped fresh cilantro
6 (6-inch) corn tortillas
Vegetable cooking spray
3/4 cup (3 ounces) shredded Monterey Jack cheese with peppers
6 cups shredded iceburg lettuce
3/4 cup Grilled Corn Salsa (page 55)

Position knife blade in food processor bowl. Drop garlic through food chute with processor running. Process 3 seconds or until garlic is minced. Add beans, broth, onion, and salt; process until smooth, scraping sides of processor bowl once. Transfer bean mixture to a medium saucepan. Partially cover mixture, and cook over medium heat 15 minutes or until thickened, stirring frequently.

Combine sour cream and cilantro; stir well. Cover and chill.

Place tortillas on a baking sheet coated with cooking spray. Bake at 350° for 6 minutes; turn tortillas over, and bake 6 to 8 additional minutes or until crisp.

Place 1 tortilla on each individual serving plate. Spoon bean mixture evenly over tortillas; top each with cheese. Arrange lettuce over cheese. Top each tostada with 2 tablespoons Grilled Corn Salsa and 1 tablespoon sour cream mixture. Yield: 6 servings.

Per Serving

Calories 275 (20% Calories from Fat)	Carbohydrate 32.3 g	Cholesterol 11 mg
Fat 6.0 g (Saturated Fat 2.9 g)	Protein 15.5 g	Sodium 273 mg

Polenta with Mushroom-Tomato Sauce

Polenta's Humble Roots
If you like grits or cornbread, you'll like polenta, an Italian tradition. It has the same grainy texture and comes from the same source–ground corn. Serve polenta like you would grits, as a spoonable side dish. Or cool the cooked cornmeal mush in a skillet or pan to cut into squares or wedges which can be toasted and sometimes topped with a tasty sauce.

1 cup coarse yellow cornmeal
1 cup cold water
2 cups canned vegetable broth, undiluted
3/4 cup frozen whole-kernel corn
1/2 cup freshly grated Parmesan cheese, divided
1/4 teaspoon salt
Olive oil-flavored vegetable cooking spray
1 teaspoon olive oil
1 large onion, chopped
1 large clove garlic, minced
1/8 teaspoon dried crushed red pepper
1/2 pound fresh mushrooms, sliced
1/3 cup dry white wine
1 (14.5-ounce) can no-salt-added whole tomatoes, undrained and chopped
2 tablespoons chopped fresh parsley
1 tablespoon chopped fresh basil
1 tablespoon chopped fresh oregano
1/4 teaspoon salt
1/8 teaspoon black pepper

Combine cornmeal and water in a small bowl; set aside.

Pour vegetable broth into a medium saucepan, and bring to a boil over high heat. Add cornmeal mixture in a slow, steady stream, stirring constantly. Stir in corn. Reduce heat to medium; cook, stirring constantly, 20 minutes or until mixture pulls away from sides of pan. Add 1/4 cup cheese and 1/4 teaspoon salt, stirring until cheese melts. Spoon into an 8-inch cakepan coated with cooking spray. Set polenta aside, and let cool completely.

Coat a large nonstick skillet with cooking spray; add oil. Place over medium-high heat until hot. Add onion; sauté until tender. Add garlic and crushed red pepper; cook 1 minute. Add mushrooms; sauté until tender. Add wine and tomatoes; cook over medium-high heat, stirring constantly, until most of the liquid evaporates. Add parsley, basil, oregano, 1/4 teaspoon salt, and 1/8 teaspoon black pepper. Set aside, and keep warm.

Turn polenta out onto a cutting board; cut polenta into 6 wedges. Place polenta wedges on a baking sheet coated with cooking spray. Coat polenta lightly with cooking spray. Broil 5 1/2 inches from heat (with electric oven door partially opened) 6 minutes or until crusty and golden. Place a polenta wedge on each individual serving plate.

Top wedges evenly with mushroom mixture and remaining ¼ cup Parmesan cheese. Serve warm. Yield: 6 servings.

Per Serving
Calories 253 (23% Calories from Fat) Carbohydrate 37.1 g Cholesterol 11 mg
Fat 6.4 g (Saturated Fat 3.0 g) Protein 11.1 g Sodium 475 mg

Broccoli- and Cheddar-Stuffed Baked Potatoes

4 (8-ounce) baking potatoes
2 cups fresh broccoli flowerets, chopped
½ cup plain low-fat yogurt
2 teaspoons reduced-calorie margarine
½ cup (2 ounces) shredded reduced-fat sharp Cheddar cheese, divided
3 tablespoons chopped fresh parsley
1½ teaspoons chopped fresh oregano
1½ teaspoons chopped fresh basil
¼ teaspoon salt
¼ teaspoon pepper
½ teaspoon paprika

Scrub potatoes; prick each several times with a fork. Bake at 400° for 1 hour or until done. Cool slightly.

Cook broccoli in boiling water 3 to 5 minutes or until tender; drain well.

Cut a 1-inch-wide lengthwise strip from top of each potato; carefully scoop out potato pulp, leaving ¼-inch-thick shells. Set shells aside. Place pulp, yogurt, and margarine in a medium bowl; mash until smooth. Add broccoli, ¼ cup plus 2 tablespoons cheese, and next 5 ingredients; stir well. Fill potato shells with broccoli mixture. Place potatoes in an ungreased 9-inch square pan. Bake at 400° for 25 minutes. Remove from oven, and sprinkle potatoes with remaining 2 tablespoons cheese and paprika. Return to oven, and bake 5 additional minutes or until cheese melts. Yield: 4 servings.

Per Serving
Calories 282 (15% Calories from Fat) Carbohydrate 49.6 g Cholesterol 11 mg
Fat 4.8 g (Saturated Fat 2.0 g) Protein 12.7 g Sodium 314 mg

Vegetable Garden Couscous

Harissa, a thick, blistering hot red chile paste, is often served as a condiment with couscous in the Middle East. Find canned harissa in ethnic markets, or make your own; it keeps well in the refrigerator.

Tune in to Turmeric
This bold-flavored, bright gold spice is a basic ingredient in curry powders—and the reason they're all golden yellow.

2 (14½-ounce) cans vegetable broth, undiluted
4 small round red potatoes, peeled and quartered
4 medium carrots, scraped and cut into 1½-inch pieces
Vegetable cooking spray
1 tablespoon margarine
1 large onion, chopped
2 large cloves garlic, minced
1 teaspoon ground ginger
½ teaspoon ground turmeric
½ teaspoon ground cumin
¼ teaspoon ground cinnamon
3 tablespoons all-purpose flour
1 tablespoon Harissa (page 66)
4 ounces fresh green beans, halved diagonally
1 large sweet red pepper, seeded and cut into 1-inch pieces
3 tablespoons raisins
2 small zucchini, cut into ½-inch pieces
½ teaspoon salt, divided
¼ teaspoon pepper
¼ cup chopped fresh parsley
¼ cup chopped fresh cilantro
2 tablespoons fresh lemon juice
1 cup couscous, uncooked
2 tablespoons sliced almonds, toasted
Harissa (optional)

Combine first 3 ingredients in a large saucepan. Bring to a boil; cover, reduce heat, and simmer 15 minutes or until tender. Remove vegetables with a slotted spoon; keep warm. Reserve 3 cups broth; set aside.

Coat a large nonstick skillet with cooking spray; add margarine. Place over medium heat until margarine melts. Add onion, and sauté 3 to 5 minutes or until tender. Add garlic; sauté 30 seconds.

Add ginger and next 4 ingredients; stir well. (Mixture will be dry.) Gradually add 1½ cups of the reserved broth, stirring constantly. Cook, stirring constantly, 2 minutes or until thickened and bubbly. Stir in 1 tablespoon Harissa.

Add beans, red pepper, and raisins. Bring to a boil; cover, reduce heat, and simmer 5 minutes or until beans are tender. Add zucchini

Vegetable Garden Couscous

and reserved potato and carrot. Cook, covered, 5 minutes or until zucchini is tender. Add $\frac{1}{4}$ teaspoon salt and next 4 ingredients; stir mixture well.

Bring remaining $1\frac{1}{2}$ cups broth and remaining $\frac{1}{4}$ teaspoon salt to a boil in a medium saucepan; stir in couscous. Remove from heat; cover and let stand 5 minutes. Fluff couscous with a fork. Place couscous on a serving dish. Spoon vegetable mixture over couscous; sprinkle evenly with almonds. Serve with additional Harissa, if desired. Yield: 4 servings.

Per Serving

Calories 411 (16% Calories from Fat)	Carbohydrate 81.4 g	Cholesterol 0 mg
Fat 7.2 g (Saturated Fat 1.0 g)	Protein 11.4 g	Sodium 837 mg

ZUCCHINI-CANNELLINI TOSS

- Vegetable cooking spray
- 2 pounds zucchini, cut into 2- x ½-inch strips
- 1 large clove garlic, minced
- 2 tablespoons dry white wine
- 2 (15-ounce) cans cannellini beans, drained
- ¼ teaspoon salt
- ⅛ teaspoon pepper
- ½ cup slivered fresh basil
- 2 tablespoons chopped fresh oregano
- 2 cups hot cooked couscous
- 3 tablespoons freshly grated Parmigiano Reggiano cheese

Coat a large nonstick skillet with cooking spray; place over high heat until hot. Add zucchini; sauté 4 minutes or until lightly browned, stirring frequently. Add garlic, and sauté 1 minute. Add wine; cook 2 minutes. Add beans, salt, and pepper. Reduce heat to medium, and cook 4 minutes or until thoroughly heated. Add basil and oregano; toss. Spoon evenly over couscous; sprinkle with cheese. Yield: 4 (1½-cup) servings.

Per Serving

Calories 329 (7% Calories from Fat)	Carbohydrate 57.5 g	Cholesterol 2 mg
Fat 2.6 g (Saturated Fat 1.0 g)	Protein 17.7 g	Sodium 307 mg

Cater to Couscous

Serve couscous (KOOS-koos) instead of strands of pasta one night; you'll like the change in texture. This bland bead-like pasta from the Middle East takes on flavor easily. Find it in boxes on the pasta or rice aisles.

Vegetable Fried Rice

Although tofu itself tastes rather bland, it takes on the flavor of food with which it's cooked. The smooth, creamy cakes made from soybean curd are low in calories and have no cholesterol. Tofu's texture is similar to that of a thick custard.

1 egg
1/8 teaspoon salt
1 tablespoon low-sodium soy sauce
1 teaspoon peanut oil
1/2 teaspoon brown sugar
Vegetable cooking spray
1 cup sliced celery
1/2 cup sliced onion, cut in half
1 cup sliced fresh mushrooms
1 (6-ounce) package smoked tofu, crumbled
2 cloves garlic, crushed
3 cups cooked long-grain rice (cooked without salt or fat)
1 cup frozen English peas, thawed

Combine egg and salt, beating with a wire whisk until frothy. Set aside. Combine soy sauce, oil, and sugar. Set aside.

Coat a wok with cooking spray. Heat at medium-high (375°) until hot. Add celery and onion; stir-fry 2 minutes. Add mushrooms, tofu, and garlic; stir-fry 1 minute.

Push vegetable mixture up sides of wok, forming a well in center. Pour egg mixture into well, and stir-fry until set. Add rice, and stir-fry 1 minute. Add soy sauce mixture and peas; stir-fry 2 minutes. Serve immediately. Yield: 6 (1-cup) servings.

Per Serving

Calories 202 (9% Calories from Fat)	Carbohydrate 31.2 g	Cholesterol 37 mg
Fat 2.0 g (Saturated Fat 0.8 g)	Protein 10.9 g	Sodium 204 mg

How to Handle Tofu

Store tofu covered in water in the refrigerator up to a week and change the water each day. You can freeze it for up to 3 months, but this will cause the texture to become a bit chewier.

Parmesan Rice Pilaf in Artichokes

- 4 medium artichokes
- 1 teaspoon lemon juice
- Vegetable cooking spray
- 1 teaspoon olive oil
- ⅓ cup minced onion
- 2 tablespoons minced celery
- 1 cup water
- ½ cup basmati rice
- ¼ cup minced sun-dried tomatoes
- 1½ teaspoons dried Italian seasoning, divided
- 1 tablespoon chopped ripe olives
- ½ cup plain nonfat yogurt
- 2 teaspoons all-purpose flour
- 2 tablespoons grated Parmesan cheese

Wash artichokes by plunging up and down in cold water. Cut off stem ends, and trim about ½ inch from top of each artichoke. Remove any loose bottom leaves. With scissors, trim away about one-fourth of each outer leaf. Brush top and edges of leaves with lemon juice to prevent discoloration.

Place artichokes in a large Dutch oven; add water to depth of 1 inch. Bring to a boil; cover, reduce heat, and simmer 25 minutes or until artichokes are almost tender. Spread leaves apart; scrape out the fuzzy thistle center (choke) with a spoon, and discard thistle. Set artichokes aside.

Coat a medium saucepan with cooking spray; add oil. Place over medium-high heat until hot. Add onion and celery; sauté until tender. Add 1 cup water, rice, tomato, and 1 teaspoon Italian seasoning. Bring to a boil; cover, reduce heat, and simmer 20 minutes or until rice is tender and liquid is absorbed. Stir in olives.

Spoon rice mixture into artichoke cavities. Combine yogurt and flour. Spoon over rice mixture. Sprinkle with cheese and remaining ½ teaspoon Italian seasoning. Arrange artichokes in a 13- x 9- x 2-inch baking dish. Cover and bake at 350° for 20 minutes. Bake, uncovered, 5 additional minutes or until thoroughly heated. Yield: 4 servings.

Per Serving

Calories 287 (11% Calories from Fat) Carbohydrate 58.0 g Cholesterol 3 mg
Fat 3.4 g (Saturated Fat 1.0 g) Protein 12.5 g Sodium 427 mg

Popcorn Rice

That's the nickname of basmati rice, an aromatic rice variety, because it smells like hot popped corn when it cooks.

Italian Risotto with Roasted Red Peppers and Peas

Arborio rice is a must for risotto, an Italian dish featuring creamy, broth-cooked rice.

3 large sweet red peppers
2 cups canned vegetable broth, undiluted
2 cups water
1 teaspoon olive oil
1 cup Arborio rice, uncooked
1 (10-ounce) package frozen English peas, thawed
¼ cup freshly grated Parmesan cheese
3 tablespoons chopped fresh basil
3 tablespoons chopped fresh parsley
1 tablespoon lemon juice
⅛ teaspoon freshly ground pepper

Cut peppers in half lengthwise; remove and discard seeds and membranes. Place peppers, skin side up, on a baking sheet, and flatten with palm of hand. Broil 5½ inches from heat (with electric oven door partially opened) 15 to 20 minutes or until charred. Place in ice water until cool; peel and discard skins. Chop and set aside.

Combine broth and water in a saucepan; place over medium heat. Cover and bring to a simmer; reduce heat to low, and keep warm. (Do not boil.)

Heat oil in a medium saucepan over medium-high heat until hot; add rice. Cook 2 minutes or until rice is lightly browned, stirring constantly. Reduce heat to medium-low.

Add 1 cup of simmering broth mixture to rice, stirring constantly until most of liquid is absorbed. Add remaining broth, ½ cup at a time, cooking and stirring constantly until each ½ cup addition is absorbed (about 30 minutes). (Rice will be tender and will have a creamy consistency.)

Add peas; cook, stirring constantly, until thoroughly heated. Add chopped pepper, cheese, and remaining ingredients; cook, stirring constantly, until thoroughly heated. Yield: 4 (1½-cup) servings.

Per Serving

Calories 308 (11% Calories from Fat)	Carbohydrate 56.4 g	Cholesterol 4 mg
Fat 3.8 g (Saturated Fat 1.0 g)	Protein 10.3 g	Sodium 643 mg

Mushroom-Pepper Pizza

2½ teaspoons rapid rise yeast
2 cups bread flour
1 teaspoon salt
1 teaspoon olive oil
¾ cup plus 3 tablespoons water
3 tablespoons bread flour, divided
Vegetable cooking spray
1 tablespoon cornmeal
1 cup thinly sliced fresh mushrooms
½ cup thinly sliced onion
6 cloves garlic, thinly sliced
1 large sweet red pepper, thinly sliced
1 teaspoon garlic-flavored olive oil
1 tablespoon chopped fresh oregano
¼ teaspoon salt
¼ teaspoon black pepper
¼ teaspoon ground red pepper
1¼ cups (5 ounces) shredded reduced-fat Cheddar cheese

Combine first 3 ingredients in a large mixing bowl; stir well. Combine olive oil and water in a saucepan; heat to 120° to 130°.

Gradually add liquid mixture to flour mixture, beating well at low speed of an electric mixer. Beat 2 additional minutes at medium speed.

Sprinkle 2 tablespoons bread flour evenly over work surface.

Turn dough out onto floured surface, and knead until smooth and elastic (about 10 minutes). Place in a bowl coated with cooking spray, turning to coat top. Cover and let rise in a warm place (85°), free from drafts, 45 minutes or until doubled in bulk.

Sprinkle remaining 1 tablespoon bread flour evenly over work surface. Punch dough down; roll to a 14-inch circle on floured work surface. Transfer dough to a 14-inch pizza pan coated with cooking spray and sprinkled with cornmeal. Set aside.

Combine mushrooms and next 3 ingredients in a large bowl. Add garlic-flavored olive oil; toss well. Add oregano and next 3 ingredients; stir well. Arrange vegetable mixture evenly over pizza crust; sprinkle cheese evenly over vegetables. Bake at 425° for 15 to 20 minutes. Cut into wedges. Yield: 8 servings.

Per Serving

Calories 222 (22% Calories from Fat)	Carbohydrate 32.1 g	Cholesterol 11 mg
Fat 5.4 g (Saturated Fat 2.3 g)	Protein 11.0 g	Sodium 499 mg

Middle Eastern Pita Sandwiches

2 cups seeded and chopped tomato
1 cup peeled and chopped cucumber
¼ cup chopped green onions
1½ tablespoons chopped fresh parsley
1½ tablespoons chopped fresh mint
2 tablespoons balsamic vinegar
½ teaspoon dried oregano
¼ teaspoon pepper
Hummus
6 (7-inch) pita bread rounds
2 cups shredded iceberg lettuce
¼ cup plus 2 tablespoons thinly sliced radishes
¼ cup plus 2 tablespoons sliced ripe olives
½ cup crumbled feta cheese

Combine first 8 ingredients. Cover; chill 2 hours. Spread ¼ cup Hummus on each pita round. Sprinkle lettuce, radishes, and olives across centers of pitas. Top with tomato mixture; sprinkle with cheese. Roll up pitas; secure with wooden picks. Yield: 6 servings.

Per Serving
Calories 313 (20% Calories from Fat) Carbohydrate 50.7 g Cholesterol 13 mg
Fat 7.0 g (Saturated Fat 2.5 g) Protein 10.6 g Sodium 371 mg

Dip into Hummus

Hummus (HOOM-uhs) is a thick sauce made from garbanzo beans (sometimes called chick-peas) which is often served with pita wedges as a dip.

Hummus

2 cloves garlic, minced
1 (15-ounce) can garbanzo beans, drained
3 tablespoons lemon juice
2 tablespoons plain nonfat yogurt
½ teaspoon ground cumin
½ teaspoon olive oil
¼ teaspoon ground coriander
¼ teaspoon ground red pepper

Position knife blade in food processor bowl. Add all ingredients; process until smooth, stopping once to scrape down sides. Transfer to a bowl. Cover; chill at least 2 hours. Yield: 1½ cups.

Per Serving
Calories 81 (17% Calories from Fat) Carbohydrate 13.5 g Cholesterol 0 mg
Fat 1.5 g (Saturated Fat 0.2 g) Protein 4.3 g Sodium 92 mg

Texas-Grilled Sirloin with Fresh Tomato Salsa

MEATS

If you're tired of serving plain roast turkey every holiday, then fire up the grill and cook the bird over the coals. You'll free up your oven for the rest of the meal and may even start a new family tradition. Just ask Foods Editor Deborah Lowery: "One Thanksgiving

POULTRY

I grill-smoked a turkey breast using hickory chips. Now the family wants a smoked turkey for every holiday," she says. "They say it tastes so much better."

Another benefit of grilling is that the fat drips away as the meat cooks over coals—a great low-fat cooking technique. And if you don't have any aromatic wood chips, that's okay—the meat will still taste delicious. To experiment with more flavors, toss a few fresh herb sprigs on the coals.

SEAFOOD

Marinating and packing on spice rubs before cooking are two other ways to improve the taste. Marinades and spice blends of all flavors line the grocery shelves these days, so buy a few to try, or use our marinade and spice blend recipes from the chapter beginning on page 10. Spices, herbs, and salsas are three more ways to fire up flavorful entrées your family will beg you to serve again. But don't take our word for it; try the recipes, and see for yourself.

GREEN PEPPERCORN STEAKS

4 (4-ounce) beef tenderloin steaks
3 tablespoons green peppercorns, drained and crushed
Vegetable cooking spray
2 bunches watercress, torn
1/4 cup Cognac
1/2 cup canned no-salt-added beef broth, undiluted
1/4 teaspoon salt

Smoke Alarm
Don't lean into the smoke when you sear steaks seasoned with peppercorns; the pepper smoke can sting your eyes.

Trim fat from tenderloin steaks. Gently press crushed green peppercorns into both sides of steaks; let stand at room temperature 20 minutes.

Coat a large nonstick skillet with cooking spray; place skillet over medium-high heat until hot. Add watercress, and cook, stirring constantly, 1 to 2 minutes or until watercress wilts. Remove watercress from skillet; set aside, and keep warm.

Coat skillet with cooking spray; place over high heat until very hot. Add steaks, and cook 6 to 8 minutes on each side or to desired degree of doneness. Remove steaks from skillet. Set steaks aside, and keep warm.

Remove skillet from heat; add Cognac, and ignite with a long match. When flame dies down, add beef broth and salt. Bring to a boil; reduce heat, and simmer 2 to 3 minutes or until broth mixture is reduced by half.

Place watercress evenly on 4 individual serving plates; place steaks on watercress. Pour broth mixture over steaks and watercress. Yield: 4 servings.

Per Serving

Calories 180 (38% Calories from Fat)	Carbohydrate 1.5 g	Cholesterol 70 mg
Fat 7.6 g (Saturated Fat 3.0 g)	Protein 24.6 g	Sodium 476 mg

Texas-Grilled Sirloin with Fresh Tomato Salsa

Hickory chips
1 pound lean boneless top sirloin steak
1/4 cup fresh lime juice
2 tablespoons chopped fresh oregano
1 tablespoon chopped fresh rosemary
1 teaspoon cayenne pepper
1 teaspoon pepper
1 teaspoon sugar
1 large clove garlic, crushed
Vegetable cooking spray
Fresh Tomato Salsa (page 50)
Fresh rosemary sprigs (optional)
Lime slices (optional)

Soak hickory chips in water at least 30 minutes.

Trim fat from steak. Combine steak and next 7 ingredients in a large heavy-duty, zip-top plastic bag; seal bag, and shake well. Marinate in refrigerator at least 8 hours, turning steak occasionally.

Remove steak from marinade; discard marinade. Coat grill rack with cooking spray; place on grill over medium-hot coals (350° to 400°). Place steak on rack; grill, covered, 5 to 6 minutes on each side or to desired degree of doneness. Let steak stand 5 minutes. Cut diagonally across grain into thin slices; arrange on individual serving plates. Serve with Fresh Tomato Salsa. If desired, garnish with fresh rosemary sprigs and lime slices. Yield: 4 servings.

Per Serving
Calories 203 (30% Calories from Fat) Carbohydrate 8.6 g Cholesterol 76 mg
Fat 6.7 g (Saturated Fat 2.5 g) Protein 27.1 g Sodium 214 mg

Out of Oregano?

Then substitute marjoram. And vice-versa. You can do this because oregano is actually a wild variety of marjoram. And though the flavor of marjoram is a little more delicate than that of oregano, the flavors are similar enough to be interchanged.

Basil Beef Burgers

1 pound ground round
Sun-Dried Tomato Pesto Spread, divided
½ cup chopped fresh basil
3 tablespoons minced green onions
2 tablespoons freshly grated Parmesan cheese
¼ teaspoon pepper
Vegetable cooking spray
4 green leaf lettuce leaves
3 plum tomatoes, sliced
4 thin slices sweet onion
4 kaiser rolls, split and toasted

Basil Beef Burgers

Combine beef, ¼ cup plus 2 tablespoons Sun-Dried Tomato Pesto Spread, basil, and next 3 ingredients; shape mixture into 4 patties.

Coat a large nonstick skillet with cooking spray. Place over medium heat until hot. Add patties, and cook 5 minutes on each side or until done.

Place a lettuce leaf, 3 slices tomato, and an onion slice on bottom half of each roll; top with patties. Spread remaining Sun-Dried Tomato Pesto Spread evenly over patties. Top with remaining roll halves. Yield: 4 servings.

Per Serving

Calories 457 (31% Calories from Fat)	Carbohydrate 42.3 g	Cholesterol 75 mg
Fat 15.9 g (Saturated Fat 4.2 g)	Protein 36.0 g	Sodium 727 mg

Sun-Dried Tomato Pesto Spread

12 sun-dried tomatoes
¾ cup boiling water
2 cloves garlic
¼ cup freshly grated Parmesan cheese
¼ cup chopped fresh parsley
2 tablespoons slivered almonds, toasted
1 teaspoon dried basil
1 teaspoon vegetable oil

Combine tomatoes and boiling water in a small bowl; cover and let stand 30 minutes. Drain, reserving 1 tablespoon of liquid.

Position knife blade in food processor bowl. Drop garlic through food chute with processor running, and process 3 seconds or until garlic is minced. Add reserved tomato liquid, tomatoes, cheese, and remaining ingredients. Pulse 4 times or until minced. Chill, if desired. Yield: ¾ cup.

Per Tablespoon
Calories 27 (56% Calories from Fat) Carbohydrate 1.9 g Cholesterol 2 mg
Fat 1.7 g (Saturated Fat 0.5 g) Protein 1.5 g Sodium 88 mg

Zucchini-Beef Parmigiana

½ pound ground round
1¾ cups chopped onion
1 large clove garlic, minced
2 (14½-ounce) cans no-salt-added whole tomatoes, undrained and chopped
⅓ cup dry white wine
3 tablespoons no-salt-added tomato paste
1½ teaspoons dried oregano
1½ teaspoons dried basil
1 teaspoon fennel seeds
½ teaspoon salt
¼ teaspoon pepper
8 medium zucchini (about 2½ pounds)
Olive oil-flavored vegetable cooking spray
¼ cup plus 2 tablespoons grated fat-free Parmesan cheese, divided

Combine beef, onion, and garlic in a skillet; cook over medium heat until browned, stirring well. Add tomatoes and next 7 ingredients, stirring well. Bring to a boil. Reduce heat; simmer, uncovered, 1 hour and 20 minutes or until sauce is reduced to 4 cups, stirring occasionally.

Cut zucchini in half crosswise; cut each half into 5 lengthwise slices. Coat with spray; place on baking sheets. Broil 5½ inches from heat (with electric oven door partially opened) 6 minutes on each side.

Spoon 1⅓ cups sauce in a 13- x 9- x 2-inch baking dish. Place half of zucchini slices over sauce, overlapping slightly. Spoon 1⅓ cups sauce over zucchini; sprinkle with 2 tablespoons cheese. Place remaining zucchini over cheese; top with remaining 1⅓ cups sauce, and sprinkle with remaining ¼ cup cheese.

Bake, uncovered, at 350° for 25 minutes or until lightly browned and bubbly. Let stand 10 minutes before serving. Yield: 6 servings.

Per Serving
Calories 172 (27% Calories from Fat) Carbohydrate 19.0 g Cholesterol 28 mg
Fat 5.2 g (Saturated Fat 1.9 g) Protein 15.6 g Sodium 283 mg

Fragrant Fennel

If it smells a little like anise and tastes a little like licorice, it must be fennel. Fennel seeds are used in several types of cuisines to season salami, pork, fish, tomato sauces, vegetarian dishes, and breads. The seeds can even be chewed as a breath freshener.

Grilled Mint-Lamb Chops

- 8 (5-ounce) lean lamb loin chops (1 inch thick)
- ½ cup grated onion
- ¼ cup plus 1 tablespoon chopped fresh mint, divided
- 1 large clove garlic, pressed
- ½ teaspoon pepper
- Vegetable cooking spray

Mint to Be
You can change the flavor of your favorite mint-seasoned recipe by varying the type of mint used in the recipe. Try apple mint, peppermint, spearmint, pineapple mint, or lemon-flavored basil mint.

Trim fat from chops. Combine onion, 3 tablespoons mint, garlic, and pepper in a large heavy-duty, zip-top plastic bag. Add chops; seal bag, and shake until chops are well coated. Marinate chops in refrigerator at least 3 hours, turning bag occasionally.

Remove chops from marinade; discard marinade. Coat grill rack with cooking spray; place on grill over medium-hot coals (350° to 400°). Place chops on rack; grill, covered, 5 minutes on each side or to desired degree of doneness.

To serve, place 2 chops on each individual serving plate. Sprinkle chops evenly with remaining 2 tablespoons mint. Yield: 4 servings.

Per Serving

Calories 238 (40% Calories from Fat)	Carbohydrate 1.5 g	Cholesterol 101 mg
Fat 10.5 g (Saturated Fat 3.7 g)	Protein 32.1 g	Sodium 90 mg

Gingered Pork Chops

- 4 (6-ounce) lean center-cut loin pork chops (½ inch thick)
- ¼ cup peeled, minced gingerroot
- 1 tablespoon minced garlic
- 2 tablespoons molasses
- 1 tablespoon dry sherry
- 1 tablespoon balsamic vinegar
- Vegetable cooking spray

Trim fat from chops; set aside.

Position knife blade in mini-food processor bowl, and add gingerroot, garlic, molasses, sherry, and vinegar. Process mixture 10 seconds or until mixture is smooth, scraping sides of processor bowl once. Pour marinade mixture into a heavy-duty, zip-top plastic bag. Add chops to marinade; seal bag, and shake until chops are well coated. Marinate chops in refrigerator at least 4 hours, turning bag occasionally.

Coat grill rack with cooking spray; place on grill over medium-hot coals (350° to 400°). Place chops on rack; grill, covered, 5 minutes on each side or until done. Yield: 4 servings.

Per Serving
Calories 279 (43% Calories from Fat) Carbohydrate 8.9 g Cholesterol 90 mg
Fat 13.2 g (Saturated Fat 0 g) Protein 28.7 g Sodium 74 mg

Pork Medallions with Glazed Apples

Cooked apples are a popular addition to savory pork dishes. To get the best flavor, use a tart, slightly acidic apple such as Granny Smith, Golden Delicious, or Newtown Pippin. However, any good, all-purpose cooking apple will do.

Vegetable cooking spray
1 teaspoon vegetable oil
1 (1-pound) pork tenderloin, cut into 1/4-inch-thick slices
2 large Granny Smith apples, peeled, cored, and cut into 1/4-inch-thick rings
1/3 cup frozen unsweetened apple juice concentrate, thawed and undiluted
2 teaspoons Dijon mustard
1/4 teaspoon salt
1/4 teaspoon pepper

Coat a large nonstick skillet with cooking spray; add oil. Place over medium-high heat until hot. Add pork slices, and cook until browned on both sides, turning once. Drain and pat dry with paper towels. Set pork aside.

Coat skillet with cooking spray; place over medium-high heat until hot. Add apples; sauté until tender. Add apple juice concentrate, and bring to a boil. Stir in mustard, salt, and pepper; add pork. Cook until thoroughly heated. Serve immediately. Yield: 4 servings.

Per Serving
Calories 220 (24% Calories from Fat) Carbohydrate 16.7 g Cholesterol 79 mg
Fat 5.9 g (Saturated Fat 1.7 g) Protein 24.7 g Sodium 278 mg

Go with Granny

Tart, greened-skinned Granny Smith apples are extremely juicy, crisp, and firm—just right to use in baked recipes or to serve with strong cheeses. Keep slices from turning brown by dipping them in an equal mixture of lemon juice and water.

Pork Loin with Roasted
Peppers and Penne

Pork Loin with Roasted Peppers and Penne

1 large sweet red pepper
1 large sweet yellow pepper
1 large green pepper
1 large onion, sliced
Vegetable cooking spray
8 ounces penne (short tubular pasta), uncooked
1 pound lean boneless pork loin
1 cup sliced fresh mushrooms
1 large clove garlic, minced
1 (14½-ounce) can no-salt-added whole tomatoes, undrained and chopped
½ cup dry white wine
1 teaspoon sugar
½ teaspoon salt
½ cup slivered fresh basil
2 tablespoons chopped fresh oregano

Seed peppers, and cut into 1-inch pieces. Place pepper and onion in a 15- x 10- x 1-inch jellyroll pan coated with cooking spray. Coat pepper mixture with cooking spray. Bake, uncovered, at 475° for 15 to 20 minutes or until vegetables are tender and browned, stirring occasionally. Set aside.

Cook pasta according to package directions, omitting salt and fat; drain well. Set aside, and keep warm.

Trim fat from pork; slice pork into ¼-inch slices. Coat a nonstick skillet with cooking spray; place over medium-high heat until hot. Add half of pork slices, and cook 1 to 2 minutes on each side; remove from skillet. Set aside, and keep warm. Repeat with remaining pork slices. Wipe drippings from skillet with a paper towel.

Coat skillet with cooking spray; place over medium-high heat until hot. Add mushrooms and garlic; sauté 1 to 2 minutes or until lightly browned. Add tomatoes and next 3 ingredients. Bring to a boil; reduce heat, and simmer, uncovered, 5 minutes. Return pork slices to skillet, and cook until thoroughly heated. Remove from heat, and stir in roasted pepper mixture, basil, and oregano.

Combine pasta and pork mixture in a large serving bowl, tossing gently. Serve warm. Yield: 5 servings.

Per Serving
Calories 431 (24% Calories from Fat) Carbohydrate 51.1 g Cholesterol 61 mg
Fat 11.7 g (Saturated Fat 3.6 g) Protein 26.9 g Sodium 303 mg

Sicilian Pizza

- 1 package active dry yeast
- 1/4 cup warm water (105° to 115°)
- 1 teaspoon sugar
- 2 teaspoons olive oil
- 2 cups all-purpose flour
- 1 cup whole wheat flour
- 1/4 teaspoon salt
- 3/4 cup lukewarm water (95° to 100°)
- Vegetable cooking spray
- 1 tablespoon all-purpose flour
- 6 ounces lean ground chicken
- 3/4 teaspoon fennel seeds, crushed
- 1/4 teaspoon salt
- 1 cup seeded and chopped plum tomato
- 4 ounces fresh mushrooms, thinly sliced
- 1 1/2 tablespoons chopped fresh oregano
- 3/4 cup (3 ounces) shredded part-skim mozzarella cheese
- 1/2 cup (2 ounces) freshly grated Parmesan cheese

Plum Good Tomatoes
A plum tomato is small, pear-shaped, and full of flavor. Roma is one of the most popular plum tomato varieties.

Combine yeast and 1/4 cup warm water in a 1-cup liquid measuring cup; add sugar, and let stand 5 minutes. Add oil.

Position knife blade in food processor bowl; add yeast mixture, 2 cups all-purpose flour, whole wheat flour, and 1/4 teaspoon salt. Process 30 seconds, stopping once to scrape down sides. Pour 3/4 cup lukewarm water through food chute with processor running; process until blended and dough is soft.

Turn dough out onto a work surface, and knead until smooth (about 2 minutes). Place in a large bowl coated with cooking spray, turning to coat top. Cover and let rise in a warm place (85°), free from drafts, 45 minutes or until doubled in bulk.

Punch dough down. Sprinkle 1 tablespoon all-purpose flour over work surface. Turn dough out onto floured surface, and knead lightly 4 or 5 times; roll into a 15- x 10-inch rectangle. Place dough into a 15- x 10- x 1-inch jellyroll pan coated with cooking spray.

Cover and let rise in a warm place, free from drafts, 30 minutes or until doubled in bulk. Coat dough with cooking spray. Bake at 450° for 10 minutes; set aside.

Coat a large nonstick skillet with cooking spray, and place over medium-high heat until hot. Add chicken, fennel seeds, and 1/4 teaspoon salt; cook, stirring constantly, until chicken is done. Drain.

Sprinkle tomato evenly over crust, leaving a 1/2-inch border. Spread chicken mixture evenly over tomato. Arrange mushrooms over chicken mixture; sprinkle oregano and cheeses evenly over pizza. Bake at 450° for 10 minutes. Yield: 8 servings.

Per Serving
Calories 278 (20% Calories from Fat) Carbohydrate 39.1 g Cholesterol 26 mg
Fat 6.2 g (Saturated Fat 2.7 g) Protein 16.9 g Sodium 327 mg

Chicken Enchiladas

Vegetable cooking spray
3/4 pound skinned, boned chicken breast halves, cut into 1/2-inch pieces
1 cup chopped green pepper
1/2 cup chopped onion
1 jalapeño pepper, seeded and minced
1 (16-ounce) can fat-free refried black beans
3 tablespoons Mexican Seasoning Blend (page 25), divided
2 (8-ounce) cans no-salt-added tomato sauce
1/2 cup low-sodium vegetable juice
12 (8-inch) fat-free flour tortillas
3/4 cup (3 ounces) shredded reduced-fat sharp Cheddar cheese
Nonfat sour cream (optional)
Thinly sliced green onions (optional)

Coat a large nonstick skillet with cooking spray; place over medium heat until hot. Add chicken and next 3 ingredients; cook until chicken is done, stirring occasionally. Stir in black beans and 1 tablespoon Mexican Seasoning Blend.

Combine remaining 2 tablespoons Mexican Seasoning Blend, tomato sauce, and vegetable juice; stir well. Spoon 1/3 cup tomato mixture into a 13- x 9- x 2-inch baking dish coated with cooking spray. Set remaining tomato mixture aside.

Spoon 1/4 cup chicken mixture down center of each tortilla. Roll up tortillas; place, seam side down, in dish. Pour remaining tomato mixture over tortillas. Cover and bake at 350° for 25 minutes. Uncover and sprinkle with cheese; bake 5 additional minutes or until cheese melts. If desired, garnish each enchilada with 1 tablespoon sour cream and green onions. Yield: 6 servings.

Per Serving
Calories 475 (8% Calories from Fat) Carbohydrate 77.1 g Cholesterol 42 mg
Fat 4.2 g (Saturated Fat 2.0 g) Protein 31.7 g Sodium 1105 mg

No Jalapeños?

You can substitute serranos or canned green chiles for jalapeños in almost any recipe.

Chicken Tamale in a Skillet

- 3 (4-ounce) skinned, boned chicken breast halves
- 2 cups water
- Vegetable cooking spray
- 1 cup finely chopped onion
- 1 large clove garlic, minced
- 2 tablespoons water
- ½ teaspoon dried oregano
- ½ teaspoon ground cumin
- 1 (14½-ounce) can no-salt-added whole tomatoes, undrained and chopped
- 1 cup fresh or frozen corn kernels, thawed
- 1 tablespoon chili powder
- ¼ teaspoon salt
- ⅛ teaspoon pepper
- ½ cup plus 1 tablespoon coarse yellow cornmeal
- ½ cup canned no-salt-added chicken broth, undiluted
- ⅓ cup plain low-fat yogurt
- ¼ cup sliced ripe olives, drained
- ¼ cup (1 ounce) shredded reduced-fat sharp Cheddar cheese
- ¼ cup chopped fresh cilantro

Combine chicken and 2 cups water in a medium saucepan. Bring to a boil; cover, reduce heat, and simmer 15 minutes or until chicken is tender. Remove chicken from water; drain and finely shred. Discard water.

Coat a medium nonstick skillet with cooking spray. Place over medium-high heat until hot; add onion, and sauté until crisp-tender. Add garlic and next 3 ingredients; cook 2 minutes. Stir in chicken, tomatoes, and next 4 ingredients. Bring to a boil; reduce heat, and simmer 5 minutes.

Combine cornmeal, broth, and yogurt in a small bowl. Pour ⅔ cup cornmeal mixture into chicken mixture, and simmer 5 minutes. Smooth top of mixture, and arrange sliced olives over top. Drizzle remaining cornmeal mixture over top, and sprinkle with cheese. Cover, reduce heat, and simmer 20 minutes. Remove from heat, and let stand, covered, 10 minutes. Sprinkle with cilantro, and serve immediately. Yield: 4 servings.

Per Serving

Calories 315 (19% Calories from Fat)	Carbohydrate 37.8 g	Cholesterol 60 mg
Fat 6.6 g (Saturated Fat 2.0 g)	Protein 27.7 g	Sodium 378 mg

Chili Versus Chile

In this book, if it's chili powder with an "i," use the blend of 15 or more spices most often used for chili (the stew). If the ingredient is the rusty red chile powder with an "e," then look for red powder made from ground red chiles.

Chicken Fajitas

- 4 (4-ounce) skinned, boned chicken breast halves, cut crosswise into thin strips
- 2 teaspoons vegetable oil
- 1 tablespoon fresh lime juice
- 1 teaspoon ground cumin
- 1 (14½-ounce) can no-salt-added whole tomatoes, drained and chopped
- 1 (4-ounce) can chopped green chiles, drained
- 2 green onions, sliced
- 3 tablespoons chopped fresh cilantro
- ¼ teaspoon salt
- ¼ teaspoon pepper
- 8 (6-inch) flour tortillas
- Vegetable cooking spray
- ½ cup low-fat sour cream
- 1 lime, cut into 8 wedges

Place chicken strips in a heavy-duty, zip-top plastic bag. Combine oil, lime juice, and cumin; pour over chicken. Seal bag, and shake until chicken is well coated. Marinate chicken in refrigerator at least 30 minutes, turning bag occasionally.

Combine tomatoes and next 5 ingredients in a small bowl; stir well. Set aside.

Wrap tortillas in heavy-duty aluminum foil. Bake at 350° for 10 minutes or until thoroughly heated. Set aside; keep warm.

Remove chicken from marinade, discarding marinade.

Coat a large nonstick skillet with cooking spray; place skillet over medium-high heat until hot. Add chicken, and cook 5 to 7 minutes or until done, stirring occasionally.

Place chicken evenly down centers of tortillas. Top each with 2 tablespoons tomato mixture and 1 tablespoon sour cream; roll up tortillas. Top with lime wedges and remaining tomato mixture. Serve immediately. Yield: 4 servings.

Per Serving

Calories 434 (24% Calories from Fat)	Carbohydrate 47.7 g	Cholesterol 77 mg
Fat 11.4 g (Saturated Fat 3.6 g)	Protein 34.3 g	Sodium 816 mg

Onion Options

Tiny *pearl onions* are best pickled or added to soups and stews. Choose mild, sweet *scallions* for stir-fries or to use raw in salads. In flavor, *shallots* are a cross between garlic and onions. *White* and *yellow onions* are the most common onions; they have a pungent flavor and keep well.

AROMATIC-HERBED CHICKEN

Turn to page 222 for an Indian menu that features this recipe.

6 (4-ounce) skinned, boned chicken breast halves
½ teaspoon salt
1 teaspoon grated lemon rind
2 tablespoons fresh lemon juice
Vegetable cooking spray
2 cups finely chopped onion
1 tablespoon minced garlic
1 tablespoon peeled, grated gingerroot
½ teaspoon ground cardamom
1 (3-inch) stick cinnamon
4 whole cloves
2 teaspoons vegetable oil
1 teaspoon cumin seeds
1 teaspoon coriander seeds
½ teaspoon ground turmeric
½ teaspoon ground red pepper
1 (14½-ounce) can no-salt-added stewed tomatoes
2 tablespoons chopped fresh cilantro

Place chicken in a shallow dish; sprinkle with salt. Combine lemon rind and juice; drizzle lemon mixture over chicken. Cover and marinate in refrigerator 30 minutes.

Coat a large nonstick skillet with cooking spray; place skillet over medium-high heat until hot. Add onion, and cook 4 to 5 minutes or until tender, stirring frequently. Add garlic and gingerroot; cook 2 minutes. Stir in cardamom, cinnamon, and cloves; cook 2 additional minutes. Remove from skillet; set aside.

Coat skillet with cooking spray; add oil. Place over medium-high heat until hot. Add chicken, and cook 5 minutes; turn chicken, and sprinkle with cumin and next 3 ingredients. Cook 5 additional minutes or until golden. Add onion mixture and tomatoes; stir well. Cover, reduce heat, and simmer 25 minutes or until chicken is tender. Remove and discard cinnamon stick and whole cloves. Add cilantro the last 5 minutes of cooking. Yield: 6 servings.

Per Serving

Calories 185 (17% Calories from Fat)	Carbohydrate 10.4 g	Cholesterol 66 mg
Fat 3.4 g (Saturated Fat 0.7 g)	Protein 27.8 g	Sodium 284 mg

Capturing Cardamom Flavor

It's peppery and tastes almost sweet. These unusual flavor characteristics make cardamom a wonderful seasoning for beverages, breads, entrées, and desserts. To bring out the best flavor for savory recipes, buy cardamom pods (they're on the supermarket spice racks); then split them, and take out the sticky, brown seeds. Add the seeds to a hot skillet, and stir while they cook until they're roasted.

Hickory-Grilled Jerk Chicken

When Jamaicans barbecue, they call it jerk. This style of outdoor cooking is best known for its hot habañero chiles and the oak, pecan, or hickory wood smoke flavor.

Hickory chips
Wet Jerk Rub (page 21), divided
6 (4-ounce) skinned, boned chicken breast halves
Vegetable cooking spray
4 cups cooked long-grain rice (cooked without salt or fat)
3 tablespoons fresh lime juice
2 tablespoons peeled, grated gingerroot
½ teaspoon freshly grated nutmeg
¼ teaspoon salt

Soak hickory chips in water at least 30 minutes; drain.

Set aside ½ cup Wet Jerk Rub. Coat chicken with remaining 1 cup Wet Jerk Rub. Place chicken in a large heavy-duty, zip-top plastic bag; seal bag, and marinate in refrigerator 8 hours.

Preheat gas grill to medium-hot (350° to 400°) using both burners. After preheating, turn left burner off. Place hickory chips in a disposable aluminum foil pan or an aluminum foil packet poked with holes on grill over right burner. Coat grill rack with cooking spray; place on grill over medium-hot coals. Place chicken on rack over left burner. Grill, uncovered, 30 minutes or until done, turning frequently. Transfer chicken to a platter, and keep warm.

Combine rice and remaining ingredients; toss gently. Spoon rice mixture evenly onto individual serving plates. Top rice with chicken. Serve immediately with reserved Wet Jerk Rub. Yield: 6 servings.

Per Serving

Calories 375 (21% Calories from Fat)	Carbohydrate 43.4 g	Cholesterol 72 mg
Fat 8.6 g (Saturated Fat 1.9 g)	Protein 31.0 g	Sodium 955 mg

Grilled Chicken Fettuccine Alfredo with Mushrooms

Spice Advice
To keep dried spices tasting fresh up to three years, keep them in a cool, dry place away from heat or light. In our test kitchens, we store them in the freezer.

- **3 (4-ounce) skinned, boned chicken breast halves**
- **1/3 cup plain low-fat yogurt**
- **1 teaspoon dried basil, divided**
- **1 teaspoon dried oregano, divided**
- **Vegetable cooking spray**
- **1 teaspoon olive oil**
- **1 cup finely chopped onion**
- **1/2 cup chopped sweet red pepper**
- **2 cloves garlic, minced**
- **5 cups sliced fresh mushrooms (about 3/4 pound)**
- **1/3 cup frozen English peas, thawed**
- **1/2 cup dry white wine**
- **2 tablespoons all-purpose flour**
- **1 1/2 cups canned low-sodium chicken broth, undiluted**
- **3 ounces Neufchâtel cheese, cut into cubes**
- **1/2 teaspoon salt**
- **1/4 teaspoon freshly grated nutmeg**
- **1/3 cup chopped fresh parsley**
- **1/4 cup grated Parmesan cheese**
- **8 ounces fettuccine, uncooked**

Combine chicken, yogurt, 1/2 teaspoon basil, and 1/2 teaspoon oregano in a shallow dish; stir well. Cover and marinate in refrigerator 30 minutes.

Coat a large nonstick skillet with cooking spray; add oil. Place over medium heat until hot. Add onion and red pepper; cook, stirring constantly, 3 to 5 minutes. Add remaining 1/2 teaspoon basil and 1/2 teaspoon oregano; stir in garlic. Cook 1 minute, stirring frequently. Add mushrooms and peas. Cook over medium-high heat 3 to 4 minutes or until mushrooms begin to brown, stirring frequently. Add wine; cook over medium heat until liquid evaporates, stirring occasionally. Sprinkle with flour, stirring well. Add broth; bring just to a simmer over low heat, stirring frequently. Add Neufchâtel cheese, salt, and nutmeg. Cook 3 to 5 minutes or until cheese melts and mixture is smooth, stirring frequently. Remove from heat; stir in parsley and Parmesan cheese. Set aside, and keep warm.

Cook pasta according to package directions, omitting salt and fat, and drain well. Combine pasta and vegetable mixture, and toss well. Set aside, and keep warm. Remove chicken from marinade, discarding marinade.

Coat grill rack with cooking spray; place on grill over medium-hot coals (350° to 400°). Place chicken on rack; grill, covered, 3 to 4 minutes on each side or until chicken is done.

Remove chicken from grill; let stand 5 minutes. Slice diagonally across grain into thin strips.

Spoon pasta mixture onto a serving platter; top with chicken strips. Serve immediately. Yield: 4 servings.

Per Serving
Calories 382 (28% Calories from Fat) Carbohydrate 32.1 g Cholesterol 75 mg
Fat 12.0 g (Saturated Fat 5.3 g) Protein 32.1 g Sodium 582 mg

Greek Feta Chicken

1 (8-ounce) carton plain low-fat yogurt
1 tablespoon lemon juice
½ teaspoon dried oregano
½ teaspoon dried rosemary
¼ teaspoon pepper
1 large clove garlic, minced
4 (4-ounce) skinned, boned chicken breast halves
Vegetable cooking spray
¼ cup plus 1 tablespoon crumbled feta cheese
1 tablespoon chopped fresh parsley

Combine first 6 ingredients in a large heavy-duty, zip-top plastic bag; add chicken. Seal bag, and shake until chicken is well coated. Marinate chicken in refrigerator 30 minutes.

Remove chicken from marinade, reserving marinade. Place chicken on a rack in a broiler pan coated with cooking spray. Broil 5½ inches from heat (with electric oven door partially opened) 7 minutes. Turn chicken; spoon reserved marinade over chicken, and top with feta cheese. Broil 7 minutes or until done. Sprinkle with parsley. Yield: 4 servings.

Per Serving
Calories 195 (22% Calories from Fat) Carbohydrate 5.7 g Cholesterol 79 mg
Fat 4.8 g (Saturated Fat 2.5 g) Protein 30.9 g Sodium 233 mg

Finding Feta

Find this favorite Greek cheese made from goat, sheep, or cow's milk packed in brine in jars or shrink-wrapped in the supermarket's dairy case.

Lemon-Sage Roasted Chicken and Vegetables

1 (6-pound) roasting chicken
½ teaspoon salt
¼ teaspoon pepper
3 lemons, divided
¼ cup tightly packed fresh sage leaves, divided
1 medium onion, thinly sliced and separated into rings
6 cloves garlic, peeled and halved
Vegetable cooking spray
6 medium-size red potatoes, unpeeled and quartered
1 large sweet potato, peeled and cut into sixths
3 carrots, scraped and cut into 2-inch pieces
1 purple onion, peeled and cut into sixths
1 tablespoon brown sugar
1 teaspoon grated lemon rind
1½ cups canned no-salt-added chicken broth, undiluted
2 tablespoons all-purpose flour
1 tablespoon Dijon mustard
1 tablespoon fresh lemon juice
Fresh sage sprigs (optional)
Lemon wedges (optional)

Getting Under the Skin
Don't take that skin off the chicken . . . yet. Use it to hold herbs, citrus slices, or flavorful vegetables next to the meat while it cooks. When you remove the skin, the flavor is still in the meat. And because chicken does not absorb much fat from the skin during cooking, most of the fat is gone after the skin is removed.

Trim excess fat from chicken. Remove giblets and neck; reserve for another use. Rinse chicken thoroughly under cold water, and pat dry with paper towels. Sprinkle chicken with salt and pepper.

Carefully separate skin from body of chicken at neck area, working down to breast and thigh area. Thinly slice 1 lemon. Place lemon slices and 3 tablespoons sage leaves between skin and meat of chicken. Cut remaining 2 lemons in half; place in cavity of chicken. Truss chicken. Insert meat thermometer into meaty part of thigh, making sure it does not touch bone.

Place remaining sage leaves, onion, and garlic in a 17- x 11- x 2½-inch roasting pan coated with cooking spray. Place chicken, breast side up, on top. Combine red potatoes and next 3 ingredients in a bowl. Combine brown sugar and lemon rind. Sprinkle over vegetables; toss gently. Arrange vegetables in roasting pan around chicken.

Bake chicken and vegetables, uncovered, at 400° for 15 minutes. Reduce heat to 350°; bake, uncovered, 1 hour and 30 minutes or until vegetables are tender and meat thermometer registers 180°. Remove vegetables from pan; keep warm. Transfer chicken to a serving platter; remove and discard skin, lemon slices, and sage. Remove and discard lemon halves from cavity. Set chicken aside; keep warm.

Add chicken broth to roasting pan. Cook over high heat, deglazing pan by scraping particles that cling to bottom; cook 5 additional minutes. Pour broth mixture through a wire-mesh strainer into a 1-cup liquid measuring cup, discarding onion, sage, and garlic. Skim fat from broth; add water to make 1 cup.

Combine flour and ¼ cup broth mixture in a small saucepan, stirring until smooth. Gradually add remaining broth mixture, stirring frequently. Cook over medium heat until thickened and bubbly, stirring frequently. Stir in Dijon mustard.

Drizzle lemon juice over roasted vegetables. Arrange vegetables around chicken on a serving platter; serve with mustard mixture. If desired, garnish with sage sprigs and lemon wedges. Yield: 12 servings.

Per Serving

Calories 475 (15% Calories from Fat)	Carbohydrate 45.2 g	Cholesterol 159 mg
Fat 7.7 g (Saturated Fat 1.9 g)	Protein 53.3 g	Sodium 471 mg

Lemon-Sage Roasted Chicken and Vegetables

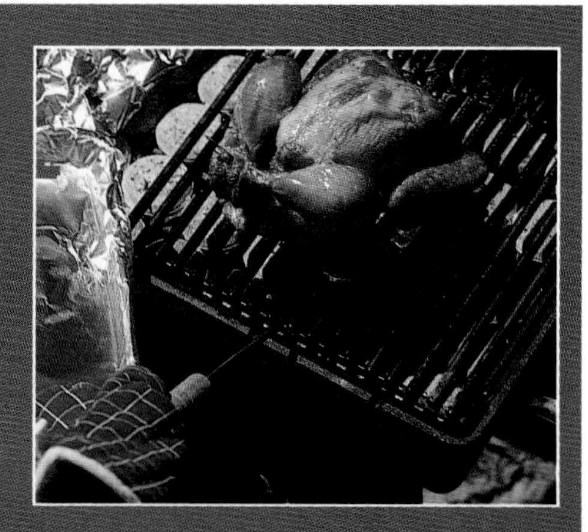

Where There's Smoke, There's Flavor

Aromatic wood chips tossed on the coals add extra flavor to smoked meats. To smoke-cook with wood chips, use one of these methods:

1. Soak the chips at least 30 minutes, and then toss them on the ashen charcoal briquettes.
2. To make the wood chips last longer on the long-cooking fire, wrap the wood chips in heavy-duty aluminum foil (no need to soak the chips). Poke holes in the foil packet, and place it on the hot briquettes or coals.

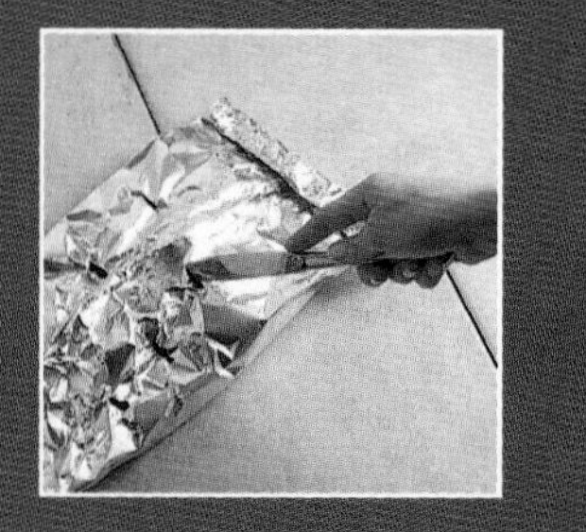

3. On a gas grill, poke holes in the bottom of a disposable foil pan, fill it with soaked wood chips, and place it on hot briquettes.

Southwestern Corn-Stuffed Turkey

1¾ cups yellow cornmeal, divided
¾ cup whole wheat flour
1 tablespoon baking powder
3 tablespoons freshly grated Parmesan cheese
2 teaspoons red chile powder
1½ teaspoons salt
⅔ cup skim milk
1 egg
2 tablespoons honey
1 teaspoon olive oil
1 jalapeño pepper, seeded and minced
1 cup minced purple onion
1 cup frozen corn kernels
Vegetable cooking spray
1 (12-pound) turkey
1 tablespoon ground red pepper
1 teaspoon salt
½ teaspoon black pepper
1 (14¼-ounce) can no-salt-added chicken broth, undiluted

Combine ¾ cup cornmeal and next 5 ingredients in a large bowl, stirring well. Combine milk and next 3 ingredients in a small bowl. Pour milk mixture into cornmeal mixture, stirring until dry ingredients are moistened. Fold in jalapeño pepper, onion, and corn.

Coat a 10-inch cast-iron skillet with cooking spray; add cornmeal mixture. Bake at 500° for 15 minutes; remove from oven, and let cool completely on a wire rack.

Trim excess fat from turkey. Remove giblets and neck from turkey; reserve for another use. Rinse turkey thoroughly under cold water, and pat dry with paper towels. Break cornbread into pieces; lightly pack into body cavity of turkey. Lightly pack any remaining cornbread into neck cavity. Pour chicken broth into each cavity. Tie ends of legs to tail with cord. Lift wingtips up and over back, and tuck under turkey. Combine remaining 1 cup cornmeal, red pepper, salt, and black pepper in a small bowl. Coat all sides of bird with cornmeal mixture.

Place turkey on a rack coated with cooking spray, and place rack in a shallow roasting pan. Insert meat thermometer into meaty portion of thigh, making sure it does not touch bone.

Bake at 500° for 20 minutes. Reduce heat to 325°, and bake 2 hours and 15 minutes or until meat thermometer registers 180°.

When turkey is two-thirds done, cut the cord holding the drumstick ends to the tail; this will ensure that the insides of the thighs are cooked. Turkey is done when drumsticks are easy to move up and down. Let stand fifteen minutes before carving. Remove skin before slicing. Yield: 14 servings.

Per Serving

Calories 298 (8% Calories from Fat)	Carbohydrate 17.0 g	Cholesterol 143 mg
Fat 2.7 g (Saturated Fat 0.9 g)	Protein 49.2 g	Sodium 373 mg

Mesquite-Smoked Turkey Breast

Mesquite chips
1 (6-pound) turkey breast, skinned
¼ cup Mexican Seasoning Blend (page 25)
Vegetable cooking spray

Soak mesquite chips in water at least 30 minutes; drain.

Rinse turkey breast thoroughly under cold water, and pat dry with paper towels. Rub Mexican Seasoning Blend inside and outside turkey breast.

Preheat gas grill to medium-hot (350° to 400°) using both burners. After preheating, turn left burner off. Place mesquite chips in a disposable aluminum foil pan or an aluminum foil packet poked with holes on grill over right burner. Coat grill rack with cooking spray; place on grill over medium-hot coals.

Insert meat thermometer into thickest part of turkey, making sure it does not touch bone. Place turkey on rack over left burner. Cook, covered, 3 hours or until meat thermometer registers 170°. Let stand 20 minutes before carving. Yield: 12 servings.

Per Serving

Calories 178 (20% Calories from Fat)	Carbohydrate 1.2 g	Cholesterol 75 mg
Fat 3.9 g (Saturated Fat 1.2 g)	Protein 32.6 g	Sodium 107 mg

Mesquite Magic

Wood from the persistent scrubby tree that pesters western ranchers is great for grilling. Buy mesquite chips or mesquite flavored briquettes to heap on the coals for extra flavor. Just soak the chips so they'll smoke, not burn.

Crispy Pan-Fried Catfish

- 1 egg white, lightly beaten
- 1 tablespoon water
- ¼ cup yellow cornmeal
- 2 tablespoons grated Parmesan cheese
- 1 tablespoon chopped fresh thyme
- ¼ teaspoon pepper
- 4 (4-ounce) farm-raised catfish fillets
- 3 tablespoons all-purpose flour
- Vegetable cooking spray
- Chopped fresh thyme (optional)
- Lemon wedges (optional)

Combine egg white and water; stir well. Combine cornmeal, Parmesan cheese, 1 tablespoon thyme, and pepper. Dredge fillets in flour; dip in egg white mixture, and dredge in cornmeal mixture.

Coat a large nonstick skillet with cooking spray, and place over medium-high heat until hot. Add fillets, and cook 3 minutes on each side or until fish flakes easily when tested with a fork. If desired, sprinkle fish with chopped fresh thyme, and garnish with lemon wedges. Yield: 4 servings.

Per Serving
Calories 202 (27% Calories from Fat) Carbohydrate 11.5 g Cholesterol 68 mg
Fat 6.0 g (Saturated Fat 1.6 g) Protein 23.9 g Sodium 132 mg

Grilled Grouper with Tomato-Papaya Salsa

- ¼ cup fresh lime juice
- ¼ cup chopped fresh cilantro, divided
- 2 teaspoons olive oil
- 4 (4-ounce) grouper fillets
- ¼ teaspoon salt
- ¼ teaspoon freshly ground pepper
- Vegetable cooking spray
- Tomato-Papaya Salsa

Combine lime juice, 2 tablespoons cilantro, and oil in a large shallow dish. Place grouper in dish, turning to coat. Cover and marinate in refrigerator 20 minutes, turning once.

Remove fillets from marinade, discarding marinade. Sprinkle with salt and pepper. Place fillets in a grilling basket coated with cooking spray.

Coat grill rack with cooking spray; place on grill over medium-hot coals (350° to 400°). Place basket on rack, and grill, uncovered, 10 minutes on each side or until fish flakes easily when tested with a fork.

Transfer grouper to a serving platter, and top evenly with Tomato-Papaya Salsa. Sprinkle with remaining 2 tablespoons cilantro. Yield: 4 servings.

Per Serving

Calories 158 (22% Calories from Fat)	Carbohydrate 8.8 g	Cholesterol 40 mg
Fat 3.8 g (Saturated Fat 0.6 g)	Protein 22.2 g	Sodium 271 mg

Tomato-Papaya Salsa

1 cup diced tomato
1 cup diced papaya
1 tablespoon plus 2 teaspoons diced purple onion
1 tablespoon chopped fresh cilantro
½ teaspoon sugar
½ teaspoon ground cumin
⅛ teaspoon salt
⅛ teaspoon freshly ground pepper
Dash of hot sauce

Combine all ingredients in a medium bowl; stir well. Serve at room temperature. Yield: 2 cups.

Per Tablespoon

Calories 4 (23% Calories from Fat)	Carbohydrate 0.9 g	Cholesterol 0 mg
Fat 0.1 g (Saturated Fat 0 g)	Protein 0.1 g	Sodium 13 mg

WHAT'S A PAPAYA?

It looks like a large, golden avocado. But when you cut into the yellow-red fruit, you'll find the center filled with gray-black seeds. When it's soft and ripe, a papaya is juicy and sweet-tart. An underripe papaya has greenish skin and feels hard when squeezed, but it will ripen quickly when it is left in a paper bag for a day or so.

Switch to Dark Sesame Oil

We do. When we want a stronger sesame flavor, we sometimes use dark instead of the more common light sesame oil in our test kitchens. Dark oil has more flavor because it's made from toasted sesame seeds.

Seared Salmon Steaks

- 4 (4-ounce) salmon fillets (1 inch thick)
- Vegetable cooking spray
- 1 teaspoon Curry Seasoning Blend (page 24)
- 2 tablespoons low-sodium soy sauce
- 2 tablespoons unsweetened orange juice
- 1 tablespoon dry sherry
- 1 teaspoon lemon juice
- ½ teaspoon dark sesame oil
- 2 green onions, thinly sliced

Coat fillets with cooking spray; sprinkle Curry Seasoning Blend evenly over fillets.

Coat a large nonstick skillet with cooking spray; place over high heat until very hot. Add fillets, and cook, uncovered, 3 minutes on each side. Cover and cook 3 minutes or until fish flakes easily when tested with a fork. Transfer to a serving platter, and keep warm.

Add soy sauce and next 3 ingredients to skillet; cook over high heat, deglazing skillet by scraping particles that cling to bottom. Add sesame oil; stir well. Pour soy sauce mixture over fish, and sprinkle with green onions. Yield: 4 servings.

Per Serving

Calories 186 (37% Calories from Fat)	Carbohydrate 2.3 g	Cholesterol 44 mg
Fat 7.6 g (Saturated Fat 1.4 g)	Protein 24.9 g	Sodium 249 mg

Citrus-Marinated Orange Roughy with Corn Relish

- 4 (4-ounce) orange roughy fillets
- Citrus Marinade (page 13)
- Vegetable cooking spray
- 1 teaspoon vegetable oil
- 1 clove garlic, minced
- 2 cups frozen whole-kernel corn, thawed
- 1 cup finely chopped sweet red pepper
- 4 cups sliced green onions
- ¼ teaspoon salt
- ¼ teaspoon pepper

Place fillets in a 13- x 9- x 2-inch baking dish. Pour Citrus Marinade over fish. Cover and marinate in refrigerator 30 minutes.

Remove fillets from marinade, discarding marinade. Coat fillets with cooking spray. Place fillets on a rack in a broiler pan coated with cooking spray. Broil 5½ inches from heat (with electric oven door partially opened) 10 minutes or until fish flakes easily when tested with a fork.

Coat a large nonstick skillet with cooking spray; add vegetable oil. Place over medium-high heat until hot. Add garlic, and sauté 30 seconds. Add corn and red pepper; increase heat to high. Cook until corn is slightly tender and charred, stirring frequently. Stir in green onions, salt, and pepper. Place vegetable mixture evenly on 4 individual serving plates. Top each with a fillet. Yield: 4 servings.

Per Serving

Calories 157 (19% Calories from Fat)	Carbohydrate 17.9 g	Cholesterol 18 mg
Fat 3.3 g (Saturated Fat 0.5 g)	Protein 16.0 g	Sodium 216 mg

Cajun-Blackened Swordfish Steaks

Don't confuse Cajun and Creole cooking. Cajun is a combination of French and Southern cuisines with an emphasis on country-style cookery. Creole cuisine relies on the use of butter, cream, and lots of tomatoes.

4 (4-ounce) swordfish steaks (½ inch thick)
Cajun Seasoning Blend (page 23)

Dredge fish in Cajun Seasoning Blend; set aside.

Place a large cast-iron skillet over medium-high heat 5 minutes or until very hot. Add fish, and cook 3 minutes. Turn fish, and cook 2 to 3 additional minutes or until fish flakes easily when tested with a fork. Fish should look charred. (You may prefer to do this procedure outside due to the small amount of smoke that is created.) Yield: 4 servings.

Per Serving

Calories 155 (30% Calories from Fat)	Carbohydrate 3.4 g	Cholesterol 44 mg
Fat 5.1 g (Saturated Fat 1.3 g)	Protein 23.3 g	Sodium 399 mg

Garlic's Great . . .

. . . but not on your hands. Get rid of garlic odor by rubbing salt or parsley vigorously between your palms.

Caper Flavor
Capers, the seasoning that looks like whole black peppercorns, is actually a sun-dried, pickled flower bud. The pungent flavor tastes best in meat and vegetable dishes. To remove some of the salty flavor, just rinse before using.

Broiled Flounder with Capered Wine Sauce

- ½ cup plus 1 tablespoon dry white wine
- 1 teaspoon lemon zest
- ⅓ cup fresh lemon juice
- 1 teaspoon dried Italian seasoning
- 4 (4-ounce) flounder fillets
- Olive oil-flavored cooking spray
- 2 cloves garlic, minced
- 1 teaspoon all-purpose flour
- ⅓ cup dry white wine
- 2 tablespoons fresh lemon juice
- 1½ tablespoons chopped fresh parsley
- 1½ teaspoons capers
- 1 tablespoon freshly grated Parmesan cheese

Combine first 4 ingredients in a heavy-duty, zip-top plastic bag. Add fish; seal bag, and shake until fish is well coated. Marinate in refrigerator 30 minutes.

Coat a small saucepan with cooking spray; place over medium heat until hot. Add garlic, and sauté 10 seconds. Add flour; cook, stirring constantly with a wire whisk, 1 minute. Gradually add ⅓ cup wine and 2 tablespoons lemon juice, stirring constantly. Cook, stirring constantly, 1 to 2 minutes or until thickened and bubbly. Stir in parsley and capers. Set aside.

Remove fish from marinade; discard marinade. Place fish on a rack in a broiler pan coated with cooking spray. Broil 5½ inches from heat (with electric oven door partially opened) 2 minutes. Sprinkle fish with cheese, and broil 2 additional minutes or until fish flakes easily when tested with a fork. Serve fish with wine sauce. Yield: 4 servings.

Per Serving

Calories 173 (16% Calories from Fat)	Carbohydrate 4.4 g	Cholesterol 63 mg
Fat 3.0 g (Saturated Fat 0.9 g)	Protein 23.2 g	Sodium 238 mg

Tilapia with Citrus-Coriander Baste

4 (4-ounce) tilapia fillets
½ teaspoon grated orange rind
¼ cup unsweetened orange juice
½ teaspoon grated lime rind
2 tablespoons fresh lime juice
½ teaspoon salt
½ teaspoon ground cumin
¼ teaspoon ground coriander
¼ teaspoon hot sauce
Vegetable cooking spray

Place fillets in a large shallow dish. Combine orange rind and next 7 ingredients; stir well. Pour over fillets in dish. Cover and marinate in refrigerator 2 hours.

Remove fillets from marinade, reserving marinade. Place fillets on a rack in a broiler pan coated with cooking spray. Broil fillets 5½ inches from heat (with electric oven door partially opened) 5 minutes on each side or until fish flakes easily when tested with a fork, basting frequently with reserved marinade. Yield: 4 servings.

Per Serving
Calories 95 (22% Calories from Fat) Carbohydrate 2.6 g Cholesterol 0 mg
Fat 2.3 g (Saturated Fat 0.4 g) Protein 15.9 g Sodium 340 mg

Cilantro's Alias

Call it coriander when it's in the form of dried whole or ground seeds. But fresh, it's simply cilantro.

Fragrant Shrimp Brochettes

Fragrant Shrimp Brochettes

Use a citrus reamer or juicer to extract the intense, natural flavor of freshly squeezed citrus juice—the flavors of bottled juices don't compare.

1½ pounds unpeeled fresh jumbo shrimp
⅓ cup fresh grapefruit juice
¼ cup coarsely chopped fresh cilantro
¼ cup coarsely chopped fresh mint
¼ cup fresh orange juice
2 tablespoons fresh lime juice
¼ teaspoon salt
¼ teaspoon cracked pepper
Olive oil-flavored vegetable cooking spray
3 cups cooked long-grain rice (cooked without salt or fat)

Peel and devein shrimp; leave tails intact. Combine grapefruit juice and next 6 ingredients in a large bowl. Add shrimp; toss well. Cover and marinate in refrigerator 30 minutes.

Remove shrimp from marinade, discarding marinade. Thread shrimp evenly onto 4 (10-inch) metal skewers. Coat shrimp with cooking spray.

Coat grill rack with cooking spray; place on grill over medium-hot coals (350° to 400°). Place skewers on rack; grill, covered, 3 minutes on each side or until shrimp turn pink. Serve over hot cooked rice. Serve immediately. Yield: 4 servings.

Per Serving

Calories 285 (5% Calories from Fat)	Carbohydrate 38.4 g	Cholesterol 221 mg
Fat 1.6 g (Saturated Fat 0.3 g)	Protein 26.9 g	Sodium 326 mg

Save Those Stems

When you've stripped rosemary stems of the fresh leaves, save the woody stems to use as kabob skewers. Trim one end of each stem into a sharp point; then soak the stems for 30 minutes. Thread fish chunks, shrimp, scallops, or chicken onto the stems before grilling or broiling, and you'll get extra herb flavor.

How to Keep Ginger

To keep fresh ginger for several weeks, wrap it in paper towels; then place it in a zip-top plastic bag in the refrigerator.

Szechuan Shrimp Stir-Fry

- 1/4 cup canned no-salt-added chicken broth, undiluted
- 1 tablespoon low-sodium soy sauce
- 1 tablespoon tomato puree
- 2 teaspoons sugar
- 1 teaspoon cornstarch
- 1 teaspoon dried crushed red pepper
- 1 1/2 pounds unpeeled medium-size fresh shrimp
- Vegetable cooking spray
- 4 green onions, cut into 1-inch pieces
- 1 tablespoon peeled, minced gingerroot
- 4 cups cooked long-grain rice (cooked without salt or fat)

Combine first 6 ingredients in a small bowl; set aside.

Peel and devein shrimp. Coat a wok with cooking spray; heat at medium-high (375°) until hot. Add shrimp, onions, and gingerroot; stir-fry 3 to 4 minutes or until shrimp turn pink. Add chicken broth mixture, and cook 1 minute or until sauce is slightly thickened and bubbly, stirring frequently. Spoon rice onto a serving platter; top with shrimp mixture. Yield: 4 servings.

Per Serving

Calories 328 (5% Calories from Fat)	Carbohydrate 53.2 g	Cholesterol 129 mg
Fat 1.9 g (Saturated Fat 0.3 g)	Protein 21.6 g	Sodium 243 mg

Spicy Shrimp with Spinach and Walnuts

1 pound unpeeled large fresh shrimp
3 tablespoons dry sherry, divided
1 tablespoon peeled, grated gingerroot
2 teaspoons cornstarch
⅓ cup canned no-salt-added chicken broth, undiluted
2 tablespoons reduced-calorie soy sauce
1 tablespoon rice wine vinegar
2 tablespoons low-sodium ketchup
2 teaspoons sugar
1 teaspoon dark sesame oil
¼ teaspoon ground red pepper
Vegetable cooking spray
2 tablespoons chopped walnuts
1 teaspoon peanut oil
1 (10-ounce) package fresh spinach
1 large clove garlic, minced
1 large sweet red pepper, cut into ½-inch strips
2 tablespoons water
6 green onions, cut into 1-inch pieces

Rice Is Nice

Rice vinegar, often used in Asian recipes, is made from fermented rice wine. Japanese versions of rice vinegar are mild-flavored and mellow. In China, the vinegar is often slightly sour.

Peel, devein, and butterfly shrimp. Combine shrimp, 1½ tablespoons sherry, and gingerroot. Cover and marinate in refrigerator 30 to 45 minutes.

Combine remaining 1½ tablespoons sherry, cornstarch, chicken broth, soy sauce, and vinegar; stir well. Add ketchup and next 3 ingredients. Set aside.

Coat a wok or large nonstick skillet with cooking spray. Heat at medium-high (375°) until hot. Add walnuts, and stir-fry 30 seconds. Remove walnuts from wok, and set aside.

Drizzle peanut oil around top of wok, coating sides. Add spinach to wok; stir-fry 2 minutes. Remove to a serving platter; keep warm.

Add garlic to wok; stir-fry 10 seconds. Add sweet red pepper and 2 tablespoons water; stir-fry 2 minutes. Add shrimp mixture and green onions; stir-fry 3 to 4 minutes. Add cornstarch mixture; stir-fry until mixture is slightly thickened and bubbly. Spoon over spinach, and sprinkle with walnuts. Serve immediately. Yield: 4 servings.

Per Serving
Calories 206 (29% Calories from Fat) Carbohydrate 12.4 g Cholesterol 151 mg
Fat 6.6 g (Saturated Fat 0.9 g) Protein 23.8 g Sodium 405 mg

Herb-Marinated
Tomatoes

SAVORY

Remember when the only way to cook green beans was to simmer them with fat until they were soft? Today, we cook green beans just until crisp-tender and serve them with a fresh-tasting tomato vinaigrette. In a past decade, most cooks mashed their potatoes with plenty of butter and, of course, salt. Today, whole

baked potatoes seasoned with salsa or topped with broccoli are just as likely to show up on restaurant menus—and even at fast-food joints. After a long culinary evolution, side dishes have finally stepped to the forefront to command as much attention as entrées.

Imagine what these new cooking methods can do for an annual Fourth of July cookout. Instead of plain

DISHES

corn on the cob, you can serve Basil-Wrapped Corn on the Cob (page 166) fresh from the grill. Or, in place of plain white rice, you can make a cilantro-flavored rice to go with dinner one night. Rest assured, you'll get comments. And compliments. And requests for more.

So, never fear. You can keep up the image of imaginative cook with these recipes. Most are new twists on old, familiar side dishes; they have fresh, new flavors and updated looks. If we could only do the same with our wardrobes. . . .

Asparagus in Lemon Sauce

For stronger flavor, use dark sesame oil. The seeds for this dark orange-colored oil are toasted first, giving the oil its distinct flavor.

1/3 cup canned low-sodium chicken broth, undiluted
2 teaspoons cornstarch
1/2 teaspoon grated lemon rind
2 tablespoons dry sherry
1 tablespoon lemon juice
1 tablespoon low-sodium soy sauce
1/2 teaspoon dark sesame oil
1/4 teaspoon salt
1/8 teaspoon pepper
1 pound fresh asparagus spears
Vegetable cooking spray
1 teaspoon vegetable oil
2 teaspoons peeled, minced gingerroot
1 large clove garlic, minced
2 tablespoons water
1/2 cup julienne-sliced sweet red pepper
1/2 cup canned sliced water chestnuts, drained
3 green onions, sliced

Combine first 3 ingredients in a small bowl, stirring until cornstarch dissolves. Stir in sherry and next 5 ingredients. Set aside.

Snap off tough ends of asparagus. Remove scales from stalks with a knife or vegetable peeler, if desired. Cut asparagus diagonally into 2-inch pieces.

Coat a wok with cooking spray; drizzle 1 teaspoon vegetable oil around top of wok, coating sides. Heat at medium-high (375°) until hot. Add gingerroot and garlic; stir-fry 10 seconds. Add asparagus; stir-fry 2 minutes. Add 2 tablespoons water, cooking until water evaporates. Add red pepper and water chestnuts; stir-fry 1 minute.

Add chicken broth mixture and green onions to wok; cook, stirring constantly, 1 minute or until mixture is thickened. Serve immediately. Yield: 4 (3/4-cup) servings.

Per Serving
Calories 74 (28% Calories from Fat) | Carbohydrate 12.0 g | Cholesterol 0 mg
Fat 2.3 g (Saturated Fat 0.3 g) | Protein 2.4 g | Sodium 257 mg

Sweet on Sherry

Sherry, a wine that's fortified with a bit of brandy, is often savored as a drink before or after dinner. Sometimes it's added to recipes for mellow, sweet, and nutty flavor. Sherry comes in a range of colors, flavors, and prices. It also varies in degree of sweetness. Medium sherry (sometimes called milk sherry) is darker and sweeter than dry sherry; cream or golden sherry is the sweetest.

If you need a substitute, then use 1 to 2 teaspoons of vanilla extract for 2 tablespoons of sherry.

Gingered Broccoli with Toasted Sesame Seeds

2 teaspoons sesame seeds
4 cups broccoli flowerets
1 small sweet red pepper, cut into 1- x 1/4-inch strips
Vegetable cooking spray
1 tablespoon peeled, minced gingerroot
1 clove garlic, minced
1/2 teaspoon dark sesame oil
1/4 teaspoon salt

Place sesame seeds in a small nonstick skillet; cook over medium heat, stirring constantly, 1 to 2 minutes or until seeds are golden. Remove from heat.

Cook broccoli in boiling water to cover 3 to 4 minutes; add red pepper. Cook 30 seconds; drain, reserving 1/3 cup liquid.

Coat a large nonstick skillet with cooking spray; place over medium heat until hot. Add gingerroot and garlic; sauté 30 seconds. Add reserved liquid; bring to a boil. Add broccoli mixture, sesame oil, and salt; toss gently. Transfer to a serving platter, and sprinkle with toasted sesame seeds. Serve immediately. Yield: 4 (1-cup) servings.

Per Serving
Calories 66 (29% Calories from Fat) Carbohydrate 10.2 g Cholesterol 0 mg
Fat 2.1 g (Saturated Fat 0.3 g) Protein 5.0 g Sodium 187 mg

Green Beans in Chunky Tomato Vinaigrette

1 pound fresh green beans
Chunky Tomato Vinaigrette (page 40)

Wash beans; trim ends, and remove strings. Cut into 2-inch pieces. Arrange beans in a vegetable steamer over boiling water. Cover and steam 5 to 7 minutes or until crisp-tender; drain.

Combine green beans and Chunky Tomato Vinaigrette in a large bowl; toss gently. Cover; chill 1 hour. Yield: 5 (1-cup) servings.

Per Serving
Calories 70 (39% Calories from Fat) Carbohydrate 10.7 g Cholesterol 0 mg
Fat 3.0 g (Saturated Fat 0.4 g) Protein 2.3 g Sodium 12 mg

Lemon-Herbed Green Beans

1 pound fresh green beans
Olive oil-flavored vegetable cooking spray
½ teaspoon olive oil
1 clove garlic, minced
1½ teaspoons chopped fresh oregano
3 tablespoons water
1 tablespoon fresh lemon juice
¼ teaspoon salt
⅛ teaspoon pepper
1 tablespoon freshly grated Parmesan cheese

Wash beans; remove ends. Cook in boiling water to cover 5 minutes or until crisp-tender; drain and set aside.

Coat a large nonstick skillet with cooking spray; add oil. Place over medium-high heat until hot. Add garlic and oregano; cook, stirring constantly, 1 minute. Add green beans and 3 tablespoons water; bring to a boil. Remove from heat. Add lemon juice, salt, and pepper; toss well. Transfer to a serving platter; sprinkle with cheese. Serve immediately. Yield: 4 (1-cup) servings.

Per Serving

Calories 56 (29% Calories from Fat)	Carbohydrate 8.4 g	Cholesterol 2 mg
Fat 1.8 g (Saturated Fat 0.7 g)	Protein 3.3 g	Sodium 210 mg

Get More Lemon Juice

You'll squeeze more juice from a lemon if you let it come to room temperature before you juice it. If you forget to set it out on the counter ahead of time, microwave the whole lemon for about 10 seconds. Once the lemon reaches room temperature, press and roll it on the counter with the palm of your hand. If you're going to need grated rind, be sure to grate the rind before juicing the fruit.

Spicy Pinto Beans

1 cup dried pinto beans
4¼ cups cold water
1 teaspoon olive oil
1 cup chopped onion
2 medium cloves garlic, crushed
½ cup diced reduced-fat, low-salt ham
3 jalapeño peppers, seeded and chopped
2 tablespoons red wine vinegar
2 teaspoons brown sugar
¼ teaspoon salt
¼ teaspoon pepper

Sort and wash beans; place beans in a large saucepan. Cover with water to a depth of 2 inches above beans. Bring to a boil; cover, remove from heat, and let stand for 1 hour. Drain beans, and return to saucepan; add 4¼ cups water. Bring to a boil; cover, reduce heat, and simmer, partially covered, 2 hours or until tender.

Heat oil in a large nonstick skillet over medium-high heat until hot. Add onion, and sauté 5 minutes. Add garlic, ham, and chopped pepper; sauté 5 additional minutes. Add onion mixture to beans in saucepan. Add vinegar and remaining ingredients; stir well. Bring to a boil; cover, reduce heat, and simmer 20 minutes. Yield: 4 (¾-cup) servings.

Per Serving
Calories 118 (19% Calories from Fat) Carbohydrate 16.6 g Cholesterol 10 mg
Fat 2.5 g (Saturated Fat 0.7 g) Protein 8.3 g Sodium 314 mg

Caraway Brussels Sprouts with Carrots

10 ounces fresh brussels sprouts
1½ cups sliced carrot
1 teaspoon caraway seeds
1 tablespoon lemon juice
2 teaspoons margarine
1 teaspoon sugar
¼ teaspoon salt
⅛ teaspoon pepper

Wash brussels sprouts thoroughly, and remove discolored leaves. Cut off stem ends. Cut brussels sprouts in half vertically.

Combine brussels sprouts, carrot, and caraway seeds in a large saucepan; add water to cover. Bring to a boil. Cover, reduce heat, and simmer 5 minutes or until vegetables are tender. Drain; return mixture to pan. Add lemon juice and remaining ingredients, stirring gently until margarine melts. Serve immediately. Yield: 7 (½-cup) servings.

Per Serving
Calories 41 (29% Calories from Fat) Carbohydrate 6.9 g Cholesterol 0 mg
Fat 1.3 g (Saturated Fat 0.3 g) Protein 1.6 g Sodium 115 mg

Nutty Caraway

Caraway seeds come from an herb in the parsley family and have a distinct nutty flavor. To keep the flavor at its freshest, store the seeds in an airtight container in a cool dark place for up to six months.

Lime-Glazed Carrots

- 1 pound carrots, scraped and diagonally cut into 1/4-inch slices
- 1/2 cup water
- 1 tablespoon sugar
- 1 1/2 tablespoons fresh lime juice
- 2 teaspoons margarine
- 1/4 teaspoon salt

Cook carrot in a small amount of boiling water 4 minutes or until crisp-tender; drain and return to saucepan. Add 1/2 cup water and sugar; bring to a boil. Reduce heat, and simmer, uncovered, 9 minutes or until liquid evaporates and carrot is tender. Stir in lime juice, margarine, and salt. Yield: 3 (1/2-cup) servings.

Per Serving
Calories 81 (30% Calories from Fat) Carbohydrate 14.5 g Cholesterol 0 mg
Fat 2.7 g (Saturated Fat 0.5 g) Protein 1.0 g Sodium 258 mg

Basil-Wrapped Corn on the Cob

Basically Basil
Basil comes in cinnamon, lemon, anise, spice, and purple varieties. All of these types have the basic warm spicy smell and flavor of the most popular one—sweet basil. You can add an extra flavor kick by substituting any of the basils with the spicy-sounding names.

- 4 ears fresh corn
- 2 teaspoons reduced-calorie margarine, melted
- 1/4 teaspoon salt
- 1/4 teaspoon freshly ground pepper
- 24 large fresh basil leaves

Remove husks and silk from corn. Combine margarine, salt, and pepper in a small bowl, stirring well. Brush margarine mixture over corn. Place each ear on a piece of heavy-duty aluminum foil. Place 3 basil leaves under each ear of corn and 3 leaves over each ear. Roll foil lengthwise around each ear; twist at ends to seal.

Place foil-wrapped corn on a baking sheet. Bake at 450° for 15 minutes or until tender. Yield: 4 servings.

Note: You can also grill this corn. Just prepare as directed above. Then, instead of baking, grill corn over medium-hot coals 15 to 20 minutes or until corn is tender, turning every 5 minutes.

Per Serving
Calories 106 (20% Calories from Fat) Carbohydrate 22.1 g Cholesterol 0 mg
Fat 2.4 g (Saturated Fat 0.3 g) Protein 3.1 g Sodium 180 mg

Green Beans in Chunky Tomato Vinaigrette

Basil-Wrapped Corn on the Cob

Crimini mushrooms have a robust, earthy flavor. *Button* and *white* mushrooms are delicious in salads or sautéed. *Shiitakes* come dried or fresh; they are best cooked and have a meaty flavor. *Portobellos* are great for meatless recipes because of their meaty texture and full-bodied flavor.

Trio of Sautéed Mushrooms

- Olive oil-flavored vegetable cooking spray
- 1 teaspoon olive oil
- 8 ounces fresh crimini mushrooms, stemmed
- 8 ounces portobello mushrooms, stemmed
- 4 ounces small fresh shiitake mushrooms, stemmed
- 1 large clove garlic, minced
- 1/3 cup dry white wine
- 2 teaspoons chopped fresh thyme
- 1/4 teaspoon salt
- 1/8 teaspoon pepper

Coat a large nonstick skillet with cooking spray; add oil. Place over medium-high heat until hot. Add mushrooms and garlic; sauté 4 minutes, stirring occasionally.

Add wine; cook, covered, 2 minutes. Uncover and cook 2 additional minutes or until liquid evaporates. Sprinkle mushroom mixture with thyme, salt, and pepper; toss well. Serve immediately. Yield: 4 (3/4-cup) servings.

Per Serving
Calories 89 (19% Calories from Fat) Carbohydrate 13.4 g Cholesterol 0 mg
Fat 1.9 g (Saturated Fat 0.3 g) Protein 4.1 g Sodium 156 mg

Roasted Peppers with Balsamic Vinaigrette

- 4 poblano chiles
- 2 large sweet red peppers
- 4 large yellow squash
- Vegetable cooking spray
- 1/4 cup balsamic vinegar
- 2 teaspoons olive oil
- 1/4 teaspoon salt
- 1/4 teaspoon pepper

Cut poblano chiles and red peppers in half lengthwise; remove and discard seeds and membranes. Place, skin side up, on a baking sheet; flatten with palm of hand. Cut squash in half lengthwise; coat squash with cooking spray. Place on baking sheet, cut side down. Broil peppers and squash 5 1/2 inches from heat (with electric door partially opened) 15 to 20 minutes or until peppers are charred.

Place peppers in ice water until cool. Broil squash 5 to 10 additional minutes or until charred. Place squash in ice water until cool. Remove peppers and squash from water; peel and discard skins. Cut into ½-inch strips.

Combine vinegar and remaining ingredients in a small bowl; stir well. Combine pepper strips and squash in a bowl; add vinegar mixture, and toss gently. Cover and chill until ready to serve. Serve with a slotted spoon. Yield: 7 (½-cup) servings.

Per Serving
Calories 64 (25% Calories from Fat) Carbohydrate 11.8 g Cholesterol 0 mg
Fat 1.8 g (Saturated Fat 0.3 g) Protein 2.6 g Sodium 91 mg

HERB-CRUSTED POTATO WEDGES

These baked potato wedges dusted with Parmesan cheese and herbs are a delicious alternative to French fries. Serve them with the Basil Beef Burgers on page 132.

2 pounds baking potatoes
1 tablespoon olive oil
3 tablespoons grated Parmesan cheese
1 tablespoon chopped fresh oregano
1 tablespoon chopped fresh thyme
2 teaspoons chopped fresh rosemary
¼ teaspoon freshly ground pepper
Olive oil-flavored vegetable cooking spray

About Thyme

Delicate thyme and other fresh herbs will keep a few days in the refrigerator if you wrap cut sprigs in a wet paper towel and store them in a zip-top plastic bag.

Scrub potatoes. Cut each potato into 8 wedges; brush with olive oil.

Combine Parmesan cheese and next 4 ingredients in a large zip-top plastic bag. Add potato wedges; seal bag, and shake to coat well. Place potato wedges, skin side down, in a single layer on a 15- x 10- x 1-inch jellyroll pan coated with cooking spray. Bake at 375° for 50 minutes or until tender and lightly browned, turning once. Yield: 8 servings.

Per Serving
Calories 110 (20% Calories from Fat) Carbohydrate 19.2 g Cholesterol 1 mg
Fat 2.5 g (Saturated Fat 0.6 g) Protein 3.3 g Sodium 43 mg

Roasting Peppers: Three Easy Steps

To roast peppers for extra flavor, follow the steps below:

Step 1: Place halved, seeded peppers, skin side up, on a baking sheet, and flatten them with the palm of your hand. Then broil them 5½ inches from the heat until blackened and charred. (It takes 12 to 15 minutes.)

Step 2: Remove roasted peppers from the baking sheet, and plunge them in ice water until cool.

Step 3: Peel and discard the blackened skins. The roasted pepper beneath the skins will be soft and slippery.

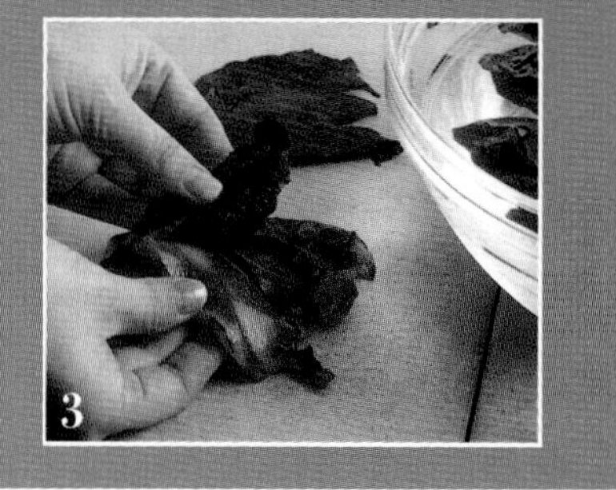

Potatoes with Roasted Poblano Chiles

1½ pounds round red potatoes (4 to 6 large)
1 pound fresh poblano chiles (4 to 5 large)
Vegetable cooking spray
½ cup plus 2 tablespoons finely chopped onion
1 large clove garlic, minced
1 teaspoon dried oregano
½ teaspoon ground cumin
¼ teaspoon salt
¼ teaspoon pepper
¼ teaspoon chopped fresh cilantro

Cook potatoes in boiling water to cover 25 minutes or until tender. Drain and let cool slightly. Cube potatoes; cover and set aside.

Cut chiles in half lengthwise; remove and discard seeds and membranes. Place chiles, skin side up, on a baking sheet, and flatten with palm of hand. Broil 5½ inches from heat (with electric oven door partially opened) 12 to 15 minutes or until charred. Place in ice water until cool; peel and discard skins. Coarsely chop chiles.

Coat a large nonstick skillet with cooking spray; place skillet over medium-high heat until hot. Add onion, garlic, oregano, and cumin; sauté 3 minutes or until onion is tender. Add cubed potato; cook until golden, turning potato gently with a metal spatula. Add chopped chile, salt, and ¼ teaspoon pepper; cook just until thoroughly heated. Transfer to a serving bowl, and sprinkle with cilantro. Serve immediately. Yield: 4 (1-cup) servings.

Per Serving

Calories 186 (3% Calories from Fat)	Carbohydrate 42.5 g	Cholesterol 0 mg
Fat 0.6 g (Saturated Fat 0.1 g)	Protein 4.8 g	Sodium 160 mg

Stuffed Mashed Potatoes with Chives

4 medium baking potatoes
Vegetable cooking spray
2 tablespoons skim milk
4 ounces nonfat cream cheese
2 tablespoons chopped fresh chives
1 tablespoon minced onion
¼ teaspoon salt
⅛ teaspoon pepper
¼ teaspoon paprika

Scrub potatoes; coat with cooking spray. Bake at 400° for 55 minutes or until soft. Cool slightly. Cut potatoes in half lengthwise, and carefully scoop out potato pulp, leaving ¼-inch-thick shells. Set shells aside. Place pulp in a small bowl; mash until smooth. Add milk and next 5 ingredients; stir well. Return mashed potato mixture to shells. Sprinkle with paprika; serve immediately. Yield: 4 servings.

Per Serving

Calories 186 (2% Calories from Fat)	Carbohydrate 36.7 g	Cholesterol 5 mg
Fat 0.4 g (Saturated Fat 0.1 g)	Protein 9.0 g	Sodium 335 mg

Herb-Marinated Tomatoes

2 large tomatoes, cut into ½-inch slices
2 tablespoons chopped fresh basil
1 tablespoon chopped fresh parsley
1 tablespoon chopped fresh oregano
1 tablespoon fresh lemon juice
1 teaspoon balsamic vinegar
¼ teaspoon salt
¼ teaspoon freshly ground pepper

Arrange tomato on a platter, slightly overlapping slices. Sprinkle with basil, parsley, and oregano.

Combine lemon juice and vinegar; drizzle over tomatoes. Cover and chill 2 hours. Sprinkle with salt and pepper. Yield: 4 servings.

Per Serving

Calories 39 (16% Calories from Fat)	Carbohydrate 8.8 g	Cholesterol 0 mg
Fat 0.7 g (Saturated Fat 0.1 g)	Protein 1.6 g	Sodium 162 mg

Turn on the Light

The light balsamic vinegar, that is. If you want the rich, mellow flavor of balsamic vinegar without the traditionally dark color, use the light-colored version. It has all of the flavor and looks great on light-colored vegetables. Find it on the vinegar aisle in most supermarkets.

Rosemary Roasted Vegetables

1 pound round red potatoes, cut into 1-inch pieces
1 tablespoon dried rosemary, crushed
2 tablespoons water
1 tablespoon olive oil
½ teaspoon freshly ground pepper
¼ teaspoon salt
Vegetable cooking spray
1 large sweet red pepper, seeded and cut into 1-inch pieces
1 medium eggplant (½ pound), cut into 1-inch pieces
8 cloves garlic

Place potato in a large bowl. Combine rosemary and next 4 ingredients; stir well. Pour one-third of oil mixture over potato; toss well.

Place potato in one end of a large roasting pan coated with cooking spray. Bake at 450° for 8 minutes. Place red pepper in bowl; add half of remaining oil mixture. Toss well; place red pepper next to potato, and bake 5 minutes. Place eggplant and garlic in bowl; add remaining oil mixture, and toss well. Add to potato and red pepper, and bake 20 additional minutes or until vegetables are tender. Arrange vegetables on a serving platter. Serve immediately. Yield: 4 (1-cup) servings.

Per Serving
Calories 155 (24% Calories from Fat) Carbohydrate 27.5 g Cholesterol 0 mg
Fat 4.2 g (Saturated Fat 0.5 g) Protein 4.0 g Sodium 160 mg

Yellow Rice with Black Beans and Corn

Use this recipe in the authentic South Florida supper on page 226.

Vegetable cooking spray
1 teaspoon olive oil
1 cup diced onion
2 cloves garlic, crushed
1 cup long-grain rice, uncooked
2 cups water
1/4 teaspoon threads of saffron
1/2 cup canned no-salt-added black beans, drained
1/2 cup frozen whole kernel corn, thawed
1/4 teaspoon salt
1/4 teaspoon freshly ground pepper

Coat a large nonstick skillet with cooking spray; add oil. Place over medium-high heat until hot. Add onion and garlic; sauté 2 minutes. Add rice, and sauté 2 minutes. Add water and saffron. Cover, reduce heat, and simmer 20 to 25 minutes or until liquid is absorbed and rice is tender. Stir in black beans and corn; cook 5 minutes or until thoroughly heated. Add salt and pepper. Yield: 4 (1-cup) servings.

Per Serving
Calories 234 (7% Calories from Fat) Carbohydrate 48.0 g Cholesterol 0 mg
Fat 1.8 g (Saturated Fat 0.3 g) Protein 6.0 g Sodium 155 mg

Threads of Flavor

It's easy to understand why saffron is the most expensive spice in the world: It takes the stigmas of over 250,000 crocus flowers to get a pound of saffron. The thread-like spice adds a sunny yellow color to food and is often used in breads. Grind the threads with a mortar and pestle just before using. Add it to food near the end of cooking time to keep the flavor pronounced.

Pesto Rice Cups

The pesto mixture that flavors the rice in this recipe has the traditional Italian flavors of pine nuts, basil, and Parmesan. But you save on fat and calories by using oil-free Italian dressing instead of olive oil. Serve these rice cups as part of the Italian menu on page 219.

1 large sweet red pepper
4 sun-dried tomatoes
Olive oil-flavored vegetable cooking spray
2 teaspoons reduced-calorie margarine
1 cup long-grain rice, uncooked
1 cup sliced green onions
1¾ cups low-sodium chicken broth
4 cloves garlic
2 tablespoons pine nuts
1½ cups tightly packed fresh basil leaves
½ cup chopped fresh parsley
⅓ cup grated Parmesan cheese
½ cup commercial oil-free Italian dressing
Parsley sprigs (optional)

Cut pepper in half lengthwise; remove and discard seeds and membrane. Place pepper, skin side up, on a baking sheet; flatten with palm of hand. Broil pepper 5½ inches from heat (with electric oven door partially opened) 15 to 20 minutes or until pepper is charred. Place pepper in ice water until cool; peel and discard skin. Dice roasted pepper.

Cover sun-dried tomatoes with boiling water, and let stand 5 minutes. Drain.

Coat a large nonstick skillet with cooking spray; place over medium-high heat until hot. Add margarine; heat until margarine melts. Add rice, and sauté 3 to 4 minutes or until golden, stirring frequently. Add green onions, and sauté 1 minute. Reserve 3 tablespoons diced red pepper; add remaining pepper to rice mixture. Add chicken broth; bring to a boil. Cover, reduce heat, and simmer 20 minutes or until liquid is absorbed. Remove from heat; uncover and let stand 10 minutes.

Position knife blade in food processor bowl. Drop garlic, pine nuts, and tomatoes through food chute with processor running; process 5 seconds or until garlic is minced. Add basil and chopped parsley; process 10 seconds or until herbs are minced. Add Parmesan cheese, and process until blended. Slowly pour Italian dressing through food chute with processor running, blending until mixture is smooth.

Stir pesto mixture gently into rice mixture, and heat thoroughly. Sprinkle reserved red pepper evenly into 6 (3/4-cup) molds. Spoon rice mixture into molds, packing gently with the back of a spoon. Unmold onto individual serving plates. Garnish with parsley sprigs, if desired. Yield: 6 (3/4-cup) servings.

Per Serving
Calories 208 (24% Calories from Fat) Carbohydrate 33.9 g Cholesterol 4 mg
Fat 5.6 g (Saturated Fat 1.4 g) Protein 6.8 g Sodium 399 mg

Cilantro Rice

If you don't like the flavor of cilantro, use fresh parsley instead.

Vegetable cooking spray
1 teaspoon vegetable oil
1½ cups long-grain rice, uncooked
1 cup chopped onion
½ cup chopped green pepper
2¾ cups canned low-sodium chicken broth, undiluted
½ teaspoon salt
½ teaspoon dried oregano
1 bay leaf
⅓ cup chopped fresh cilantro

Coat a large saucepan with cooking spray; add oil. Place pan over medium-high heat until hot. Add rice; sauté until rice is golden. Add onion and pepper; sauté 2 to 3 minutes or until vegetables are tender. Add chicken broth and next 3 ingredients. Bring to a boil. Cover, reduce heat, and simmer 20 minutes. Remove from heat; let stand 5 minutes or until liquid is absorbed. Remove and discard bay leaf. Stir in cilantro. Yield: 6 (1-cup) servings.

Per Serving
Calories 216 (8% Calories from Fat) Carbohydrate 43.7 g Cholesterol 0 mg
Fat 2.0 g (Saturated Fat 0.4 g) Protein 5.1 g Sodium 236 mg

Cilantro: An Acquired Taste

The pungent, citrus-like flavor of cilantro, the herb that is used to season many southwestern recipes, sometimes takes getting used to. If you've never tasted it, give yourself a few tries before you decide whether or not you like it. It wilts quickly, so keep cut stems in water in the refrigerator with a plastic bag over the leaves. Change the water every other day.

Zesty Citrus Oil-Free Dressing

Chunky Herbed Blue Cheese Dressing

Soups

Chili is sort of like barbecue. Everyone has a favorite recipe *and* a different opinion of which place sells the best bowl of it. Most chili lovers can't even agree on how hot it should be. So that's why you have a choice of chilis in this chapter. You purists will love Chili Ranchero (page 184) with chunks of steak (no beans). If you're afraid of a little heat, then just turn to page 186, and cook up a pot of Coward's Chili (with beans).

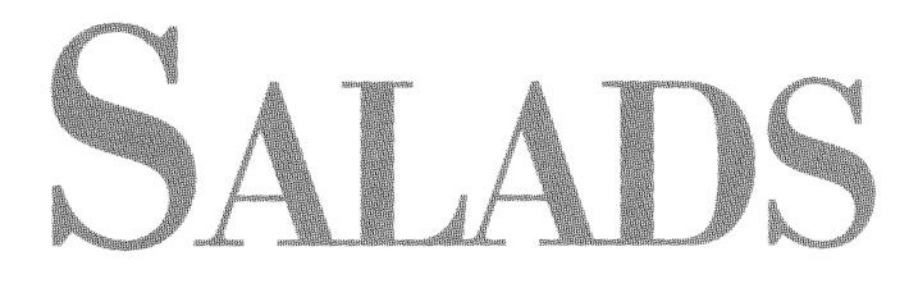

Aside from getting a variety of chili and other soups and stews in this chapter, you'll also find lots of flavor choices for salads and salad dressings. Everyone wants a really good chicken salad recipe. Our answer is Currant Chicken Salad (page 194). Or, if you're more into the leafy green type, try Grilled Chicken on Baby Greens (page 193)—it's a meal in itself.

Dressings

Looking for a different dressing? If you like vinaigrettes, try our smooth-tasting Balsamic Currant Vinaigrette (page 197) on your salad greens. And if you prefer creamy dressings, you're in for a treat. Our Chunky Herbed Blue Cheese Dressing on the same page gives you a guilt-free salad with less than one gram of fat in each tablespoon.

Cilantro-Lime Soup

Serve this soup in the southwestern menu on page 225.

1 teaspoon olive oil
1 medium-size yellow onion, peeled and quartered
4 cloves garlic, chopped
8 cups canned no-salt-added chicken broth, undiluted
1 (14½-ounce) can no-salt-added whole tomatoes, undrained and chopped
2 teaspoons grated lime rind
¼ cup fresh lime juice
2 teaspoons red chile powder
1 teaspoon dried oregano
¼ teaspoon salt
¼ teaspoon freshly ground pepper
6 (6-inch) corn tortillas, cut into ¼-inch strips
Vegetable cooking spray
½ cup chopped fresh cilantro

Heat oil in a large Dutch oven over medium-high heat until hot. Add onion and garlic; sauté until tender. Add broth and next 7 ingredients. Bring to a boil; reduce heat, and simmer 20 minutes.

Place tortilla strips on a baking sheet coated with cooking spray. Bake at 350° for 10 minutes or until crisp and lightly browned. Set aside to cool.

Stir cilantro into hot broth mixture. To serve, ladle soup into individual bowls, and top evenly with tortilla strips. Yield: 10 (1-cup) servings.

Per Serving

Calories 64 (13% Calories from Fat)	Carbohydrate 11.1 g	Cholesterol 0 mg
Fat 0.9 g (Saturated Fat 0.1 g)	Protein 1.7 g	Sodium 88 mg

HEARTY LENTIL SOUP

1 teaspoon olive oil
½ pound dried lentils
1 cup coarsely chopped onion
1 teaspoon chili powder
2 cups peeled, cubed potato
⅓ cup diced carrot
½ cup chopped 96% fat-free, low-sodium ham
7 cups water
1 (14¼-ounce) can no-salt-added chicken broth, undiluted
1 teaspoon dry mustard
1 teaspoon peeled, grated gingerroot
½ teaspoon ground coriander
½ teaspoon dried thyme
4 bay leaves
2 cloves garlic, crushed
¼ teaspoon salt
¼ teaspoon freshly ground pepper
¼ cup plus 3 tablespoons plain nonfat yogurt

Heat oil in a large Dutch oven over medium heat until hot. Add lentils, onion, and chili powder; sauté 2 minutes or until lentils are golden. Add potato and next 10 ingredients. Bring to a boil; reduce heat, and simmer, uncovered, 2 hours, stirring occasionally. Stir in salt and pepper. Remove and discard bay leaves. Ladle soup into individual bowls. Top each serving with 1 tablespoon yogurt. Yield: 7 (1-cup) servings.

Per Serving
Calories 182 (8% Calories from Fat) Carbohydrate 29.5 g Cholesterol 6 mg
Fat 1.6 g (Saturated Fat 0.2 g) Protein 13.5 g Sodium 196 mg

Confused About Coriander?

In the fresh form it's also called cilantro, a powerful leaf herb with a pungent lemon-like flavor that is often used with other bold flavors. But the seeds, ground or whole, have a mild, sweet, and peppery flavor.

Pondering Pepper Powders

The ground red pepper (sometimes called cayenne pepper) found on the spice rack is made from pungent peppers such as cayenne. Red chile powder (not to be confused with chili powder which is a blend of pepper and other spices) is the ground form of one of several types of dried red chiles and varies in heat depending on the type of chile used. Crushed red pepper flakes are made when dried red chiles are crushed along with the seeds. This version is used as a spice and a tableside condiment.

Tomato-Egg Flower Soup

Turn to page 220 for a Chinese menu that includes this soup.

1 (14¼-ounce) can no-salt-added chicken broth
1 (14½-ounce) can no-salt-added whole tomatoes, undrained and chopped
1 teaspoon low-sodium soy sauce
1 egg white
¼ teaspoon sesame oil
¼ teaspoon salt
¼ teaspoon freshly ground pepper
1 green onion, diagonally sliced

Combine broth and tomatoes in a large saucepan; bring to a boil. Remove saucepan from heat; add soy sauce.

Combine egg white and sesame oil. Stir hot broth mixture vigorously with a wire whisk while gradually adding egg white mixture. Add salt and pepper.

To serve, ladle soup into individual bowls. Top each serving with sliced green onion. Yield: 4 (1-cup) servings.

Per Serving
Calories 37 (7% Calories from Fat) | Carbohydrate 5.7 g | Cholesterol 0 mg
Fat 0.3 g (Saturated Fat 0 g) | Protein 1.9 g | Sodium 208 mg

Potato-Carrot Soup

4½ cups water
6 medium carrots, scraped and cut into 2-inch pieces
2 stalks celery, cut into 2-inch pieces
2¾ cups peeled, cubed baking potato (about 1 pound)
1 cup coarsely chopped onion
¼ cup minced fresh parsley
½ teaspoon paprika
¼ teaspoon salt
¼ teaspoon black pepper
⅛ teaspoon ground red pepper

Combine first 5 ingredients in a large saucepan; bring to a boil. Reduce heat; simmer, uncovered, 40 minutes or until vegetables are tender.

Pour half of mixture into container of an electric blender; cover and process until smooth. Repeat procedure with remaining vegetable mixture. Return pureed mixture to saucepan; add parsley and remaining ingredients. Cook until thoroughly heated. Serve warm, or cover and chill. Yield: 6 (1-cup) servings.

Per Serving

Calories 69 (4% Calories from Fat)	Carbohydrate 15.2 g	Cholesterol 0 mg
Fat 0.3 g (Saturated Fat 0 g)	Protein 2.6 g	Sodium 135 mg

Peppery Pea Soup

1 (16-ounce) package frozen English peas, thawed
1 large yellow onion, cut into eighths
1 medium baking potato, peeled and cut into fourths
1 medium carrot, scraped and cut into fourths
½ cup chopped lean cooked ham
2½ cups evaporated skimmed milk
½ cup water
½ teaspoon ground celery seeds
½ teaspoon dried thyme
½ teaspoon freshly ground pepper
¼ teaspoon salt
6 cloves garlic
¼ cup nonfat sour cream
¾ cup diced tomato

Combine first 12 ingredients in a Dutch oven; bring to a boil. Cover, reduce heat, and simmer 30 minutes or until vegetables are tender. Transfer mixture in batches to container of an electric blender. Cover and process until smooth. Return puree to Dutch oven. Cook over medium heat just until thoroughly heated (do not boil).

Ladle soup into individual bowls. Top each serving with 2 teaspoons sour cream and 2 tablespoons diced tomato. Yield: 6 (1-cup) servings.

Per Serving

Calories 216 (6% Calories from Fat)	Carbohydrate 34.6 g	Cholesterol 13 mg
Fat 1.5 g (Saturated Fat 0.2 g)	Protein 16.9 g	Sodium 520 mg

Pork Stew with Spoonbread

Spoonbread is more like a soft pudding made from cornmeal than a bread. Serve a scoop atop any meat stew for a hearty, down-home flavor.

1 pound lean boneless pork loin
Vegetable cooking spray
1½ cups chopped onion
¾ cup chopped celery
1 tablespoon all-purpose flour
½ teaspoon salt
½ teaspoon ground allspice
¼ teaspoon freshly ground black pepper
¼ teaspoon ground mace
4 cups canned no-salt-added chicken broth, undiluted
2 (14½-ounce) cans no-salt-added tomatoes, undrained and chopped
1 medium turnip, peeled and cut into ½-inch slices
3 medium carrots, scraped and cut into ½-inch slices
1 medium parsnip, scraped and cut into ½-inch slices
1¾ cups chopped baking potato
1 cup coarsely chopped crimini mushrooms
1 cup frozen whole kernel corn, thawed
2 tablespoons bourbon
⅛ teaspoon ground red pepper
Spoonbread

Trim fat from pork; cut pork into ½-inch cubes. Coat a Dutch oven with cooking spray; place over medium-high until hot. Add pork, and cook until pork is browned on all sides, stirring frequently. Drain and pat dry with paper towels. Wipe drippings from Dutch oven.

Coat Dutch oven with cooking spray; place over medium-high heat until hot. Add onion and celery; sauté until tender. Add pork, flour, and next 4 ingredients; cook 2 minutes. Add chicken broth and tomatoes, deglazing Dutch oven by scraping particles that cling to bottom. Add turnip and next 5 ingredients. Bring to a boil; reduce heat, and simmer, uncovered, 45 minutes or until vegetables are tender, stirring frequently. Just before serving, add bourbon and red pepper. Ladle stew into individual bowls. Top each with a serving of Spoonbread. Yield: 11 (1-cup) servings.

Per Serving
Calories 165 (26% Calories from Fat) Carbohydrate 17.5 g Cholesterol 32 mg
Fat 4.7 g (Saturated Fat 1.6 g) Protein 11.1 g Sodium 178 mg

Crimini Means Flavor

Crimini mushrooms taste earthy and robust and look like a dark version of fresh button mushrooms. You can substitute button mushrooms if you must, but the flavor won't be as strong.

Spoonbread

1 cup white cornmeal
1½ cups boiling water
1 teaspoon margarine, softened
2 eggs, separated
1 cup nonfat buttermilk
1 tablespoon sugar
1 teaspoon baking powder
½ teaspoon salt
¼ teaspoon baking soda
Vegetable cooking spray

Combine cornmeal and boiling water in a large bowl; stir with a wire whisk until well blended. Add margarine, egg yolks, and next 5 ingredients, stirring until dry ingredients are moistened.

Beat egg whites at high speed of an electric mixer just until stiff peaks form. Gently fold egg white into cornmeal mixture. Coat an 11- x 7- x 1½-inch baking dish with cooking spray. Pour batter into prepared dish. Bake at 375° for 28 to 30 minutes or until golden. Yield: 11 servings.

Per Serving

Calories 80 (26% Calories from Fat)	Carbohydrate 13.0 g	Cholesterol 41 mg
Fat 1.6 g (Saturated Fat 0.5 g)	Protein 3.1 g	Sodium 175 mg

Chili Ranchero

This hot and spicy chili goes great with the Cheese and Tomato Quesadillas that are pictured with it on the next page. *See page 77 for the quesadilla recipe, or turn to page 218 to find a Mexican meal that features both of these recipes.*

1½ pounds lean boneless top round steak
Vegetable cooking spray
2 cups chopped onion
2 large cloves garlic, minced
1 teaspoon dried oregano
1 teaspoon ground cumin
2 tablespoons chili powder
2 teaspoons unsweetened cocoa
½ teaspoon salt
2 cups canned no-salt-added beef broth, undiluted
1 (14½-ounce) can no-salt-added whole tomatoes, undrained and chopped
2¼ cups frozen whole kernel corn, thawed
1½ cups chopped sweet red pepper
Fresh cilantro sprigs (optional)

Trim fat from steak; cut steak into 1-inch pieces. Coat a Dutch oven with cooking spray; place over medium-high heat until hot. Add steak; cook 4 minutes or until browned on all sides, stirring frequently. Drain and pat dry with paper towels. Wipe drippings from Dutch oven with a paper towel.

Coat Dutch oven with cooking spray. Place over medium-high heat until hot. Add onion and garlic; sauté until tender. Add oregano and cumin; cook, stirring constantly, 1 minute. Add chili powder, cocoa, and salt, and cook mixture, stirring constantly, 1 additional minute. Add steak, beef broth, and tomatoes; bring to a boil. Cover, reduce heat, and simmer 1½ hours or until beef is tender.

Uncover; add corn and red pepper, and simmer 20 additional minutes.

To serve, ladle into individual serving bowls; sprinkle with cilantro, if desired. Yield: 6 (1¼-cup) servings.

Per Serving

Calories 276 (23% Calories from Fat)	Carbohydrate 21.8 g	Cholesterol 75 mg
Fat 7.0 g (Saturated Fat 2.2 g)	Protein 32.1 g	Sodium 292 mg

So Many Ways to Use Garlic

Sautéed garlic takes on a mellow roasted flavor; oven-roasted cloves are mellow and almost sweet; whole cloves add a nutty flavor when simmered in soups or studded into meats before cooking; and crushed or chopped garlic is strong and sharp. But for just a little garlic flavor, slice the clove, and rub the cut side onto a bread slice or onto the surface of a salad bowl before filling it.

Cheese and Tomato Quesadillas

Chili Ranchero

Coward's Chili

This chili is for all you cowards who prefer mild rather than wild flavor when it comes to heat.

1½ pounds ground round
2 cups chopped green pepper
2 cups coarsely chopped yellow onion
2 teaspoons chili powder
½ teaspoon ground cumin
2 (15-ounce) cans kidney beans, drained
2 (14½-ounce) cans no-salt-added tomatoes, undrained and chopped
2 (8-ounce) cans no-salt-added tomato sauce
1 (6-ounce) can no-salt-added tomato paste
1 cup water
½ teaspoon salt
¼ teaspoon freshly ground pepper

Cook ground round, green pepper, and onion in a Dutch oven over medium-high heat until beef is browned, stirring until it crumbles. Drain beef mixture, and pat dry with paper towels. Wipe drippings from Dutch oven with a paper towel.

Return beef mixture to Dutch oven. Stir in chili powder and cumin. Cook, stirring constantly, 1 minute. Add beans and remaining ingredients. Bring to a boil; cover, reduce heat, and simmer 2 hours, stirring occasionally. Yield: 11 (1-cup) servings.

Per Serving
Calories 210 (18% Calories from Fat) Carbohydrate 24.7 g Cholesterol 38 mg
Fat 4.2 g (Saturated Fat 1.4 g) Protein 19.3 g Sodium 304 mg

Crazy for Cumin

Strong and slightly bitter cumin is a mainstay in most warm cuisines. Cumin is an essential ingredient in southwestern chilis, Indian garam masalas, and curry powders.

Jicama-Orange Salad

Turn to page 218 for a Mexican menu that includes this salad.

2 cups julienne-sliced jicama
5 oranges, peeled and sectioned
¼ cup sliced green onions
¼ cup chopped fresh cilantro
3 tablespoons nonfat sour cream
1½ tablespoons fresh lime juice
1½ teaspoons vegetable oil
⅛ teaspoon salt

Combine first 4 ingredients in a medium bowl, and toss well. Cover and chill.

Combine sour cream, lime juice, oil, and salt in a small bowl; stir with a wire whisk. Just before serving, drain jicama mixture. Pour dressing over jicama mixture; toss gently. Yield: 6 (½-cup) servings.

Per Serving
Calories 64 (18% Calories from Fat) Carbohydrate 12.3 g Cholesterol 0 mg
Fat 1.3 g (Saturated Fat 0.3 g) Protein 1.6 g Sodium 57 mg

Hailing Jicama

The beauty of jicama (HEE-kama) is that rather than imparting a unique flavor of its own, it takes on the flavor of the ingredients in any mixture. The ugly, brown-skinned vegetable has a crisp, white flesh similar to, but sweeter than, turnips. Jicama is a common ingredient in Mexican and southwestern recipes.

Fragrant Garden Tabbouleh

Middle Easterners serve traditional tabbouleh (tah-BOO-luh) chilled and with a crisp bread for scooping up every delicious morsel. You can serve it in an authentic Mediterranean menu like the one on page 223.

⅔ cup bulgur (cracked wheat), uncooked
2 cups boiling water
1 medium cucumber, peeled, seeded, and cut into ½-inch pieces
1 medium-size green pepper, cut into ½-inch pieces
1 medium tomato, seeded and cut into ½-inch pieces
¾ cup chopped fresh parsley
½ cup chopped fresh mint
½ cup thinly sliced green onions
¼ cup fresh lemon juice
1 tablespoon olive oil
½ teaspoon salt
¼ teaspoon pepper

Combine bulgur and water in a bowl; let stand 30 minutes. Drain and squeeze in several layers of damp cheesecloth or dry paper towels.

Place bulgur in a large bowl; add cucumber and remaining ingredients, tossing well. Serve immediately, or cover and chill thoroughly. Yield: 4 (1-cup) servings.

Per Serving
Calories 161 (23% Calories from Fat) Carbohydrate 29.4 g Cholesterol 0 mg
Fat 4.2 g (Saturated Fat 0.6 g) Protein 4.9 g Sodium 308 mg

Rice Salad with Roasted Chiles

Chunky Herbed Blue Cheese Dressing

Grilled Chicken on Baby Greens

Couscous Salad with Creamy Roast Garlic Dressing

Although there are several varieties of parsley, flat-leaf (sometimes called Italian) parsley is one of the strongest flavored.

1 large head garlic
1½ cups canned low-sodium chicken broth, undiluted
1 cup couscous, uncooked
2 tablespoons nonfat mayonnaise
2 tablespoons red wine vinegar
¼ teaspoon salt
¼ teaspoon freshly ground pepper
¾ cup chopped sweet red pepper
½ cup chopped fresh flat-leaf parsley
¼ cup finely chopped celery

Gently peel outer skin from garlic. Cut off top one-third of head, and discard. Place garlic, cut side up, in center of a piece of heavy-duty aluminum foil. Fold aluminum foil over garlic, sealing tightly. Bake at 400° for 40 minutes or until garlic is soft. Remove from oven; let cool 10 minutes. Separate cloves, and squeeze to extract pulp.

Bring chicken broth to a boil in a medium saucepan. Remove from heat. Add couscous; cover and let stand 5 minutes or until couscous is tender and liquid is absorbed. Fluff couscous with a fork, and transfer to a serving bowl.

Combine mayonnaise and next 3 ingredients in a small bowl; stir well. Add garlic; stir well.

Combine couscous, red pepper, parsley, and celery in a large bowl; add mayonnaise mixture, and toss well. Cover and chill 3 hours. Yield: 4 (1-cup) servings.

Note: To save time, you can substitute commercial roasted garlic for fresh roasted garlic.

Per Serving
Calories 104 (9% Calories from Fat) Carbohydrate 20.7 g Cholesterol 0 mg
Fat 1.0 g (Saturated Fat 0.1 g) Protein 4.4 g Sodium 296 mg

Cooking in Flavor
This technique works with pasta and rice: Simply add some broth to the water when you cook them, and you've cooked in flavor without adding much fat.

Rice Salad with Roasted Chiles

If you don't have fresh chiles or the time to roast them, substitute frozen roasted chiles. A mail order source is on page 230.

4 whole fresh green chiles (about 10 ounces)
1 cup chopped sweet red pepper
1 medium cucumber, peeled, thinly sliced, and cut in half
2 cups cooked long-grain rice (cooked without salt or fat)
½ cup frozen whole-kernel corn, thawed
½ teaspoon grated lime rind
2½ teaspoons fresh lime juice
3 tablespoons minced shallots
2 tablespoons chopped fresh cilantro
2 tablespoons red wine vinegar
2 tablespoons olive oil
1 tablespoon water
¼ teaspoon salt
¼ teaspoon freshly ground pepper
¼ teaspoon brown sugar

Cut chiles in half lengthwise; remove and discard seeds and membranes. Place chiles, skin side up, on a baking sheet, and flatten with palm of hand. Broil 5½ inches from heat (with electric oven door partially opened) 10 to 15 minutes or until charred. Place chiles in ice water until cool. Remove from water; peel and discard skins.

Chop chiles, and place in a large bowl. Add red pepper and next 5 ingredients; toss well.

Combine shallots and remaining ingredients in a jar. Cover tightly, and shake vigorously. Pour over rice mixture; toss gently. Cover and chill thoroughly. Yield: 5 (1-cup) servings.

Per Serving
Calories 125 (22% Calories from Fat) Carbohydrate 23.1 g Cholesterol 0 mg
Fat 3.0 g (Saturated Fat 0.4 g) Protein 2.6 g Sodium 124 mg

Superbly Sectioned Oranges

Here's how our home economists get those beautiful citrus sections you see in our photographs: Peel away the orange (or grapefruit) skin and membrane with a sharp knife. Carefully slide the knife blade vertically along the inside of the membrane encasing each orange section. Beautiful citrus sections will lift right out.

Fruited Spinach-Pasta Salad

3 cups uncooked farfalle (bow tie pasta)
4 cups fresh spinach leaves, stemmed and chopped
4 oranges, peeled and sectioned
½ cup coarsely chopped red onion
1 (6-ounce) can frozen orange juice concentrate, thawed
½ cup nonfat mayonnaise
1 tablespoon paprika
Lettuce leaves

Cook pasta according to package directions, omitting salt and fat; drain. Combine pasta and next 3 ingredients in a bowl; toss gently. Combine concentrate, mayonnaise, and paprika; stir with a wire whisk. Pour over pasta; toss. Serve over lettuce. Yield: 7 (1-cup) servings.

Per Serving
Calories 160 (4% Calories from Fat) Carbohydrate 34.9 g Cholesterol 0 mg
Fat 0.7 g (Saturated Fat 0.1 g) Protein 4.5 g Sodium 235 mg

Thai Barbecue Beef Salad

2 tablespoons fish sauce
1 jalapeño pepper, seeded
2 cloves garlic
3 tablespoons fresh lime juice
1 tablespoon brown sugar
1 tablespoon lime zest
1 tablespoon Spicy Southwest Chile Oil (page 33)
4 shallots, thinly sliced lengthwise
½ cup lightly packed fresh mint, chopped
¼ cup chopped green onions
1½ teaspoons peeled, grated gingerroot
1 pound sirloin steak (1½ inches thick)
½ teaspoon freshly ground pepper
¼ teaspoon salt
Vegetable cooking spray
8 cups mixed salad greens
3 tablespoons chopped fresh cilantro
½ cup diced sweet red pepper

Combine first 3 ingredients in container of an electric blender; cover and process until smooth. Add lime juice and sugar; cover and process until smooth. Stir in lime zest.

Divide mixture in half. Stir Spicy Southwest Chile Oil into one half of sauce mixture. Add shallots, mint, green onions, and gingerroot to remaining half of sauce mixture. Set aside.

Sprinkle steak evenly with ½ teaspoon pepper and salt. Coat grill rack with cooking spray; place on grill over medium-hot coals (350° to 400°). Place steak on rack; grill, covered, 8 minutes on each side or to desired degree of doneness. Remove steak from grill; let stand 5 minutes. Slice steak diagonally across the grain into ¼-inch-thick slices; cut slices into ¼-inch-thick strips. Combine steak strips and shallot mixture; cover and chill thoroughly.

Combine mixed greens and oil mixture; toss well. Arrange on salad plates; top with steak strip mixture. Sprinkle with cilantro and red pepper. Yield: 6 servings.

What Makes It Thai?
Chiles, garlic, ginger, lime, curry, cilantro, cumin, and basil are some of the most prominent ingredients in Thai cooking. It's no wonder much of the food is hot—Thailand grows 10 of the world's hottest chiles.

Per Serving
Calories 161 (32% Calories from Fat) Carbohydrate 7.2 g Cholesterol 55 mg
Fat 5.7 g (Saturated Fat 1.9 g) Protein 20.2 g Sodium 527 mg

Grilled Chicken on Baby Greens

4 (4-ounce) skinned, boned chicken breast halves
¾ cup plus 2 tablespoons Citrus Marinade (page 13), divided
Vegetable cooking spray
8 cups mixed baby salad greens
1 medium-size orange, peeled and sectioned
1 medium grapefruit, peeled and sectioned
1 small purple onion, thinly sliced and separated into rings

Place chicken in a large heavy-duty, zip-top plastic bag; add ½ cup Citrus Marinade. Seal bag, and marinate in refrigerator 2 hours.

Coat grill rack with cooking spray; place on grill over medium-hot coals (350° to 400°). Remove chicken from marinade, discarding marinade. Place chicken on rack; grill, covered, 4 to 5 minutes on each side or until done. Cut chicken into thin slices.

Place 2 cups salad greens on each salad plate. Arrange orange sections, grapefruit sections, and onion rings over salad greens. Top each salad with chicken slices. Drizzle with remaining ¼ cup plus 2 tablespoons Citrus Marinade. Yield: 4 servings.

Per Serving
Calories 239 (26% Calories from Fat) Carbohydrate 16.2 g Cholesterol 72 mg
Fat 6.8 g (Saturated Fat 1.5 g) Protein 27.8 g Sodium 84 mg

Currant Chicken Salad

Toast the almonds in this recipe by spreading about 1/4 cup of nuts in a glass pieplate; then microwave at HIGH for 2 to 4 minutes, stirring at the end of every minute.

2 1/2 cups chopped cooked chicken breast
1 cup cubed fresh pineapple
1 cup seedless red grapes
1/2 cup sliced celery
1/4 cup Balsamic Currant Vinaigrette (page 197)
1/4 teaspoon salt
1/4 teaspoon freshly ground pepper
Red leaf lettuce
2 tablespoons slivered almonds, toasted

Combine first 4 ingredients; toss well. Add Balsamic Currant Vinaigrette, salt, and pepper; toss well. Cover; chill 1 hour.

Line individual salad plates with lettuce. Top with chicken mixture; sprinkle with almonds. Yield: 4 (1 1/4-cup) servings.

Per Serving
Calories 222 (21% Calories from Fat) Carbohydrate 14.0 g Cholesterol 78 mg
Fat 5.3 g (Saturated Fat 1.1 g) Protein 29.7 g Sodium 233 mg

Turkey and Star Anise Salad

For a crisp but still flavorful salad, use Romaine lettuce instead of Boston lettuce as the base of this salad.

1 pound boneless turkey breast, skinned
1 (14 1/4-ounce) can no-salt-added chicken broth
3 tablespoons chili powder
2 whole star anise
2 tablespoons dark brown sugar
1 tablespoon dried oregano
1 sweet red pepper, cut into thin strips
2/3 cup green onions, diagonally sliced
1/2 cup fresh cilantro leaves
2 tablespoons rice wine vinegar
1 teaspoon peanut oil
1/4 teaspoon salt
1/4 teaspoon freshly ground pepper
8 cups torn Boston lettuce (about 2 heads)

Star of Flavor

Sweet and licorice-like, star anise is used mostly in Chinese cooking to season poultry, pork, and fish. The star-shaped dried fruit of an evergreen tree is most often used whole or broken into pieces. Toss a star anise or two in the water when you simmer rice or when you simmer soups with an Oriental flavor.

Turkey and Star Anise Salad

Place first 6 ingredients in a Dutch oven. Bring to a boil; reduce heat, and simmer, uncovered, 40 minutes or until turkey is done. Remove turkey; strain broth mixture, and set broth aside. Shred turkey. Combine turkey, red pepper, green onions, and cilantro. Cover and chill at least 2 hours.

Bring reserved broth to a boil, and reduce to ½ cup. Remove from heat. Combine broth, vinegar, oil, salt, and pepper. Cover and chill dressing.

Arrange lettuce on individual salad plates. Arrange turkey mixture over lettuce. Drizzle dressing over salads. Yield: 4 (1½-cup) servings.

Per Serving

Calories 220 (24% Calories from Fat)	Carbohydrate 13.9 g	Cholesterol 59 mg
Fat 5.9 g (Saturated Fat 1.3 g)	Protein 28.6 g	Sodium 303 mg

Check the Fat Grams

Don't be misled by the percentage of calories from fat in several of these salad dressings. Look at the total grams of fat per serving as well as the percentage to determine if it is a healthy recipe. Even though this dressing has 58% calories from fat, it still has less than one gram of fat per serving—and that's quite good.

Blueberry Dressing

½ cup fresh or frozen blueberries, thawed
½ cup water
1 tablespoon plus 1 teaspoon sugar
1 tablespoon olive oil
½ teaspoon lemon rind
¼ cup lemon juice
¼ teaspoon salt
¼ teaspoon freshly ground pepper

Combine all ingredients in a small bowl, stirring well. Cover and chill thoroughly. Serve over steamed asparagus, fresh fruit salads, or grilled or poached chicken. Store dressing in refrigerator up to 3 days. Yield: 1 cup.

Per Tablespoon

Calories 14 (58% Calories from Fat)	Carbohydrate 2.0 g	Cholesterol 0 mg
Fat 0.9 g (Saturated Fat 0.1 g)	Protein 0.1 g	Sodium 37 mg

Zesty Citrus Oil-Free Dressing

2 tablespoons orange zest
½ cup plus 2 tablespoons fresh orange juice
2 tablespoons powdered fruit pectin
2 tablespoons honey
1 teaspoon poppy seeds

Combine all ingredients in a small jar; cover tightly, and shake vigorously. Chill thoroughly. Serve with salad greens, fresh fruit, melons, angel food cake, or grilled fish. Store in refrigerator up to 3 days. Yield: ¾ cup.

Per Tablespoon

Calories 22 (8% Calories from Fat)	Carbohydrate 5.3 g	Cholesterol 0 mg
Fat 0.2 g (Saturated Fat 0 g)	Protein 0.2 g	Sodium 0 mg

Balsamic Currant Vinaigrette

- 2 tablespoons currants
- ¼ cup balsamic vinegar
- 3 cloves garlic, crushed
- 2 tablespoons water
- 1 teaspoon Dijon mustard
- 1 teaspoon olive oil
- ¼ teaspoon sugar
- ¼ teaspoon freshly ground pepper

Combine currants and vinegar in a jar; cover and let stand 30 minutes. Add garlic and remaining ingredients. Cover tightly, and shake vigorously. Chill, if desired. Serve with salad greens. Yield: ½ cup.

Note: See Currant Chicken Salad (page 194).

Per Tablespoon

Calories 14 (45% Calories from Fat)	Carbohydrate 2.0 g	Cholesterol 0 mg
Fat 0.7 g (Saturated Fat 0.1 g)	Protein 0.1 g	Sodium 20 mg

Chunky Herbed Blue Cheese Dressing

- 1 cup nonfat buttermilk
- 1 cup 1% low-fat cottage cheese
- ¼ cup reduced-calorie mayonnaise
- 1 tablespoon white wine vinegar
- ¼ teaspoon salt
- ¼ teaspoon ground white pepper
- ⅓ cup plus 1 tablespoon crumbled blue cheese
- 2 tablespoons finely chopped fresh basil

Combine first 6 ingredients in container of an electric blender; cover and process until smooth, stopping once to scrape down sides.

Transfer mixture to a small bowl. Stir in blue cheese and basil. Cover and chill at least 2 hours. Serve with salad greens or assorted fresh vegetables. Yield: 2½ cups.

Per Tablespoon

Calories 15 (54% Calories from Fat)	Carbohydrate 0.6 g	Cholesterol 2 mg
Fat 0.9 g (Saturated Fat 0.3 g)	Protein 1.2 g	Sodium 75 mg

Mix greens to get great salad flavor. For a bitter taste, use dandelion, turnip or collard greens, romaine, or radicchio. Beet greens taste like beets; kale flavor is similar to cabbage; watercress and arugula are peppery-flavored; and Boston lettuce is sweet and succulent.

Lemon-Lime Cake

CAKES

When Margaret Willoughby was running her Norfolk, Virginia, household in 1800, she planned dessert only for rare and special occasions. Sugar, spices, and other dessert flavoring ingredients were expensive and hard to get. So she and her friends turned to other means of adding flavor to their cakes, cookies, and pies. They

COOKIES

poured a little rosewater into cakes and cookies. They cooked with fresh herbs in season and even achieved a great lemon flavor by making a syrup from lemon balm.

One of Mrs. Willoughby's favorite recipes was rose geranium pound cake. This deliciously rich cake had a hint of lemon from baking rose geranium leaves (the herb, not the often-potted flower) right into the

PIES

cake. One of our editors tried the recipe after a visit to the historic Willoughby home and wondered if rose geranium would make a low-fat pound cake taste just as delicious. So we tried it and achieved mouth-watering results—without all the eggs and butter of the original cake—that you'll see in this chapter on page 208. Mrs. Willoughby would be pleased.

And you'll surely be pleased with the other recipes to follow. We gave so many of these desserts high marks that we can't even pick a favorite.

Mimosa Fruit Cup with Cracked Sugar

- ¼ cup sugar
- 1½ teaspoons water
- 2 cups seedless green grapes, halved
- 2 cups fresh strawberry halves
- 1 cup sliced fresh plums
- 1 cup fresh orange sections (about 2 medium oranges)
- ½ cup champagne, chilled
- ¼ cup frozen orange juice concentrate, thawed and undiluted
- 2 tablespoons sugar
- 10 commercial waffle cone bowls
- ½ cup plus 2 tablespoons frozen reduced-calorie whipped topping, thawed

Combine ¼ cup sugar and water in a small saucepan, and cook over medium heat until golden, stirring occasionally. Pour mixture onto an aluminum foil-lined baking sheet. Tilt baking sheet to spread mixture to ¼-inch thickness. Cool completely; break into small pieces.

Combine grapes and next 3 ingredients in a large bowl; toss gently. Combine champagne, orange juice concentrate, and 2 tablespoons sugar; stir well. Pour over fruit mixture; toss gently. Cover and chill 30 minutes, stirring occasionally.

Spoon fruit mixture into waffle cone bowls; dollop each serving with 1 tablespoon whipped topping. Sprinkle with cracked sugar. Serve immediately. Yield: 10 (½-cup) servings.

Per Serving

Calories 156 (11% Calories from Fat)	Carbohydrate 24.2 g	Cholesterol 0 mg
Fat 1.9 g (Saturated Fat 0.1 g)	Protein 1.0 g	Sodium 29 mg

Keep Them Crisp

Walnuts need to be toasted to stay crisp when they're mixed into liquid mixtures like sauces. To toast them, first drop the nuts into rapidly boiling water, and boil them for 3 minutes. Drain; then spread the nuts on a baking sheet. Bake the walnuts at 350° for 12 to 15 minutes or until they turn golden. Be sure to stir often during baking so the nuts will toast evenly without burning.

Grilled Banana-Walnut Quesadillas

- 2 tablespoons sugar
- ½ teaspoon ground cinnamon
- ⅛ teaspoon ground nutmeg
- 4 (8-inch) fat-free flour tortillas
- Butter-flavored vegetable cooking spray
- 2 cups coarsely chopped banana
- 2 teaspoons lemon juice
- ¼ cup chopped walnuts, toasted
- 1 cup frozen nonfat vanilla yogurt
- ¼ cup fat-free caramel topping

Grilled Banana-Walnut Quesadillas

Combine first 3 ingredients in a small bowl; set aside.

Coat one side of each tortilla with cooking spray; sprinkle coated sides evenly with 1 tablespoon sugar mixture.

Combine banana, lemon juice, and remaining sugar mixture; toss gently. Spoon banana mixture evenly onto plain sides of tortillas, arranging just off center of each. Sprinkle each with 1 tablespoon walnuts.

Coat grill rack with cooking spray; place on grill over medium-hot coals (350° to 400°). Place tortillas on rack; grill, uncovered, 30 seconds or until bottoms of tortillas are golden. Fold each tortilla in half; cook 30 seconds or until thoroughly heated.

Spoon 1/4 cup nonfat frozen yogurt onto each quesadilla; drizzle caramel topping evenly over quesadillas. Yield: 4 servings.

Per Serving

Calories 316 (14% Calories from Fat)	Carbohydrate 64.0 g	Cholesterol 3 mg
Fat 5.0 g (Saturated Fat 0.5 g)	Protein 6.3 g	Sodium 370 mg

Caramel Peach Trifle

Vanilla Pudding
1/4 cup fat-free caramel topping
1 (15-ounce) loaf fat-free pound cake
1/4 cup Praline Liqueur (page 43)
3 cups fresh or frozen sliced peaches
2 cups frozen lite or reduced-calorie whipped topping, thawed
2 tablespoons chopped pecans, toasted

Combine Vanilla Pudding and caramel topping in a small bowl; set mixture aside.

Cut cake into 1-inch cubes. Arrange half of cake cubes in a 3-quart trifle bowl; brush with half of Praline Liqueur. Spread half of peach slices over cake. Spoon half of pudding mixture over peach slices. Top with half of whipped topping. Repeat layers with remaining cake cubes, Praline Liqueur, peaches, pudding mixture, and whipped topping. Cover and chill at least 4 hours. Sprinkle with pecans. Yield: 12 servings.

Per Serving
Calories 234 (13% Calories from Fat) Carbohydrate 44.7 g Cholesterol 20 mg
Fat 3.5 g (Saturated Fat 0.7 g) Protein 4.4 g Sodium 170 mg

Use Your Beans

Your vanilla beans, that is. Even though these beans produced by orchids are expensive, you can use them more than once. If you use the seeds from the center of the bean in a recipe, don't toss the pod after you remove the seeds. Instead, let the pod dry for a couple of days; then place it in a jar of sugar to give the sugar a delicate aroma and flavor.

Vanilla Pudding

1 (6-inch) vanilla bean, split
3 cups low-fat milk
1/4 cup plus 2 tablespoons sugar
3 1/2 tablespoons cornstarch
3 tablespoons water
1 egg yolk, lightly beaten
1 tablespoon reduced-calorie margarine

Scrape seeds from vanilla bean. Combine vanilla seeds, vanilla bean, and milk in a large, heavy saucepan. Bring milk mixture to a boil; reduce heat, and simmer, uncovered, 20 minutes, stirring occasionally.

Combine sugar and cornstarch in a bowl. Gradually add water, stirring until smooth; add to milk mixture. Remove and discard vanilla bean.

Gradually stir 1/4 of hot milk mixture into egg yolk; add to remaining hot mixture, stirring constantly with a wire whisk. Cook over medium-low heat 20 minutes or until mixture is thickened, stirring frequently. Remove mixture from heat, and stir in margarine. Yield: 4 (½-cup) servings.

Per Serving
Calories 194 (16% Calories from Fat) Carbohydrate 34.1 g Cholesterol 58 mg
Fat 3.4 g (Saturated Fat 0.9 g) Protein 7.0 g Sodium 126 mg

Rum-Mango Frozen Yogurt

2 cups cubed mango
¼ cup sugar
¼ cup light rum
1 quart vanilla nonfat frozen yogurt, softened
Vegetable cooking spray

Combine first 3 ingredients; stir well. Cover and chill 2 hours.

Position knife blade in food processor bowl; add mango mixture. Process until smooth, scraping sides of processor bowl once. Stir in yogurt. Spoon into a 6-cup mold coated with cooking spray. Cover; freeze until firm. Unmold onto a serving plate. Yield: 6 servings.

Per Serving
Calories 218 (0% Calories from Fat) Carbohydrate 45.7 g Cholesterol 0 mg
Fat 0.1 g (Saturated Fat 0 g) Protein 5.6 g Sodium 95 mg

Grapefruit-Tequila Granita

1½ cups sugar
1⅓ cups water
¼ cup grated grapefruit rind
4 cups fresh pink grapefruit juice (about 7 large grapefruit)
¾ cup gold tequila

Combine first 3 ingredients; stir well. Bring to a boil; cook, stirring constantly, 1 minute or until sugar dissolves.

Combine sugar mixture, grapefruit juice, and tequila in a large bowl; stir well. Pour into a 13- x 9- x 2-inch baking dish. Cover; freeze 8 hours or until firm. Remove from freezer; scrape with tines of a fork until fluffy. Yield: 9 (1-cup) servings.

Per Serving
Calories 216 (0% Calories from Fat) Carbohydrate 44.0 g Cholesterol 0 mg
Fat 0.1 g (Saturated Fat 0 g) Protein 0.6 g Sodium 2 mg

How Sweet Is It?

If you want your grapefruit on the sweet side, choose naturally sweeter pink grapefruit. The fewer the seeds in the fruit, the sweeter it is.

A Good Bark to Bite

Cinnamon is actually the bark peeled from branches of a small evergreen tree that grows in tropical regions. The rolled and dried "sticks" are most often used in desserts and beverages, but its spicy sweet flavor also enhances savory meat soups and stews and dried fruit recipes.

Apple-Oatmeal Crumble

4 cups peeled, sliced Granny Smith apple
½ teaspoon grated orange rind
⅓ cup fresh orange juice
⅓ cup regular oats, uncooked
½ cup sugar
¼ cup all-purpose flour
½ teaspoon ground cinnamon
¼ teaspoon ground nutmeg
⅛ teaspoon salt
3 tablespoons reduced-calorie margarine
¼ cup plus 2 tablespoons frozen lite whipped topping, thawed

Spoon apple slices into an 8-inch square pan; sprinkle with orange rind and juice.

Combine oats and next 5 ingredients in a medium bowl; stir well. Cut in margarine with a pastry blender until mixture resembles coarse meal. Sprinkle mixture over apple. Bake at 375° for 40 to 45 minutes or until apple is tender and topping is lightly browned. Spoon into individual dessert bowls; top each serving with 1 tablespoon whipped topping. Yield: 6 servings.

Per Serving
Calories 171 (25% Calories from Fat) Carbohydrate 32.6 g Cholesterol 0 mg
Fat 4.7 g (Saturated Fat 0.6 g) Protein 1.6 g Sodium 105 mg

Grapefruit Frosted Cupcakes

1¾ cups sifted cake flour
1 cup superfine sugar
2 teaspoons baking powder
½ cup skim milk
⅓ cup vegetable oil
1 teaspoon vanilla extract
½ teaspoon grated grapefruit rind
6 egg whites
1 teaspoon cream of tartar
Grapefruit Icing

Combine first 3 ingredients in a large bowl, stirring well. Combine milk, oil, vanilla, and grapefruit rind in a small bowl, stirring well. Add milk mixture to flour mixture, stirring well.

Beat egg whites at high speed of an electric mixer just until foamy. Add cream of tartar, and beat until stiff peaks form. Gently fold one-third of beaten egg white into batter; gently fold in remaining beaten egg white.

Pour batter evenly into paper-lined muffin pans, filling two-thirds full. Bake at 350° for 18 to 20 minutes or until a wooden pick inserted in center comes out clean. Remove cupcakes from pans immediately, and let cool completely on wire racks. Spread Grapefruit Icing evenly over cupcakes. Yield: 2 dozen.

Note: If you want a delicious plain white cupcake, just omit the grapefruit juice and rind from the cupcake batter and the icing.

Per Cupcake
Calories 120 (23% Calories from Fat) Carbohydrate 21.4 g Cholesterol 0 mg
Fat 3.1 g (Saturated Fat 0.6 g) Protein 1.8 g Sodium 31 mg

Oh, So Superfine

Superfine sugar has finer granules than regular sugar, and it dissolves quickly. This makes it ideal to use in cold liquids, icings, and meringues; you won't get a gritty, grainy texture.

Grapefruit Icing

⅔ cup superfine sugar
1 egg white
1 tablespoon light corn syrup
1 tablespoon fresh grapefruit juice
⅛ teaspoon salt
2 teaspoons grated grapefruit rind

Combine first 5 ingredients in the top of a double boiler; beat at low speed of an electric mixer 30 seconds or just until blended. Place over boiling water; beat at high speed 7 minutes or until stiff peaks form. Remove from heat; stir in rind. Yield: 1¾ cups.

Per Tablespoon
Calories 25 (0% Calories from Fat) Carbohydrate 6.3 g Cholesterol 0 mg
Fat 0 g (Saturated Fat 0 g) Protein 0.1 g Sodium 16 mg

Chocolate-Peanut Butter Cake

1/4 cup reduced-fat creamy peanut butter
1/3 cup nonfat cream cheese, softened
3 tablespoons margarine, softened
1 1/2 cups sugar
1/2 cup frozen egg substitute, thawed
2 cups sifted cake flour
1/4 cup plus 2 tablespoons unsweetened cocoa
1 teaspoon baking soda
1/4 teaspoon salt
1 cup nonfat buttermilk
1 teaspoon vanilla extract
Vegetable cooking spray
Chocolate Frosting
2 tablespoons finely chopped unsalted peanuts

Beat peanut butter, cream cheese, and margarine at medium speed of an electric mixer until creamy; gradually add sugar, beating well. Add egg substitute, beating well.

Combine flour and next 3 ingredients; stir well with a wire whisk. Add to peanut butter mixture alternately with buttermilk, beginning and ending with flour mixture. Mix batter just until blended after each addition. Stir in vanilla.

Pour batter into a 13- x 9- x 2-inch pan coated with cooking spray. Bake at 350° for 30 to 35 minutes or until a wooden pick inserted in center comes out clean. Cool completely on a wire rack. Spread Chocolate Frosting over cooled cake, and sprinkle with chopped peanuts. Yield: 15 servings.

Per Serving

Calories 319 (16% Calories from Fat)	Carbohydrate 59.4 g	Cholesterol 3 mg
Fat 5.7 g (Saturated Fat 1.2 g)	Protein 7.2 g	Sodium 308 mg

Chocolate Frosting

1/4 cup plus 2 tablespoons evaporated skimmed milk
2 tablespoons reduced-fat creamy peanut butter
3 cups sifted powdered sugar
1/4 cup unsweetened cocoa
1/4 teaspoon salt
1 teaspoon vanilla extract

Combine evaporated milk and peanut butter in a small saucepan; cook over low heat until peanut butter melts and mixture is smooth.

Combine milk mixture with powdered sugar and remaining ingredients, stirring until frosting is cool. Yield: 1⅓ cups.

Per Serving

Calories 83 (2% Calories from Fat)	Carbohydrate 18.8 g	Cholesterol 0 mg
Fat 1.0 g (Saturated Fat 0.2 g)	Protein 1.0 g	Sodium 40 mg

Lemon-Lime Cake

½ cup reduced-calorie margarine, softened
¾ cup sugar
¾ cup Lemon-Vanilla Sugar (page 29)
2 cups sifted cake flour
2½ teaspoons baking powder
1 tablespoon grated lime rind
½ teaspoon salt
⅔ cup skim milk
¼ cup lemon juice
4 egg whites
½ teaspoon cream of tartar
Vegetable cooking spray
1 teaspoon powdered sugar

Beat margarine at medium speed of an electric mixer until creamy; gradually add ¾ cup sugar and Lemon-Vanilla Sugar, beating well.

Combine flour and next 3 ingredients, and stir well. Combine milk and lemon juice. Add flour mixture to margarine mixture alternately with milk mixture, beginning and ending with flour mixture. Mix after each addition.

Beat egg whites and cream of tartar at high speed of an electric mixer until stiff peaks form. Fold beaten egg white into batter.

Spoon batter into an 8-inch angel food cake pan or a 9- x 5- x 3-inch loaf pan coated with cooking spray. Bake at 350° for 45 to 50 minutes or until a wooden pick inserted in center comes out clean. Cool in pan on a wire rack 10 minutes. Remove from pan, and let cool completely on wire rack. Sift powdered sugar over cooled cake. Yield: 10 servings.

Note: To make cupcakes, fill paper-lined muffin pans three-fourths full. Bake at 350° for 15 minutes. Yield: 20 cupcakes.

Per Serving

Calories 248 (22% Calories from Fat)	Carbohydrate 46.2 g	Cholesterol 0 mg
Fat 6.1 g (Saturated Fat 0.8 g)	Protein 3.7 g	Sodium 236 mg

What's an Angel Food Cake Pan?

It's smaller than a typical 10-inch tube pan or a Bundt pan. The smaller pan size allows you to bake less cake batter into a tall, stately-looking dessert. Find this smaller size tube pan with a rounded bottom wherever you find cake decorating supplies—in discount, department, or cooking supply stores.

Low-Fat Pound Cake Secrets

Think there's no way to make pound cake taste good without the butter, eggs, and cream of traditional recipes? It's simple, really. Try these fat-reducing tips on your own favorite pound cake recipe:

- Use egg whites or egg substitute instead of whole eggs. (You may have to add an extra white.)
- Replace butter with reduced-calorie margarine.
- Use cake flour instead of all-purpose flour. (It makes a lower-fat cake more tender.)
- Substitute nonfat buttermilk for cream; you'll get a rich flavor without the fat. (When you use buttermilk, make sure that baking soda is one of the leavening ingredients.)

Rose Geranium Pound Cake

Rose geranium leaves come from an herb which imparts an aromatic citrus or nutmeg flavor. Buy rose geranium plants at your local nursery or wherever you buy potted herbs.

6 large rose geranium leaves
Vegetable cooking spray
3/4 cup reduced-calorie margarine, softened
3 cups sugar
8 egg whites
1 1/2 cups nonfat buttermilk
2 teaspoons vanilla extract
4 1/2 cups sifted cake flour
3/4 teaspoon baking soda
1/4 teaspoon baking powder
1/4 teaspoon salt

Coat geranium leaves with cooking spray; arrange leaves, dull side up, in bottom of a 10-inch tube pan lined with wax paper and coated with cooking spray and flour. Set aside.

Beat margarine at medium speed of an electric mixer until creamy; gradually add sugar, beating well. Add egg whites; beat well.

Combine buttermilk and vanilla, stirring well. Combine cake flour and remaining ingredients; add to margarine mixture alternately with buttermilk mixture, beginning and ending with flour mixture. Mix after each addition. Spoon batter into tube pan. Bake at 325° for 1 hour and 35 minutes or until a wooden pick inserted in center comes out clean. Cool in pan 10 minutes. Remove cake from pan, and let cool completely on a wire rack. Yield: 16 servings.

Per Serving
Calories 319 (16% Calories from Fat) Carbohydrate 62.8 g Cholesterol 1 mg
Fat 5.8 g (Saturated Fat 0.1 g) Protein 5.0 g Sodium 229 mg

Rose Geranium Pound Cake

MEXICAN MOCHA ANGEL FOOD CAKE

1 (14½-ounce) package angel food cake mix
¼ cup Mexican Mocha Spice Mix, divided (page 29)

Prepare cake batter according to package directions. Spoon one-third of batter into an ungreased 10-inch tube pan. Sprinkle with 2 tablespoons Mexican Mocha Spice Mix. Repeat layers; top with remaining one-third batter. Gently swirl batter with a knife. Bake according to package directions. Yield: 16 servings.

Per Serving

Calories 106 (2% Calories from Fat)	Carbohydrate 23.8 g	Cholesterol 0 mg
Fat 0.2 g (Saturated Fat 0.1 g)	Protein 2.5 g	Sodium 190 mg

LEMON MERINGUE PIE

1 cup all-purpose flour
1 teaspoon sugar
¼ teaspoon salt
¼ cup margarine
⅔ cup plus 3 tablespoons nonfat buttermilk, divided
¾ cup sugar
¼ cup plus 2 tablespoons cornstarch
⅛ teaspoon salt
1 cup water
½ cup frozen egg substitute, thawed
2 teaspoons grated lemon rind
½ cup fresh lemon juice
5 egg whites
½ teaspoon cream of tartar
½ teaspoon vanilla extract
¼ cup sugar

Combine first 3 ingredients in a bowl; cut in margarine with a pastry blender until mixture resembles coarse meal and is pale yellow (about 3½ minutes). Sprinkle 3 tablespoons buttermilk over surface; toss with a fork until dry ingredients are moistened and mixture is crumbly.

Gently press mixture into a 4-inch circle on heavy-duty plastic wrap; cover with additional heavy-duty plastic wrap, and chill 15 minutes. Roll dough, still covered, to a 10½-inch circle. Remove plastic wrap, and fit dough into a 9-inch pieplate. Roll edges under, and flute. Prick bottom of pastry with a fork. Bake at 450° for 10 minutes or until lightly browned; cool completely on a wire rack.

Lemon Meringue Pie

Combine ¾ cup sugar, cornstarch, and ⅛ teaspoon salt in a saucepan; gradually stir in water and remaining ⅔ cup buttermilk. Cook over medium heat, stirring constantly, until mixture comes to a boil. Cook, stirring constantly, 1 minute. Remove from heat.

Gradually stir about one-fourth of hot mixture into egg substitute; add to remaining hot mixture, stirring constantly. Cook over medium heat, stirring constantly, 2 minutes or until thickened. Remove from heat; stir in lemon rind and lemon juice. Spoon into pastry shell.

Beat egg whites, cream of tartar, and vanilla at high speed of an electric mixer until foamy. Gradually add ¼ cup sugar, 1 tablespoon at a time, beating until stiff peaks form and sugar dissolves (2 to 4 minutes). Spread meringue mixture over hot filling, sealing to edge of pastry. Bake at 325° for 25 minutes or until golden. Cool completely on a wire rack. Yield: 8 servings.

Per Serving
Calories 259 (21% Calories from Fat) Carbohydrate 46.0 g Cholesterol 1 mg
Fat 5.9 g (Saturated Fat 1.2 g) Protein 6.1 g Sodium 254 mg

Pick a Lemon
The best lemons are heavy for their size. If you plan to extract the juice, look for small, thin-skinned ones—they'll have less white pith and more juice.

Nutmeg Flavor Plus
Mace is the yellow-orange lacy outer coating of a whole nutmeg and tastes like a stronger version of nutmeg. It's great to flavor anything sweet, as well as savory sauces, chicken, or fish.

LEMON 'N' SPICE APPLE PIE

1 cup all-purpose flour
1 tablespoon sugar
1/8 teaspoon salt
1/2 teaspoon grated lemon rind
1/4 cup reduced-calorie margarine, chilled
3 tablespoons water
1 tablespoon fresh lemon juice
1/4 cup Lemon-Vanilla Sugar (page 29)
1 1/2 tablespoons cornstarch
1/2 cup all-purpose flour
1/3 cup Lemon-Vanilla Sugar
1/2 teaspoon ground cinnamon
1/4 teaspoon ground ginger
1/8 teaspoon ground mace
3 tablespoons reduced-calorie margarine, chilled
3 cups peeled, sliced Golden Delicious apple
3 cups peeled, sliced Granny Smith apple
2 tablespoons water
1/2 cup frozen lite or reduced-calorie whipped topping, thawed

Combine 1 cup all-purpose flour, sugar, salt, and lemon rind in a medium bowl. Cut in 1/4 cup margarine with a pastry blender until mixture resembles coarse meal.

Combine 3 tablespoons water and lemon juice; add to flour mixture. Toss with a fork just until dry ingredients are moistened. Gently press mixture into a 4-inch circle on heavy-duty plastic wrap; cover with additional plastic wrap, and chill 15 minutes.

Roll dough, still covered, into an 11-inch circle. Place dough in freezer for 5 minutes or until plastic wrap can easily be removed. Remove top sheet of plastic wrap. Invert and fit dough into a 9-inch pieplate. Remove remaining sheet of plastic wrap. Fold edges of dough under, and flute. (Do not prick.) Bake at 375° for 12 minutes or until golden.

Combine 1/4 cup Lemon-Vanilla Sugar and cornstarch in a small bowl; stir well. Set aside.

Combine 1/2 cup flour, 1/3 cup Lemon-Vanilla Sugar, cinnamon, ginger, and mace in a small bowl. Cut 3 tablespoons margarine into spice mixture with a pastry blender until mixture resembles coarse meal; set spice topping aside.

Combine apple slices and 2 tablespoons water in a large saucepan. Bring to a boil; reduce heat, and simmer, uncovered, 7 minutes or until apple is tender, stirring frequently. Remove from heat; stir in cornstarch mixture. Cook 1 minute or until thickened, stirring frequently. Cool mixture slightly.

Spoon apple mixture into prepared pastry shell. Sprinkle with spice topping. Bake at 375° for 20 minutes or until topping is golden. Slice and serve warm or at room temperature. Top each serving with 1 tablespoon whipped topping. Yield: 8 servings.

Per Serving

Calories 257 (26% Calories from Fat)	Carbohydrate 47.2 g	Cholesterol 0 mg
Fat 7.4 g (Saturated Fat 1.1 g)	Protein 2.7 g	Sodium 135 mg

Chocolate-Mint Biscotti

1¾ cups all-purpose flour
1 cup sugar
⅓ cup unsweetened cocoa
¾ teaspoon baking soda
¼ teaspoon salt
⅓ cup mint chocolate morsels, chopped
3 tablespoons slivered almonds, chopped and toasted
2 eggs
1 egg white
2 tablespoons crème de menthe
1 tablespoon all-purpose flour
Vegetable cooking spray

Combine first 7 ingredients in a large bowl; set aside. Combine eggs, egg white, and crème de menthe, stirring well with a wire whisk. Slowly add egg mixture to flour mixture, stirring by hand until dry ingredients are moistened. (Mixture will be very stiff.)

Sprinkle 1 tablespoon flour evenly over work surface. Turn dough out onto floured surface, and knead lightly 7 or 8 times. Divide dough in half; shape each half into an 8-inch log. Place logs, 4 inches apart, on a baking sheet coated with cooking spray. Bake at 325° for 40 minutes; remove from oven, and let cool 15 minutes.

Carefully cut each log diagonally into 15 (½-inch) slices, and place, cut sides down, on baking sheet. Reduce oven temperature to 300°, and bake for 18 minutes. (Cookies will be slightly soft in center but will harden as they cool.) Remove from baking sheet, and let cool completely on wire racks. Yield: 2½ dozen.

Per Cookie

Calories 80 (16% Calories from Fat)	Carbohydrate 14.6 g	Cholesterol 15 mg
Fat 1.4 g (Saturated Fat 0.5 g)	Protein 1.8 g	Sodium 58 mg

Not Just for Pie

Pumpkin pie spice is a blend of cinnamon, ginger, nutmeg, allspice, and cloves. If you don't have any on your spice shelf, you can blend together the five ground spices. But go easy on the allspice and cloves; they are more powerful in flavor than the others.

Spiced Heart Cookies

- **1/4 cup plus 2 tablespoons reduced-calorie margarine, softened**
- **2/3 cup sugar**
- **1/4 cup molasses**
- **1 egg white**
- **2 1/3 cups all-purpose flour**
- **1 1/2 teaspoons baking soda**
- **1/4 teaspoon salt**
- **1 3/4 teaspoons ground cinnamon**
- **3/4 teaspoon pumpkin pie spice**
- **Vegetable cooking spray**
- **1 tablespoon sugar**

Beat margarine at medium speed of an electric mixer until creamy; gradually add 2/3 cup sugar, beating well. Add molasses and egg white; mix well.

Combine flour and next 4 ingredients, stirring well. Gradually add flour mixture to creamed mixture, mixing well. Shape into a ball; cover and chill at least 1 hour.

Divide dough into 2 portions. Roll 1 portion between 2 sheets of heavy-duty plastic wrap to 1/4-inch thickness. Remove top sheet of plastic wrap; cut with a 2-inch heart-shaped cookie cutter. Place on a cookie sheet coated with cooking spray. Repeat procedure with remaining dough. Sprinkle cookies evenly with 1 tablespoon sugar. Bake at 350° for 10 to 12 minutes or until golden. Cool on wire racks. Yield: 28 cookies.

Per Cookie

Calories 80 (19% Calories from Fat)	Carbohydrate 15.3 g	Cholesterol 0 mg
Fat 1.7 g (Saturated Fat 0.2 g)	Protein 1.2 g	Sodium 115 mg

Mint-Cream Cheese Brownies

- 1 cup sugar
- 2/3 cup unsweetened cocoa
- 1/3 cup all-purpose flour
- 1/2 teaspoon baking powder
- 4 egg whites, lightly beaten
- 1/4 cup vegetable oil
- 1 teaspoon vanilla extract
- 1/4 teaspoon peppermint extract
- Vegetable cooking spray
- 6 ounces nonfat cream cheese
- 3 tablespoons sugar
- 1 tablespoon all-purpose flour
- 1 egg white
- 1/2 teaspoon vanilla extract
- 1/4 teaspoon peppermint extract

Combine first 4 ingredients in a large mixing bowl; stir well. Combine 4 egg whites and next 3 ingredients in a small bowl; add to dry ingredients, stirring well. Spread batter in an 8-inch square pan coated with cooking spray.

Combine cream cheese and remaining ingredients in a medium bowl. Beat at low speed of an electric mixer until smooth. Spoon cream cheese mixture by tablespoonfuls over cocoa mixture. Cut through cream cheese and cocoa mixtures with a knife to create a marbled effect. Bake at 350° for 22 minutes or until wooden pick inserted in center comes out almost clean. Let cool in pan on a wire rack. Cut into bars. Yield: 12 brownies.

Per Brownie

Calories 174 (27% Calories from Fat)	Carbohydrate 26.0 g	Cholesterol 3 mg
Fat 5.2 g (Saturated Fat 1.2 g)	Protein 5.2 g	Sodium 109 mg

Make a Cup of Extract

It's easier to buy vanilla extract off the shelf, but you can make your own for fun. Place a couple of vanilla beans in a jar with 1 cup of brandy or vodka, and let the mixture sit for 2 to 3 months. When you've used all the extract, use the same beans, and add more liquor to make another batch.

HIGH-FLAVOR

Surely you've noticed. As you've thumbed through this book, you've probably realized that we've found the best ways to flavor food by using food traditions that have been enjoyed for centuries in regions around the world. In the preceding chapters, we've given you a culinary world tour with Mexican salsas, Italian pastas, and even a Jamaican hot and herby jerk rub.

But we know you may be hesitant to put together an entire meal from a specific cuisine. (Many readers

MENUS

tell us that they'd rather clean the house than plan a menu.) So we've done the hard part for you.

We've picked recipes from chapters throughout the book and combined them to create international menus. All of the recipes within a menu complement each other—so you can't miss. You'll also see some "non-recipe" dishes like cooked rice and steamed green beans included in the menus.

And to make it even easier for you, we've calculated the total calories and the percentage of calories from fat per serving. No need to guess. This is really one world tour you can take that won't cost you in calories *or* dough (the kind you spend). And you can visit as often as you like.

HOT, HEARTY MEXICAN MEAL

Serves 6

Total Calories Per Serving: 514 (Calories from Fat: 20%)

Cheese and Tomato Quesadillas, page 77
Chili Ranchero, page 184
Jicama-Orange Salad, page 186

Open any spice cabinet in Mexico and you'll find cinnamon, chili powder, cumin, garlic, and oregano. They're staple seasonings to go with the fresh hot chiles, mostly ancho, jalapeño, and serrano. Complementing the fiery heat are refreshing limes and oranges, tomatoes chopped into salsas, avocados mashed into guacamole, and crisp, turnip-like jicama (eaten raw) sliced and served in salads. Rice and black beans (frijoles) are standards, too. For bread, no Mexican table is complete without a tortilla warmer full of homemade tortillas—unless they're rolled or stacked in the entrée.

Although Mexico has few traditional desserts, its Mexican chocolate (with a bit of cinnamon) is often an ingredient in the ones you'll find. And when used in savory sauces such as mole for chicken, Mexican chocolate brings out a succulent flavor in the meat.

HERBED ITALIAN REPAST

Serves 6

Total Calories Per Serving: 461 (Calories from Fat: 23%)

Steamed Artichokes with Lemon-Flavored Nonfat Mayonnaise (see below)
Zucchini-Beef Parmigiana, page 133
Pesto Rice Cups, page 174
12 commercial breadsticks

Garden-fresh herbs, or even aromatic dried ones like basil, fennel seeds, and oregano are likely to flavor any food from this boot-shaped country. It's also true for Italian-made fresh Parmesan cheese, fresh tomatoes and eggplant, pasta sauces made of vegetables or cream, and just-caught seafood from the Italian coast.

It is said that Italy may just have some of the world's finest produce, too; that includes artichokes, tomatoes, and zucchini. And that's why this menu features a simple no-fat dip to bring out the flavor of fresh steamed artichokes.

To steam the artichokes, wash them first by plunging them up and down in cold water. Cut off the stem ends, and trim about ½ inch from the top of each artichoke. Pluck off any loose bottom leaves. With scissors, trim away about ¼ of each outer leaf. Rub the top and edges of the leaves with a lemon wedge to keep them from turning brown.

Then place the artichokes in a large Dutch oven with about an inch of water. Cover it tightly and heat to boiling. Reduce heat, and simmer for 35 to 45 minutes or until the leaves are easy to pull out. Spread the leaves apart gently so you can reach the center; snip around the fuzzy thistle (choke), and remove it with a spoon.

To enjoy the delicate leaves as an appetizer, just stir 2 tablespoons lemon juice into 1½ cups of nonfat mayonnaise to use as a dip.

We count one-third of an artichoke and 2 tablespoons lemon mayonnaise as an appetizer serving. To complete the menu, just add a fresh fruit dessert, and Viva Italian!

SPICY-SWEET CHINESE CELEBRATION

Serves 4

Total Calories Per Serving: 504 (Calories from Fat: 13%)

Tomato-Egg Flower Soup, page 180
Spicy Shrimp with Spinach and Walnuts, page 159
4 cups steamed white rice

The especially strong flavors you taste in Chinese food are usually the result of an artful blend of fermented seasonings like soy sauce (from soy beans); spices like cloves, crystallized ginger, fennel, and star anise; and aromatic fresh herbs like cilantro. Chinese five-spice powder, a combination of some of these most popular spices, is also widely used in Chinese cooking. Shiitake mushrooms and all kinds of chile peppers contribute to the strong flavors as well. Because much of the food is fresh and cooked quickly in a wok, the pungent flavors aren't lost during a long cooking time.

Rice, of course, is a must with every meal. This bland side dish is a natural absorber of the succulent sauces and a nice complement to powerful flavors. If you want to go authentic and use chopsticks, be sure to cook up short grain rice—it sticks together in clumps and is easier to eat.

Tomato-Egg Flower Soup

Spicy Indian Dinner

Serves 6

Total Calories Per Serving: 693 (Calories from Fat: 8%)

Aromatic-Herbed Chicken, page 142
4 cups basmati rice and raisins
Cucumber and Yogurt Raita, page 63
Fresh Mint Relish, page 59
6 baked papadams

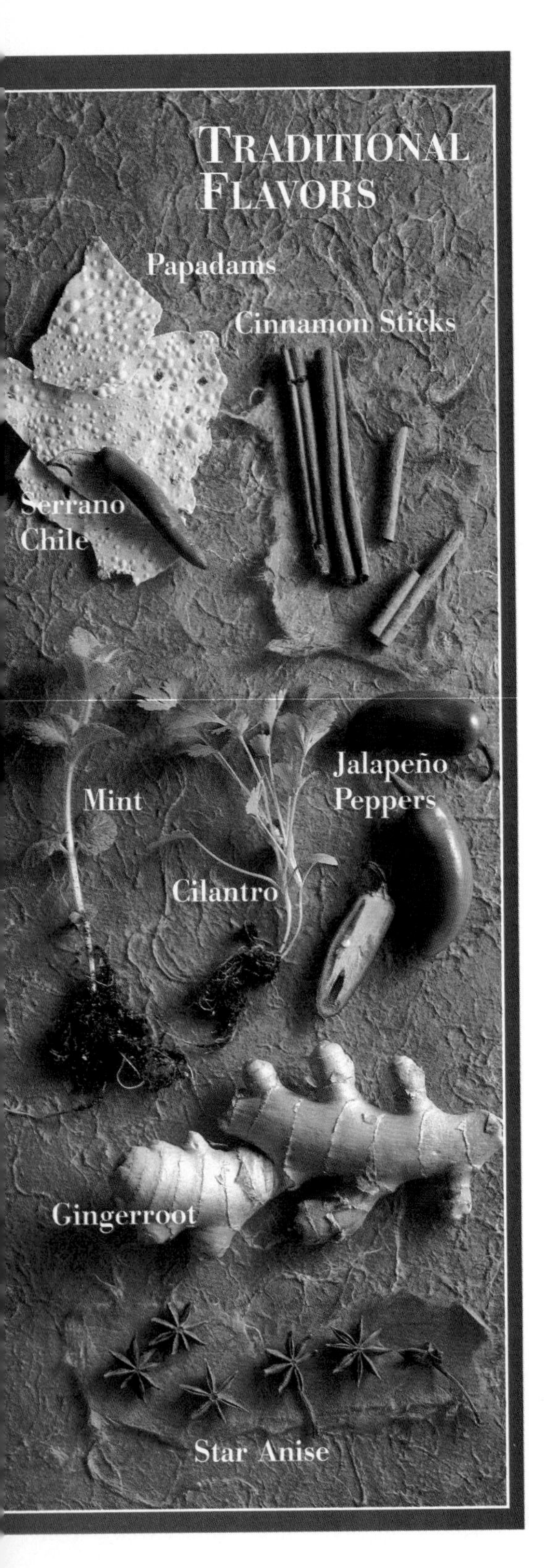

In India, there's even an occupation—a masalchi—devoted to the highly developed art of blending spices. The favorites in this earthy-tasting and often hot cuisine are too numerous to list completely, but among them are cardamom, cloves, cilantro, cinnamon, coriander, cumin, ginger, golden turmeric, mint, saffrons, and star anise. Hot chiles like jalapeño peppers and serranos blend with the spices to create the country's characteristic flavors. (A little tip from the Indians: Serve a dairy food such as the traditional yogurt-based raita with a spicy hot recipe; it cools the burn from hot chiles.)

Rice is as essential as spices to an Indian meal. In this menu, we suggest stirring raisins into cooked aromatic rice. And for the bread, spicy papadams are traditionally crisp-fried; baking them will save fat and calories. (See page 230 for a mail-order source for papadams.)

Savory Mediterranean Menu

Serves 4

Total Calories Per Serving: 464 (Calories from Fat: 17%)

Greek Feta Chicken, page 145
Fragrant Garden Tabbouleh, page 187
4 commercial pita pockets
4 cups iced mint tea

With ingredients like pungent feta cheese, garlic, herb-flavored vinegars, lemons, yogurt, and a host of fresh vegetables, the cuisine of Mediterranean countries rates high in flavor. From Greece come eggplant, feta cheese, green beans, honey, okra, and pita bread. Spain contributes fresh-tasting parsley, peppers, and sun-reddened tomatoes. Artichokes are abundant in Italy, as are garlic and onions in Portugal.

The region's blended cuisine is touted for healthful traditions and fresh flavors. Oregano, rosemary, and thyme are among the most popular herb flavorings. Mint and parsley are essential ingredients for tabbouleh, a long-time Lebanese favorite; it's a salad made of nutty, chewy dried bulgur.

Southwestern Corn-Stuffed Turkey

Sizzling Southwestern Spread

Serves 10

Total Calories Per Serving: 384 (Calories from Fat: 12%)

Cilantro-Lime Soup, page 178
Orange Slices with Pomegranate Seeds and Mint (see below)
Southwestern Corn-Stuffed Turkey, page 148
10 hot corn tortillas

Blend the fiery chiles of Mexico; the earthy-tasting corn, squash, and bean staples of native American tribes; and the beef, tomatoes, and campfire cookery favorites of Texas cowboys. The flavors melt into a truly American cuisine—southwestern. Chile de Arbol, red chile powder, crushed red pepper flakes, and chipotle are some of the hot spices that make southwestern dishes sizzle. Southwestern cooking also boasts robust tongue-tantalizers like limestone-cured blue corn, cilantro, citrus fruit (especially lime), coriander, cumin, and garlic.

Southwestern cuisine is mostly peasant-style food, and almost every meal includes a salsa of some type. Bland side dishes of rice and beans or cool, refreshing citrus sides and salads help tame the heat. To make an easy salad for this menu, sprinkle 2 teaspoons each of pomegranate seeds and chopped mint over 2 orange slices for each salad.

Dessert is optional on a typical menu, but when it is included, the flavors are most likely cinnamon, chocolate, sweet potato, or creamy flan with caramelized sugar.

Tropical South Florida Supper

Serves 4

Total Calories Per Serving: 430 (Calories from Fat: 12%)

Hearts of Palm on Greens
with Mango Vinaigrette (see below)
Grilled Grouper with Tomato-Papaya Salsa, page 150
Yellow Rice with Black Beans and Corn, page 173
3 cups sautéed green beans

Catch the freshest fish from the coastal waters. Pick the juiciest grapefruit, lemons, key limes, mangoes, oranges, papayas, passion fruit, and plantains. Sprinkle in favorites of the Carribean isles like allspice, cilantro, cloves, cumin, hot pepper sauces, and saffron. And now you've defined South Florida's cuisine. A borrowed Cuban tradition of black beans and yellow rice has become the region's own, as well.

With this menu, fresh hearts of palm typify the indigenous produce (you can buy canned or frozen hearts of palm in other areas of the country). For each salad, toss a cup of mixed greens and ¼ cup fresh or canned hearts of palm. Add two tablespoons of commercial mango vinaigrette to heighten the regional flavor.

Grilled Grouper with
Tomato-Papaya Salsa

Pictorial

Herbs, Spices, Spice Blends

Cardamom–A spicy-sweet member of the ginger family available in seeds or pods from Guatemala, India, Mexico, and Sri Lanka. Ranks as one of the most expensive spices, along with saffron and vanilla.

Chile Powder–A powder of pure pulverized dried red chiles like cayenne. Can be very hot depending on the type of chile used.

Chili Powder–A blend of different spices and seasonings, including dried chiles. Seasoning commonly used in chili con carne recipes. Sweet tasting and mildly hot.

Cilantro–The light green, feathery leaf of the coriander herb, also known as Chinese parsley. Leaves have a pungent, lemon-like flavor and are a staple in southwestern salsas and other recipes. Also commonly used in Greek, Indian, and Mexican cuisines.

Garam Masala–The dominant spice blend of northern Indian cooking. A mixture of dry roasted and ground spices including bay leaves, black peppercorns, cardamom seeds, cinnamon, cloves, coriander, cumin, and mace. Used at the end of cooking in savory recipes or sprinkled on as a condiment.

Sage–A fragrant herb with grayish-green leaves. Enjoyed for centuries for its pungent, slightly bitter flavor. Has a musty mint aroma and is popular in traditional turkey stuffings.

Star Anise–A dark brown pod shaped like a little star with pea-sized seeds in each of its eight segments. Pod and seeds are used to flavor teas, liqueurs, cakes, cookies, and breads. Has a licorice-like flavor and is common in Asian soups, stews, and marinades. Is one of five components of Chinese five-spice powder.

Turmeric–A remarkably vivid yellow spice from the ginger family with a pungent, slightly acrid flavor. Is dried and ground and is often used as a basic spice in curry powders and as a dye for cloth.

Flavorful Produce

Chiles:

- **California Green**–Long, green, blunt-tipped chile which can range from mild to hot. Is sometimes called Anaheim or New Mexican chile. The ripened red version is often strung into wreaths called ristras and allowed to dry.
- **Habañero**–Small, bright orange, lantern-shaped Mexican chile. Considered the hottest in the world. Very similar to and interchangeable with Scotch Bonnet chile. Use rubber gloves when handling.
- **Poblano**–A medium to hot chile resembling a green bell pepper and good for stuffed chile dishes. Delicious when roasted. Popular in southwestern cuisine.
- **Scotch Bonnet**–Jamaica's equivalent of the habañero chile, also blisteringly hot. Never handle without wearing rubber gloves to protect skin.

Jicama–The root of a plant native to Mexico that looks somewhat like a turnip with brown skin. Popular in salads and slaws for its crunch and sweetness. Smaller jicamas are more tender.

Kumquat–Smallest member of the citrus family. Tiny and round with a sweet rind and tart flesh. Eaten in salads after being sliced while still raw and unpeeled; or candied for preserves.

Leek–A member of the onion family, recognizable by its large, flat, green leaves. Has a mild and delicate flavor and is commonly used in vichyssoise.

GLOSSARY

Radicchio- Deep red Italian chicory with a slightly bitter taste. Often combined with other greens in salads.

Shallot–Small, tender, delicately flavored member of the onion family that looks like a tiny onion. The backbone of many French sauces.

Tomatillo–A small, green, tomato-like fruit with a tart, lemony flavor. Grows encased in a thick, husk-like covering. Used in Mexican and southwestern recipes.

HIGH-FLAVOR CHEESES

Asiago–A semifirm to hard Italian cheese with a rich, nutty, sharp flavor. Has a light yellow interior with many small holes. Can be used for cooking, grating, and snacking.

Chèvre–Zingy, strong-tasting goat cheese. Comes in many varieties, from white and creamy to dry and firm. Served dipped in brandy, rolled in chestnut leaves, crumbled in salads, or flavored with garlic, herbs, or spices. Can be found in various shapes: logs, cones, pyramids, and little rounds.

Parmigiano Reggiano–A hard cheese which is considered Italy's best Parmesan. Aged longer than regular Parmesan to develop a complex taste and melt-in-your-mouth texture. Good eaten with fresh fruit.

OTHER FOODS OF FLAVOR

Bulgur–Parched, cracked wheat product in which wheat kernels have been steamed, dried, and crushed. Commonly used in pilaf, meat, or vegetable recipes. Is traditional in Lebanese tabbouleh. Has a dark tan color with a delicate nutty flavor.

Couscous–North Africa's version of grits. A coarsely ground semolina wheat cooked and served as porridge, eaten as a salad with fragrant dressings, sweetened and mixed with fruits, or served like rice or pasta.

Curry–A hot and spicy southern Indian sauce seasoned with a traditional mixture of up to 15 spices (bright yellow turmeric is a must). Flavors of the sauce can also be found in **curry powder**, a pre-mixed blend of spices. The traditional spice mix is the basis for many Indian recipes.

Harissa–Intensely hot chile paste from Tunisia. Used with restraint to flavor soups, tomato sauces, and couscous; or–for the daring–spread on bread and eaten with verve.

Jerk–A method of Jamaican barbecue characterized by the mixture of spices and fresh herbs which are brushed on meat to be grilled over a wood fire.

Mole Sauce–Famous Mexican sauce made of chile peppers, garlic, ground sesame or pumpkin seeds, onion, and a small portion of bitter chocolate which adds richness. Served over poultry.

Papadams–Flat, round Indian crackers made of lentil flour and spiced from mild to hot with black pepper, cumin, or chiles.

Red Beer–Ale aged in redwood barrels. Is a bit more bitter-tasting than beer.

Risotto–A creamy Italian rice dish made of arborio rice, onions, and stock often flavored with ingredients like cheeses, chicken, herbs, sausage, shrimp, vegetables, and wine.

Mail Order Sources

Breads (Ethnic)

Indian Papadams: Garlic & Chili, Black Pepper
Cinnabar Specialty Foods, Inc.
1134 W. Haining Street
Prescott, AZ 86301
800-824-4563

Maseca Corn Tortilla Mix
Don Alfonso Foods
P.O. Box 201988
Austin, TX 78720-1988
800-456-6100

Chiles

Chipotle Peppers in Adobo Sauce
Los Chileros de Nuevo Mexico
P.O. Box 6215
Santa Fe, NM 87502
505-471-6967

Dried: Ancho, Chipotle, de Arbol, Pasilla
Dried Powders: Cayenne, Habañero, Pasilla
Pre-roasted Fresh: New Mexico, Poblano
Don Alfonso Foods
P.O. Box 201988
Austin, TX 78720-1988
800-456-6100

Dried: Smoked Habañero, Smoked Jalapeño
Walnut Acres Organic Farms
Penns Creek, PA 17862
800-433-3998

Frozen: New Mexican, Poblano
Pecos Valley Spice Company
800 Rio Grande NW, Suite 14
Albuquerque, NM 87104
800-473-8226

Chutneys

Ginger-Pineapple, Mango, Peach, Pear-Cardamom, Tomato
Cinnabar Specialty Foods, Inc.
1134 W. Haining Street
Prescott, AZ 86301
800-824-4563

Flours and Meals

Blue Corn Flour
The CMC Company
P.O. Box 322
Avalon, NJ 08202
800-262-2780

Blue Corn Masa, Blue Corn Meal
Pecos Valley Spice Company
800 Rio Grande NW, Suite 14
Albuquerque, NM 87104
800-473-8226

Rye, Whole Wheat Bread Flours
Walnut Acres Organic Farms
Penns Creek, PA 17862
800-433-3998

Whole Wheat Flour
The Vermont Country Store
P.O. Box 3000
Manchester Center, VT 05252-3000
802-362-2400

Mushrooms

Dried: Porcini, Shiitake
The CMC Company
P.O. Box 322
Avalon, NJ 08202
800-262-2780

Fresh: Shiitake
Red Hill Mushrooms
P.O. Box 4234
Gettysburg, PA 17325
800-822-4003

Mustards

Cranberry & Honey, Lemon & Garlic, Lemon & Honey
Wild Thyme Farm, Route 351
Medusa, NY 12120
800-724-2877

Sweet-Hot
Kozlowski Farms
5566 Gravenstein, Hwy. 116
Forestville, CA 95436
800-473-2767

Wholegrain Champagne, Zinfandel Orange
Cuisine Perel
1064 Tibiron
San Rafael, CA 94901
415-456-4406

Oils

Citrus-Cilantro, Rosemary, Grapeseed
Cuisine Perel
1064 Tibiron
San Rafael, CA 94901
415-456-4406

Ethnic Cuisine Oils: Asian, Caribbean, Thai
Walnut Acres Organic Farms
Penns Creek, PA 17862
800-433-3998

Garlic Olive Oil, Red Chili Pepper
Wild Thyme Farm, Route 351
Medusa, NY 12120
800-724-2877

Pasta

Spinach Linguine, Tomato-Basil Fettuccine
Harvest Direct Inc.
P.O. Box 4514
Decatur, IL 62525-4514
800-835-2867

Rices

Basmati
Sultan's Delight
P.O. Box 090302
Brooklyn, NY 11209
800-852-5046

Rices *(continued)*
Organic Brown Basmati
Jaffe Bros., Inc.
P.O. Box 636
28560 Lilac Road
Valley Center, CA 92082-0636
619-749-1133

Salsas

Basil-Herb, Cilantro-Herb, Raspberry
Robert Rothschild Berry Farm
P.O. Box 311
Urbana, OH 43078
800-356-8933

Chipotle-Flavored, Habañero-Flavored
Don Alfonso Foods
P.O. Box 201988
Austin, TX 78720-1988
800-456-6100

Cilantro & Green Olive, Peach, Salsa Verde
Jardine's General Store
P.O. Box 160
Buda, TX 78610
800-544-1880

Spices and Spice Blends

Cajun & Creole Seasonings, Garam Masala Spice Mixture, Gingerroot, Gumbo Filé Powder, Mustard Seeds (Brown, Oriental, Yellow)
Penzeys, Ltd. Spice House
P.O. Box 1448
Waukesha, WI 53187
414-574-0277

Ethnic: Anise, Coriander, Mexican Oregano
Pecos Valley Spice Company
800 Rio Grande NW, Suite 14
Albuquerque, NM 87104
800-473-8226

Peppercorns: Green, Pink, Yellow
The CMC Company
P.O. Box 322
Avalon, NJ 08202
800-262-2780

Vanilla Beans
The King Arthur Flour Baker's Catalogue
P.O. Box 876
Norwich, VT 05055-0876
800-827-6836

Syrups

Pure Maple
Butternut Mountain Farm
P.O. Box 381
Johnson, Vermont 05656
800-828-2376

Tea

Red Zinger Herbal
Celestial Seasonings Direct
4500 Cherry Creek Drive So.
Suite 950
Denver, CO 80222
800-200-0832

Vinegars

Balsamic (White and Dark)
Fredericksburg Herb Farm
P.O. Drawer 927
Fredericksburg, TX 78624-0927
800-259-4372

Cinnamon & Honey-Spiced, Lemon & Garlic, Rosemary & Garlic
Wild Thyme Farm
Medusa, NY 12120
800-724-2877

Raspberry
Robert Rothschild Berry Farm
P.O. Box 311
Urbana, OH 43078
800-356-8933

Wood Chips (for Smoking)

Apple, Cherry, Hickory, Maple Sugar
Sugartown Products Company
2330 East Heil Road
P.O. Box 641
Gladwin, MI 48624
517-426-4189

Mesquite
Pecos Valley Spice Company
800 Rio Grande NW, Suite 14
Albuquerque, NM 87104
800-473-8226

Miscellaneous

Cranberries (Dried)
The King Arthur Flour Baker's Catalogue
P.O. Box 876
Norwich, VT 05055-0876
800-827-6836

Garlic (Roasted): Lemon-Dill, Riesling-Marinated
Gil's Gourmet Gallery
637 Ortiz, Suite B
Sand City, CA 93955
800-438-7480

Harissa
Sultan's Delight
P.O. Box 090302
Brooklyn, NY 11209
800-852-5046

Pesto Sauce
Gil's Gourmet Gallery
637 Ortiz, Suite B
Sand City, CA 93955
800-438-7480

Thai Green Curry Paste
Cinnabar Specialty Foods, Inc.
1134 W. Haining Street
Prescott, AZ 86301
800-824-4563

RECIPE INDEX

Subject Index

Acknowledgments & Credits

Oxmoor House wishes to thank the following merchants and individuals:

Antiques & Gardens, Birmingham, AL
Barbara Eigen Arts, Jersey City, NJ
Bridges Antiques, Birmingham, AL
Bromberg's, Birmingham, AL
Cassis and Co., New York, NY
Christine's, Birmingham, AL
Goldsmith/Corot, Inc., New York, NY
Iden Pottery, c/o Edward Russell, Valhalla, NY
Izabel Lam, Long Island City, NY
Lamb's Ears Ltd., Birmingham, AL
Los Angeles Pottery, Los Angeles, CA
M's Fabric Gallery, Birmingham, AL
Maralyn Wilson Gallery, Birmingham, AL
Pillivuyt, Salinas, CA
Robert Rothschild Berry Farms, Inc., Urbana, OH
Table Matters, Birmingham, AL

Additional photography
Josh Gibson: pages 185, 220, 221, 226, 227
Mark Gooch: pages 8-9, 48, 70-71, 132, 176, 188-189, 197, 228, 229
Brit Huckaby: pages 114, 121, 147, 156

Additional photo styling:
Kay E. Clarke: pages 220, 221, 226, 227